GLEIM®

2019 EDITION

CIA REVIEW

PART 2: PRACTICE OF INTERNAL AUDITING

by

Irvin N. Gleim, Ph.D., CPA, CIA, CMA, CFM

Revised for the 2019 CIA Exam

Gleim Publications, Inc.
PO Box 12848
University Station
Gainesville, Florida 32604
(800) 874-5346
(352) 375-0772
www.gleim.com/cia
CIA@gleim.com

For updates to the first printing of the 2019 edition of *CIA Review: Part 2*

Go To: www.gleim.com/updates

Or: Email update@gleim.com with **CIA 2 2019** in the subject line. You will receive our current update as a reply.

Updates are available until the next edition is published.

ISSN: 2638-8200

ISBN: 978-1-61854-192-5 *CIA Review: Part 1*
ISBN: 978-1-61854-193-2 *CIA Review: Part 2*
ISBN: 978-1-61854-194-9 *CIA Review: Part 3*
ISBN: 978-1-61854-199-4 *CIA Exam Guide: A System for Success*

First Printing: September 2018

ACKNOWLEDGMENTS FOR PART 2

The author is grateful for permission to reproduce the following materials copyrighted by The Institute of Internal Auditors: Certified Internal Auditor Examination Questions and Suggested Solutions (copyright © 1980-2018), excerpts from *Sawyer's Internal Auditing* (5th and 6th editions), parts of the 2018 *Certification Candidate Handbook*, and the International Professional Practices Framework.

CIA® is a Registered Trademark of The Institute of Internal Auditors, Inc. All rights reserved.

Environmental Statement -- This book is printed on recyclable, environmentally friendly groundwood paper, sourced from certified sustainable forests and produced either TCF (totally chlorine-free) or ECF (elementally chlorine-free).

ABOUT THE AUTHOR

Irvin N. Gleim is Professor Emeritus in the Fisher School of Accounting at the University of Florida and is a member of the American Accounting Association, Academy of Legal Studies in Business, American Institute of Certified Public Accountants, Association of Government Accountants, Florida Institute of Certified Public Accountants, The Institute of Internal Auditors, and the Institute of Management Accountants. He has had articles published in the *Journal of Accountancy*, *The Accounting Review*, and *The American Business Law Journal* and is author/coauthor of numerous accounting books, aviation books, and CPE courses.

REVIEWERS AND CONTRIBUTORS

Garrett W. Gleim, B.S., CGMA, received a Bachelor of Science degree from the University of Pennsylvania, The Wharton School. He also holds a CPA certificate issued by the State of Delaware. Mr. Gleim coordinated the production staff, reviewed the manuscript, and provided production assistance throughout the project.

Solomon E. Gonite, J.D., CIA, CRMA, CPA, CMA, EA, CSCA, CFE, is a graduate of the Florida State University College of Law and the Fisher School of Accounting at the University of Florida. He has practiced as an auditor (in both the private and government sectors) and as a tax practitioner. Mr. Gonite provided substantial editorial assistance throughout the project.

Grady M. Irwin, J.D., is a graduate of the University of Florida College of Law, and he has taught in the University of Florida College of Business. Mr. Irwin provided substantial editorial assistance throughout the project.

LouAnn M. Lutter, M.S. Acc., CPA, received a Master of Science in Accounting from the University of Colorado, Boulder. Previously, she was an Accounting Manager in Corporate Accounting and Shared Business Services at Caesars Entertainment. Ms. Lutter provided substantial editorial assistance throughout the project.

Joseph Mauriello, CIA, CISA, CPA, CFE, CMA, CFSA, CRMA, is a Senior Lecturer as well as the Director of the Center for Internal Auditing Excellence at the University of Texas at Dallas. He is also active in his local chapter of The IIA and currently holds the title of Past President. Professor Mauriello is the lead CIA Gleim Instruct lecturer and provided substantial editorial assistance throughout the project.

Mark S. Modas, M.S.T., CPA, received a Bachelor of Arts in Accounting from Florida Atlantic University and a Master of Science in Taxation from Nova Southeastern University. He was the Sarbanes-Oxley project manager and Internal Audit department manager at Perry Ellis International and the Director of Accounting and Financial Reporting for the School Board of Broward County, Florida. Additionally, he worked as the corporate tax compliance supervisor for Ryder Systems, Inc., and has worked as a tax practitioner in excess of 25 years. Mr. Modas provided substantial editorial assistance throughout the project.

Yiqian Zhao, MAcc., CIA, CPA, CFE, is a graduate of the Fisher School of Accounting at the University of Florida. Ms. Zhao participated in the technical editing of the manuscript.

A PERSONAL THANKS

This manual would not have been possible without the extraordinary effort and dedication of Jacob Bennett, Julie Cutlip, Ethan Good, Kelsey Hughes, Fernanda Martinez, Bree Rodriguez, Teresa Soard, Justin Stephenson, Joanne Strong, Elmer Tucker, and Candace Van Doren, who typed the entire manuscript and all revisions and drafted and laid out the diagrams, illustrations, and cover for this book.

The author also appreciates the production and editorial assistance of Sirene Dagher, Brooke Gregory, Jessica Hatker, Belea Keeney, Katie Larson, Diana León, Bryce Owen, Jake Pettifor, Shane Rapp, Drew Sheppard, and Alyssa Thomas.

The author also appreciates the critical reading assistance of Matthew Blockus, Felix Chen, Corey Connell, Cole Gabriel, Elena Hernandez, Dean Kingston, Melissa Leonard, Monica Metz, Kelly Meyer, Timothy Murphy, Amber Neumeister, Joey Noble, Cristian Prieto, Crystal Quach, Martin Salazar, and Diana Weng.

The author also appreciates the video production expertise of Gary Brooks, Matthew Church, Kristen Hennen, Andrew Johnson, and Rebecca Pope, who helped produce and edit our Gleim Instruct Video Series.

Finally, we appreciate the encouragement, support, and tolerance of our families throughout this project.

TABLE OF CONTENTS

DETAILED TABLE OF CONTENTS

PREFACE

The purpose of this book is to help **you** prepare to pass Part 2 of the CIA exam. Our overriding consideration is to provide an affordable, effective, and easy-to-use study program. This book

1. Explains how to optimize your score through learning techniques perfected by Gleim CIA.

2. Defines the subject matter tested on Part 2 of the CIA exam.

3. Outlines all of the subject matter tested on Part 2 in 9 easy-to-use study units, including all relevant authoritative pronouncements.

4. Presents multiple-choice questions from past CIA examinations to prepare you for the types of questions you will find on your CIA exams. Our answer explanations are presented to the immediate right of each question for your convenience. Use a piece of paper to cover our explanations as you study the questions. You also should practice answering these questions on your exam-emulating review course practice exams. The review course provides detailed answer explanations of both the correct and incorrect answer choices.

5. Suggests exam-taking and question-answering techniques to help you maximize your exam score.

The outline format, the spacing, and the question-and-answer formats in this book are designed to facilitate readability, learning, understanding, and success on the CIA exam. Our most successful candidates use the Gleim Premium CIA Review System*, which includes our innovative SmartAdapt technology, first-of-their-kind Gleim Instruct video lectures, the Gleim Access Until You Pass guarantee, and comprehensive exam-emulating test questions. Students who prefer to study in a group setting may attend Gleim Professor-Led Reviews, which combine the Gleim Review System with the coordination and feedback of a professor.

To maximize the efficiency and effectiveness of your CIA review program, augment your studying with the *CIA Exam Guide*. This booklet has been carefully written and organized to provide important information to assist you in passing the CIA exam.

Thank you for your interest in our materials. We deeply appreciate the comments and suggestions we have received from thousands of CIA, CMA, CPA, and EA candidates; accounting students; and faculty during the past 5 decades.

If you use Gleim materials, we want your feedback immediately after the exam upon receipt of your exam scores. The CIA exam is nondisclosed, and you must maintain the confidentiality and agree not to divulge the nature or content of any CIA question or answer under any circumstances. We ask only for information about our materials, i.e., the topics that need to be added, expanded, etc.

Please go to www.gleim.com/feedbackCIA2 to share your suggestions on how we can improve this edition.

Good Luck on the Exam,

Irvin N. Gleim

September 2018

*Visit www.gleimcia.com or call (800) 874-5346 to order.

PREPARING FOR AND TAKING THE CIA EXAM

READ THE *CIA EXAM GUIDE: A SYSTEM FOR SUCCESS*

Access the free Gleim **CIA Exam Guide** at www.gleim.com/passCIA and reference it as needed throughout your studying process to obtain a deeper understanding of the CIA exam. This booklet is your system for success.

OVERVIEW OF THE CIA EXAMINATION

The total exam is 6.5 hours of testing (including 5 minutes per part for a survey). It is divided into three parts, as follows:

CIA Exam (3-Part)			
Part	Title	Exam Length	Number of Questions
1	Essentials of Internal Auditing	2.5 hrs	125 multiple-choice
2	Practice of Internal Auditing	2 hrs	100 multiple-choice
3	Business Knowledge for Internal Auditing	2 hrs	100 multiple-choice

All CIA questions are multiple-choice. The exam is offered continually throughout the year. The CIA exam is computerized to facilitate easier and more convenient testing. Pearson VUE, the testing company that The IIA contracts to proctor the exams, has hundreds of testing centers worldwide. The online components of Gleim CIA Review provide exact exam emulations of the Pearson VUE computer screens and procedures so you feel comfortable at the testing center on exam day.

SUBJECT MATTER FOR PART 2

Below, we have provided The IIA's abbreviated CIA Exam Syllabus for Part 2. This syllabus is for the revised CIA exam that will be offered beginning January 1, 2019. The percentage coverage of each topic is indicated to its right. We adjust the content of our materials to any changes in The IIA's CIA Exam Syllabus.

Part 2: Practice of Internal Auditing

I.	Managing the Internal Audit Activity	20%
II.	Planning the Engagement	20%
III.	Performing the Engagement	40%
IV.	Communicating Engagement Results and Monitoring Progress	20%

Appendix B contains the CIA Exam Syllabus in its entirety as well as cross-references to the subunits in our text where topics are covered. Remember that we have studied the syllabus in developing our CIA Review materials. Accordingly, you do not need to spend time with Appendix B. Rather, it should give you confidence that Gleim CIA Review is the best and most comprehensive review course available to help you PASS the CIA exam.

The IIA has reported concerns from Part 2 candidates that Part 2 has tested topics that should be tested on Part 3 of the exam. The IIA has clarified that while a question in one part of the exam may appear to be testing a topic found in another part of the exam, the question is not testing those concepts. Rather, it is testing a candidate's understanding and interpretation of a concept appropriate to the part using an industry-related scenario.

The takeaway is that candidates should read each question carefully and focus on the concepts in Part 2 and how the examples relate to these concepts.

NONDISCLOSED EXAM

As part of The IIA's nondisclosure policy and to prove each candidate's willingness to adhere to this policy, a Nondisclosure Agreement and General Terms of Use must be accepted by each candidate before each part is taken. This statement is reproduced here to remind all CIA candidates about The IIA's strict policy of nondisclosure, which Gleim consistently supports and upholds.

I agree to comply with and be bound by The IIA's rules, including this nondisclosure agreement and general terms of use. I understand that The IIA's exam is confidential and secure, protected by civil and criminal laws of the United States and elsewhere. This exam is confidential and is protected by copyright law.

I have not accessed live questions that might appear on my exam. I agree not to discuss the content of the exam with anyone.

I will not record, copy, disclose, publish, or reproduce any exam questions or answers, in whole or in part, in any form or by any means before, during, or after I take an exam, including orally; in writing; in any internet chat room, message board, or forum; by SMS or text; or otherwise.

I have read, understand, and agree to the terms and conditions set forth in The IIA's Certification Candidate Handbook including fees, policies, and score invalidations for misconduct, irregularities, or breaches in The IIA's Code of Ethics.

I agree that The IIA has the right to withhold or invalidate any exam score when, in The IIA's judgement, there is a good faith basis to question the validity of a score for any reason.

I understand that if I do not agree to this nondisclosure agreement and these conditions, I will not be permitted to take the exam, and I will forfeit my exam fee.

THE IIA'S REQUIREMENTS FOR CIA DESIGNATIONS

The CIA designation is granted only by The IIA. Candidates must complete the following steps to become a CIA®:

1. Complete the appropriate certification application form and register for the part(s) you are going to take. Check the CIA blog at www.gleim.com/CIAblog for more information on the application and registration process. The CIA Review course provides a useful checklist to help you keep track of your progress and organize what you need for exam day.
2. Pass all three parts of the CIA exam within 4 years of application approval.
3. Fulfill or expect to fulfill the education and experience requirements (see the free Gleim *CIA Exam Guide*).
4. Provide a character reference proving you are of good moral character.
5. Comply with The IIA's Code of Ethics.

ELIGIBILITY PERIOD

Credits for parts passed can be retained as long as the requirements are fulfilled. However, candidates must complete the program certification process within 4 years of application approval. Candidates should note that this time period begins with application approval and not when they pass the first part. If a candidate has not completed the certification process within 4 years, all fees and exam parts will be forfeited.

Eligibility Extension: Candidates who have not successfully completed their exam(s), or who have been accepted into the program but have not taken their exam(s), have the opportunity to extend their program eligibility by 12 months. To take advantage of The IIA's one-time Certification Candidate Program Extension, candidates must pay a set fee per applicant and apply through the Candidate Management System.

Transition Information: Candidates who passed one or two parts of the exam prior to 2019 and still need to pass one or two parts will not lose credit for the part(s) already passed. Credit for any part(s) passed in the pre-2019 version of the exam remains valid for the 4-year eligibility window that begins with the application date.

MAINTAINING YOUR CIA DESIGNATION

After certification, CIAs are required to maintain and update their knowledge and skills. Practicing CIAs must complete and report 40 hours of Continuing Professional Education (CPE)–including 2 hours of ethics training–every year. The reporting deadline is December 31. Complete your CPE Reporting Form through the online Certification Candidate Management System. Processing fees vary based on location, membership status, and the method you use to report. Contact Gleim for all of your CPE needs at www.gleim.com/cpe.

GLEIM CIA REVIEW WITH SmartAdapt

Gleim CIA Review features the most comprehensive coverage of exam content and employs the most efficient learning techniques to help you study smarter and most effectively. The Gleim CIA Review System is powered by SmartAdapt technology, an innovative platform that continually zeros in on areas you should focus on when you move through the following steps for optimized CIA review:

Step 1:

Complete a Diagnostic Quiz. Your quiz results set a baseline that our SmartAdapt technology will use to create a custom learning track.

Step 2:

Solidify your knowledge by studying the suggested Knowledge Transfer Outline(s) or watching the suggested Gleim Instruct video(s).

Step 3:

Focus on weak areas and perfect your question-answering techniques by taking the adaptive quizzes that SmartAdapt directs you to.

Final Review:

After completing all study units, take the Exam Rehearsal. Then, SmartAdapt will walk you through a Final Review based on your results.

To facilitate your studies, the Gleim Premium CIA Review System uses the most comprehensive test bank of CIA exam questions on the market. Our system's content and presentation precisely mimic the whole exam environment so you feel completely at ease on test day.

GLEIM KNOWLEDGE TRANSFER OUTLINES

This edition of the Gleim *CIA Review* books has the following features to make studying easier:

1. **Examples:** We use illustrative examples, set off in shaded, bordered boxes, to make the concepts more relatable.

EXAMPLE

After gathering evidence during an audit, the auditor decides to increase the assessed control risk from the level originally planned. To achieve the same overall audit risk as originally planned, the auditor should decrease the assessed detection risk.

Audit risk is a function of inherent risk, control risk, and detection risk. The only risk the auditor directly controls is detection risk. Detection risk has an inverse relationship with control risk. Accordingly, if the auditor chooses to increase the assessed control risk, the assessed detection risk should be decreased to maintain the same overall audit risk.

---

2. **Gleim Success Tips:** These tips supplement the core exam material by suggesting how certain topics might be presented on the exam or how you should prepare for an issue.

An internal audit activity can add value to its organization by performing many types of engagements. CIA candidates must know not only the requirements of these engagements but also when and where to perform each kind of engagement.

---

3. **Guidance Designations:** In an effort to help CIA candidates better grasp The IIA authoritative literature, we have come up with visual indicators to help candidates easily identify each type of guidance.

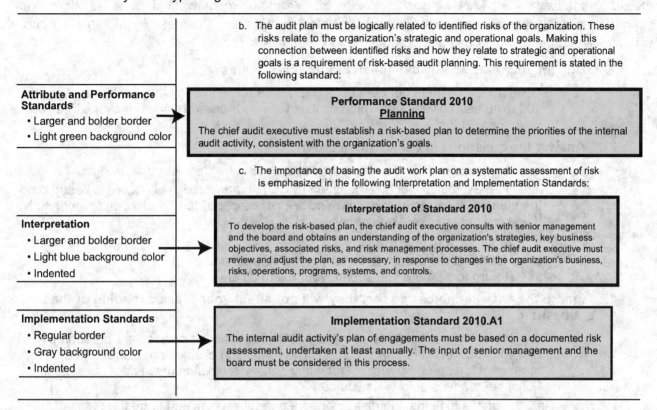

Attribute and Performance Standards
- Larger and bolder border
- Light green background color

b. The audit plan must be logically related to identified risks of the organization. These risks relate to the organization's strategic and operational goals. Making this connection between identified risks and how they relate to strategic and operational goals is a requirement of risk-based audit planning. This requirement is stated in the following standard:

> **Performance Standard 2010**
> **Planning**
>
> The chief audit executive must establish a risk-based plan to determine the priorities of the internal audit activity, consistent with the organization's goals.

c. The importance of basing the audit work plan on a systematic assessment of risk is emphasized in the following Interpretation and Implementation Standards:

Interpretation
- Larger and bolder border
- Light blue background color
- Indented

> **Interpretation of Standard 2010**
>
> To develop the risk-based plan, the chief audit executive consults with senior management and the board and obtains an understanding of the organization's strategies, key business objectives, associated risks, and risk management processes. The chief audit executive must review and adjust the plan, as necessary, in response to changes in the organization's business, risks, operations, programs, systems, and controls.

Implementation Standards
- Regular border
- Gray background color
- Indented

> **Implementation Standard 2010.A1**
>
> The internal audit activity's plan of engagements must be based on a documented risk assessment, undertaken at least annually. The input of senior management and the board must be considered in this process.

4. **Memory Aids:** We offer mnemonic devices to help you remember important concepts.

    The Seven Seas (7 Cs) is a useful memory aid. Good writing is

    1) Clear.
    2) Correct (accurate and objective).
    3) Concise.
    4) Consistent.
    5) Constructive.
    6) Coherent.
    7) Complete and timely.

TIME-BUDGETING AND QUESTION-ANSWERING TECHNIQUES FOR THE EXAM

Having a solid multiple-choice answer technique will help you maximize your score on each part of the CIA exam. Remember, knowing how to take the exam and how to answer individual questions is as important as studying/reviewing the subject matter tested on the exam. Competency in both will reduce your stress and the number of surprises you experience on exam day.

1. **Budget your time so you can finish before time expires.**

   - Spend about 1 minute per question. This would result in completing 100 questions in 100 minutes to give you 20 minutes to review your answers and questions that you have marked.

2. **Answer the questions in consecutive order.**

   - Do **not** agonize over any one item or question. Stay within your time budget.
   - Never leave a multiple-choice question (MCQ) unanswered. Your score is based on the number of correct responses. You will not be penalized for answering incorrectly. If you are unsure about a question,

      - Make an educated guess,
      - Mark it for review at the bottom of the screen, and
      - Return to it before you submit your exam as time allows.

3. **Ignore the answer choices so that they will not affect your precise reading of the question.**

   - Only one answer option is best. In the MCQs, four answer choices are presented, and you know one of them is correct. The remaining choices are distractors and are meant to appear correct at first glance. *They are called distractors for a reason.* Eliminate them as quickly as you can.
   - In computational items, the distractors are carefully calculated to be the result of common mistakes. Be careful and double-check your computations if time permits.

4. **Read the question carefully to discover exactly what is being asked.**

   - Focusing on what is required allows you to

      - Reject extraneous information
      - Concentrate on relevant facts
      - Proceed directly to determining the best answer

   - Be careful! The requirement may be an **exception** that features a negative word.

5. **Decide the correct answer before looking at the answer choices.**

6. **Read the answer choices, paying attention to small details.**

   - Even if an answer choice appears to be correct, do not skip the remaining answer choices. Each choice requires consideration because you are looking for the best answer provided.
   - Tip: Treat each answer choice like a true/false question as you analyze it.

7. **Click on the best answer.**

   - You have a 25% chance of answering the question correctly by guessing blindly, but you can improve your odds with an educated guess.
   - For many MCQs, you can eliminate two answer choices with minimal effort and increase your educated guess to a 50/50 proposition.

      - Rule out answers that you think are incorrect.
      - Speculate what The IIA is looking for and/or why the question is being asked.
      - Select the best answer or guess between equally appealing answers. Your first guess is usually the most intuitive.

LEARNING FROM YOUR MISTAKES

Learning from questions you answer incorrectly is very important. Each question you answer incorrectly is an **opportunity** to avoid missing actual test questions on your CIA exam. Thus, you should carefully study the answer explanations provided until you understand why the original answer you chose is wrong, as well as why the correct answer indicated is correct. This study technique is clearly the difference between passing and failing for many CIA candidates.

Also, you **must** determine why you answered questions incorrectly and learn how to avoid the same error in the future. Reasons for missing questions include

1. Misreading the requirement (stem)
2. Not understanding what is required
3. Making a math error
4. Applying the wrong rule or concept
5. Being distracted by one or more of the answers
6. Incorrectly eliminating answers from consideration
7. Not having any knowledge of the topic tested
8. Employing bad intuition when guessing

It is also important to verify that you answered correctly for the right reasons. Otherwise, if the material is tested on the CIA exam in a different manner, you may not answer it correctly.

HOW TO BE IN CONTROL WHILE TAKING THE EXAM

You have to be in control to be successful during exam preparation and execution. Control can also contribute greatly to your personal and other professional goals. Control is a process whereby you

1. Develop expectations, standards, budgets, and plans
2. Undertake activity, production, study, and learning
3. Measure the activity, production, output, and knowledge
4. Compare actual activity with expected and budgeted activity
5. Modify the activity, behavior, or study to better achieve the desired outcome
6. Revise expectations and standards in light of actual experience
7. Continue the process or restart the process in the future

Exercising control will ultimately develop the confidence you need to outperform most other CIA candidates and PASS the CIA exam! Obtain our *CIA Exam Guide* for a more detailed discussion of control and other exam tactics.

IF YOU HAVE QUESTIONS ABOUT GLEIM MATERIALS

Gleim has an efficient and effective way for candidates who have purchased the Premium CIA Review System to submit an inquiry and receive a response regarding Gleim materials directly through their course. This system also allows you to view your Q&A session in your Gleim Personal Classroom.

Questions regarding the **information in this introduction and/or the *CIA Exam Guide* (study suggestions, studying plans, exam specifics)** should be emailed to personalcounselor@gleim.com.

Questions concerning **orders, prices, shipments, or payments** should be sent via email to customerservice@gleim.com and will be promptly handled by our competent and courteous customer service staff.

For **technical support**, you may use our automated technical support service at www.gleim.com/support, email us at support@gleim.com, or call us at (800) 874-5346.

FEEDBACK

Please fill out our online feedback form (www.gleim.com/feedbackCIA2) immediately after you take the CIA exam so we can adapt to changes in the exam. Our approach has been approved by The IIA.

GLEIM CIA REVIEW

WE MAKE IT EASIER TO KEEP YOUR CIA MATERIALS CURRENT.

gleim.com/**CIAupdate**

Updates are available until the next edition is released.

STUDY UNIT ONE
INTERNAL AUDIT OPERATIONS

(12 pages of outline)

This study unit is the first of four covering **Domain I: Managing the Internal Audit Activity** from The IIA's CIA Exam Syllabus. This domain makes up 20% of Part 2 of the CIA exam and is tested at the **basic** and **proficient** cognitive levels. The relevant portion of the syllabus is highlighted below. (The complete syllabus is in Appendix B.)

	Managing the Internal Audit Activity (20%)		
	1. Internal Audit Operations		
	A	**Describe policies and procedures for the planning, organizing, directing, and monitoring of internal audit operations**	**Basic**
	B	**Interpret administrative activities (budgeting, resourcing, recruiting, staffing, etc.) of the internal audit activity**	**Basic**
	2. Establishing a Risk-based Internal Audit Plan		
	A	Identify sources of potential engagements (audit universe, audit cycle requirements, management requests, regulatory mandates, relevant market and industry trends, emerging issues, etc.)	Basic
	B	Identify a risk management framework to assess risks and prioritize audit engagements based on the results of a risk assessment	Basic
I	C	Interpret the types of assurance engagements (risk and control assessments, audits of third parties and contract compliance, security and privacy, performance and quality audits, key performance indicators, operational audits, financial and regulatory compliance audits)	Proficient
	D	Interpret the types of consulting engagements (training, system design, system development, due diligence, privacy, benchmarking, internal control assessment, process mapping, etc.) designed to provide advice and insight	Proficient
	E	**Describe coordination of internal audit efforts with the external auditor, regulatory oversight bodies, and other internal assurance functions, and potential reliance on other assurance providers**	**Basic**
	3. Communicating and Reporting to Senior Management and the Board		
	A	Recognize that the chief audit executive communicates the annual audit plan to senior management and the board and seeks the board's approval	Basic
	B	Identify significant risk exposures and control and governance issues for the chief audit executive to report to the board	Basic
	C	Recognize that the chief audit executive reports on the overall effectiveness of the organization's internal control and risk management processes to senior management and the board	Basic
	D	Recognize internal audit key performance indicators that the chief audit executive communicates to senior management and the board periodically	Basic

1.1 INTRODUCTION TO INTERNAL AUDITING

> ### Performance Standard 2100
> ### <u>Nature of Work</u>
>
> The internal audit activity must evaluate and contribute to the improvement of the organization's governance, risk management, and control processes using a systematic, disciplined, and risk-based approach. Internal audit credibility and value are enhanced when auditors are proactive and their evaluations offer new insights and consider future impact.

1. **Nature of Work**

   a. According to The IIA's Definition of Internal Auditing, the internal audit activity "helps an organization accomplish its objectives by bringing a systematic, disciplined approach to evaluate and improve the effectiveness of governance, risk management, and control processes."

      1) These processes are closely related. The IIA Glossary (in Appendix A) defines them as follows:

         a) **Governance** – "The combination of processes and structures implemented by the board to inform, direct, manage, and monitor the activities of the organization toward the achievement of its objectives."

         b) **Risk management** – "A process to identify, assess, manage, and control potential events or situations to provide reasonable assurance regarding the achievement of the organization's objectives."

         c) **Control** – "Any action taken by management, the board, and other parties to manage risk and increase the likelihood that established objectives and goals will be achieved. Management plans, organizes, and directs the performance of sufficient actions to provide reasonable assurance that objectives and goals will be achieved."

            i) **Control processes** – "The policies, procedures (both manual and automated), and activities that are part of a control framework, designed and operated to ensure that risks are contained within the level that an organization is willing to accept."

   b. According to IG 2100, *Nature of Work*, an understanding of the above-mentioned processes is necessary. The chief audit executive (CAE) then interviews the board and senior management about the responsibilities of each stakeholder for these processes.

      1) Ordinarily, the board is responsible for guiding governance processes, and senior management is responsible for leading risk management and control processes.

   c. An understanding of the business also is necessary, and established frameworks may be used in the auditors' evaluations.

      1) To acquire this understanding, the CAE will ordinarily review the organization's mission, strategic plan, key objectives, related risks and controls, and the minutes of the board.

   d. After discussions with the board and senior management, the CAE may document in the internal audit charter the roles and responsibilities of the board, senior management, and the internal audit activity.

   e. When determining the strategy for assessing governance, risk management, and control, the CAE typically considers (1) the maturity of these processes, (2) the seniority of the persons responsible, and (3) the organizational culture.

f.   Internal auditors may use their knowledge, experience, and best practices to provide (1) observations of weaknesses and (2) recommendations.

   1)   **Compliance** is defined in The IIA Glossary as "adherence to policies, plans, procedures, laws, regulations, contracts, or other requirements."

      a)   The internal audit activity must evaluate the risks involved in governance, operations, and information systems that relate to compliance with laws, regulations, policies, procedures, and contracts. The internal audit activity also must evaluate the controls regarding compliance.

2.   **Reasonable Assurance**

   a.   Governance, risk management, and control processes are **adequate** if management has planned and designed them to provide reasonable assurance of achieving the organization's objectives efficiently and economically.

      1)   **Efficient** performance accomplishes objectives in an accurate, timely, and economical fashion. **Economical** performance accomplishes objectives with minimal use of resources (i.e., cost) proportionate to the risk exposure.

      2)   **Reasonable assurance** is provided if the most cost-effective measures are taken in the design and implementation of controls to reduce risks and restrict expected deviations to a tolerable level.

3.   **Basic Types of Internal Audit Engagements**

   a.   The essential strategic function of the internal audit activity is to provide assurance services and consulting services. Thus, the Definition of Internal Auditing describes internal auditing as "an independent, objective assurance and consulting activity."

   b.   Separate **Implementation Standards** have been issued for assurance services and consulting services. These services are defined in The IIA Glossary as follows:

      1)   **Assurance services** – "An objective examination of evidence for the purpose of providing an independent assessment on governance, risk management, and control processes for the organization. Examples may include financial, performance, compliance, system security, and due diligence engagements."

      2)   **Consulting services** – "Advisory and related client service activities, the nature and scope of which are agreed with the client, are intended to add value and improve an organization's governance, risk management, and control processes without the internal auditor assuming management responsibility. Examples include counsel, advice, facilitation, and training."

4.   **Reporting**

   a.   Reporting to senior management and the board provides assurance about

      1)   Governance,
      2)   Risk management, and
      3)   Control.

   b.   Periodic reports also are made on the internal audit's purpose, authority, responsibility, and performance.

   c.   Reporting to senior management and the board is covered in more detail in Study Unit 4, Subunit 3.

Stop and review! You have completed the outline for this subunit. Study multiple-choice questions 1 through 4 on page 21.

1.2 INTERNAL AUDIT ADMINISTRATIVE ACTIVITIES

1.   **Overview**

a.   The chief audit executive (CAE) is responsible for management of internal audit activity resources in a manner that ensures fulfillment of its responsibilities. Like any well-managed department, the internal audit activity should operate effectively and efficiently. This can be accomplished through proper planning, which includes budgeting and human resources management.

Performance Standard 2000
Managing the Internal Audit Activity

The chief audit executive must effectively manage the internal audit activity to ensure it adds value to the organization.

Interpretation of Standard 2000

The internal audit activity is effectively managed when:

- It achieves the purpose and responsibility included in the internal audit charter.
- It conforms with the *Standards.*
- Its individual members conform with the Code of Ethics and the *Standards.*
- It considers trends and emerging issues that could impact the organization.

The internal audit activity adds value to the organization and its stakeholders when it considers strategies, objectives, and risks; strives to offer ways to enhance governance, risk management, and control processes; and objectively provides relevant assurance.

---

b.   Management oversees the day-to-day operations of the internal audit activity, including the following administrative activities:

1)   Budgeting and management accounting

2)   Human resource administration, including personnel evaluations and compensation

3)   Internal communications and information flows

4)   Administration of the internal audit activity's policies and procedures

---

Performance Standard 2040
Policies and Procedures

The chief audit executive must establish policies and procedures to guide the internal audit activity.

---

2.   **Form, Content, and Review**

Interpretation of Standard 2040

The form and content of policies and procedures are dependent upon the size and structure of the internal audit activity and the complexity of its work.

---

a.   Further guidance is provided in IG 2040, *Policies and Procedures.*

1)   A large, **mature** internal audit activity may include policies and procedures in a formal operations **manual**. If the activity is smaller or less mature, policies and procedures may reside in separate documents or an audit management software program.

2) The following **content** generally is included in an operations manual or other separate documents:

a) Policies on

   i) Purposes and responsibilities of the internal audit activity

   ii) Compliance with mandatory guidance

   iii) Independence of the internal audit activity and objectivity of internal auditors

   iv) Ethics requirements

   v) Maintaining the confidentiality of information

   vi) Retention of internal audit records

b) Procedures for

   i) Drafting the audit plan based on the risk assessment

   ii) Drafting plans and work programs for specific engagements

   iii) Performance and documentation of engagements

   iv) Communicating results of engagements

   v) Monitoring and follow-up

c) Guidance on the quality assurance and improvement programs

d) Management of the internal audit activity related to

   i) Professional training and certification

   ii) Continuing professional education

   iii) Evaluations of auditors

3) "Internal audit policies and procedures should be **reviewed** periodically, either by the CAE or an internal audit manager assigned to monitor internal audit processes and emerging issues."

3. **Budgeting**

a. The CAE is responsible for creating the operating and financial budget. Generally, the CAE, audit managers, and the internal audit activity work together to develop the budget annually. The budget is then submitted to management and the board for their review and approval.

4. **Human Resources**

a. The skill set and knowledge of the internal audit activity are essential to its ability to help the organization achieve its objectives. According to *Internal Auditing: Assurance & Consulting Services* (Redding, et al), "The CAE is responsible for hiring associates to fill the organizational structure of the internal audit function in a way that maximizes efficiency, effectively provides the necessary skill base, and makes good use of the financial budget."

b. Internal auditors should be qualified and competent. Because the selection of a superior staff is dependent on the ability to evaluate applicants, selection criteria must be well-developed.

1) Appropriate questions and forms should be prepared in advance to evaluate, among other things, the applicant's (a) technical qualifications, (b) educational background, (c) personal appearance, (d) ability to communicate, (e) maturity, (f) persuasiveness, (g) self-confidence, (h) intelligence, (i) motivation, and (j) potential to contribute to the organization.

c. Internal auditors need a diverse set of skills to perform their jobs effectively. These skills are not always apparent in a standard resumé. Developing effective interviewing techniques will ensure that the internal audit function acquires the proper set of skills, capabilities, and technical knowledge needed to accomplish its goals.

    d.   Effective interviewing methods are structured interviews and behavioral interviews.

        1)   **Structured interviews** are designed to eliminate individual bias. These interviews use a set of job-related questions with standardized answers, which then are scored by a committee of three to six members. According to *Management* (Kreitner & Cassidy, 12th edition), interviewers can use four general types of questions:

            a)   Situational – "What would you do if you saw two people arguing loudly in the work area?"

            b)   Job knowledge – "Do you know how to do an Internet search?"

            c)   Job sample simulation – "Can you show us how to compose and send an e-mail message?"

            d)   Worker requirements – "Are you able to spend 25 percent of your time on the road?"

        2)   **Behavioral interviews** determine how candidates handled past situations. Past performance is generally indicative of future performance.

Stop and review! You have completed the outline for this subunit. Study multiple-choice questions 5 through 7 on page 22.

1.3 STAKEHOLDER RELATIONSHIPS

    1.   **Stakeholder Relationships**

        a.   For internal auditors to be effective, *Sawyer's Guide for Internal Auditors*, 6th edition, states that they must build and maintain strong constructive relationships with managers and other stakeholders within the organization.

        b.   These relationships require conscious ongoing focus to ensure that risks are appropriately identified and evaluated to best meet the needs of the organization.

        c.   Internal auditors have a responsibility to work together with external auditors and other stakeholders to facilitate work efforts and compliance with regulators.

        d.   Key stakeholders include the board of directors, audit committees, management, external auditors, and regulators.

    2.   **The Board and the Audit Committee**

        a.   For the internal audit activity to achieve organizational independence, the chief audit executive (CAE) must have direct and unrestricted access to senior management and the board. Accordingly, the CAE should report administratively to senior management and functionally to the board.

        1)   The IIA defines a **board**, in part, as "[t]he highest level governing body . . . charged with the responsibility to direct and/or oversee the organization's activities and hold senior management accountable."

        b.   The **audit committee** is a subunit of the board of directors. However, not every member of the board is necessarily qualified to serve on the audit committee.

        1)   Some statutes have imposed the following significant restrictions on the membership of the audit committee:

            a)   No member may be an employee of the organization except in his or her capacity as a board member.

            b)   At least one member must be a financial expert.

        2)   Many stock exchanges require that all listed organizations have an audit committee.

        c.   To avoid creating conflict between the CEO and the audit committee, the CAE should request board establishment of policies covering the internal audit activity's relationships with the audit committee.

3. **Role of the Audit Committee**

    a.   The most important function of the audit committee is to promote the independence of the internal and external auditors by protecting them from management's influence.

    b.   The following are other functions of the audit committee regarding the internal audit activity:

        1)   Selecting or removing the CAE and setting his or her compensation

        2)   Approving the internal audit charter

        3)   Reviewing and approving the internal audit activity's work plan

        4)   Ensuring that the internal audit activity is allocated sufficient resources

        5)   Resolving disputes between the internal audit activity and management

        6)   Communicating with the CAE, who attends all audit committee meetings

        7)   Reviewing the internal audit activity's work product (e.g., interim and final engagement communications)

        8)   Ensuring that engagement results are given due consideration

        9)   Overseeing appropriate corrective action for deficiencies noted by the internal audit activity

        10)   Making appropriate inquiries of management and the CAE to determine whether audit scope or budgetary limitations impede the ability of the internal audit activity to meet its responsibilities

    c.   The following are other functions of the audit committee regarding the external auditor:

        1)   Selecting the external auditing firm and negotiating its fee

        2)   Overseeing and reviewing the work of the external auditor

        3)   Resolving disputes between the external auditor and management

        4)   Reviewing the external auditor's internal control and audit reports

4. **Relationships with Management**

    a.   According to *Sawyer's Guide for Internal Auditors*, 6th edition, internal auditors are responsible for performing their mission, maintaining their objectivity, and ensuring the internal audit activity's independence. They also should develop and maintain good working relationships with management.

    b.   Good relationships are developed by communicating effectively, resolving conflicts constructively, and using participative auditing methods.

        1)   **Participative auditing** is a collaboration between the internal auditor and management during the auditing process. The objective is to minimize conflict and build a shared interest in the engagement. People are more likely to accept changes if they have participated in the decisions and in the methods used to implement changes.

        2)   However, internal auditors are ultimately responsible for guiding and directing the audit because the responsibility for the final audit opinion is theirs.

Stop and review! You have completed the outline for this subunit. Study multiple-choice questions 8 through 10 beginning on page 22.

1.4 INTERNAL AUDIT RESOURCE REQUIREMENTS

Performance Standard 2030
Resource Management

The chief audit executive must ensure that internal audit resources are appropriate, sufficient, and effectively deployed to achieve the approved plan.

Interpretation of Standard 2030

Appropriate refers to the mix of knowledge, skills, and other competencies needed to perform the plan. Sufficient refers to the quantity of resources needed to accomplish the plan. Resources are effectively deployed when they are used in a way that optimizes the achievement of the approved plan.

---

1. **Managing Internal Audit Resources**

   a. The CAE is primarily responsible for the sufficiency and management of resources, including communication of needs and status to senior management and the board. These parties ultimately must ensure the adequacy of resources.

      1) **Resources** may include employees, service providers, financial support, and IT-based audit methods. To determine the sufficiency of resource allocation, the CAE considers relevant factors, including

         a) Communications received from management and the board;
         b) Information about ongoing and new engagements;
         c) Consequences of not completing an engagement on time; and
         d) Knowledge, skills, and competencies of the internal audit staff.

   b. The **competencies** of the internal audit staff should be appropriate for the planned activities. The CAE may conduct a documented **skills assessment** based on the needs identified in the risk assessment and audit plan.

      1) A job description summarizes the duties and qualifications required for a job. Properly formulated job descriptions provide a basis for identifying job qualifications, such as training and experience. They also facilitate recruiting the appropriate internal audit staff with the necessary attributes for the planned activities.

   c. Resources need to be sufficient for audit activities to be performed in accordance with the expectations of senior management and the board. **Resource planning** considers

      1) The audit universe,
      2) Relevant risk levels,
      3) The internal audit plan,
      4) Coverage expectations, and
      5) An estimate of unanticipated activities.

   d. Resources must be effectively **deployed** by assigning qualified auditors and developing an appropriate resourcing approach and organizational structure.

    e.   Some organizations maintain field offices to improve the internal audit function's efficiency and effectiveness.

        1)   The advantages of field offices compared with sending internal auditors from the home office include

            a)   Reduced travel time and expense,

            b)   Improved service in the operating locations served by the field offices,

            c)   Better morale of internal auditors as a result of increased authority, and

            d)   The possibility of employing persons who do not wish to travel.

    f.   The CAE considers succession planning, staff evaluation and development, and other human resource disciplines.

        1)   The CAE also addresses **resourcing needs**, including whether those skills are present.

        2)   Other ways to meet needs include external service providers, specialized consultants, or other employees of the organization.

    g.   The CAE's ongoing communications with senior management and the board include periodic summaries of resource status and adequacy, e.g., the effect of temporary vacancies and comparison of resources with the audit plan.

    h.   When selecting the appropriate audit staff, the CAE must consider these factors:

        1)   Complexity of the engagement

        2)   Experience levels of the auditors

        3)   Training needs of the auditors

        4)   Available resources

2. **Outsourcing the Internal Audit Activity**

    a.   An organization's governing body may decide that an external service provider is the most effective means of obtaining internal audit services.

        1)   In such cases, the following Performance Standard requires those performing internal audit services to remind the organization of the ultimate responsibility for maintaining an effective internal audit activity.

Performance Standard 2070
External Service Provider and Organizational Responsibility for Internal Auditing

When an external service provider serves as the internal audit activity, the provider must make the organization aware that the organization has the responsibility for maintaining an effective internal audit activity.

---

        2)   Accordingly, oversight of and responsibility for the internal audit activity must not be outsourced.

Interpretation of Standard 2070

This responsibility is demonstrated through the quality assurance and improvement program which assesses conformance with the Code of Ethics and the *Standards*.

Stop and review! You have completed the outline for this subunit. Study multiple-choice questions 11 through 16 beginning on page 23.

1.5 COORDINATION

1. **The Three Lines of Defense**

   a. According to The IIA's Position Paper, The Three Lines of Defense in Effective Risk Management and Control, the Three Lines of Defense model provides a simple and effective way to enhance communications on risk management and control by clarifying how specific duties should be assigned and coordinated within the organization.

   b. The **board of directors** and **senior management** are the primary stakeholders served by the lines, and they are the parties best positioned to help ensure that the Three Lines of Defense model is reflected in the organization's risk management and control processes.

   c. Further details are also provided in The IIA's Position Paper:

      1) Operational management

         a) Provides the **first line of defense** (functions that own and manage risk) for effective management of risk and control

         b) Develops and implements control and risk management processes

         c) Implements corrective actions to address process and control deficiencies

      2) Business-enabling functions

         a) Provide the **second line of defense** (functions that oversee risks) for effective management of risk and control

         b) Support the entity through specialized skills and typically may include various risk management, compliance, inspection, and financial control functions

         c) Are typically responsible for the ongoing monitoring of control and risk

      3) Internal auditors

         a) Provide the **third line of defense** (functions that provide independent assurance) for effective management of risk and control

         b) Provide assurance on the effectiveness of governance, risk management, and internal controls, including the manner in which the first and second lines of defense achieve risk management and control objectives

2. **Coordinating the Work of the Internal Audit Activity with Other Providers**

Performance Standard 2050
Coordination and Reliance

The chief audit executive should share information, coordinate activities, and consider relying upon the work of other internal and external assurance and consulting service providers to ensure proper coverage and minimize duplication of efforts.

Interpretation of Standard 2050

In coordinating activities, the chief audit executive may rely on the work of other assurance and consulting service providers. A consistent process for the basis of reliance should be established, and the chief audit executive should consider the competency, objectivity, and due professional care of the assurance and consulting service providers. The chief audit executive should also have a clear understanding of the scope, objectives, and results of the work performed by other providers of assurance and consulting services. Where reliance is placed on the work of others, the chief audit executive is still accountable and responsible for ensuring adequate support for conclusions and opinions reached by the internal audit activity.

a.   Further guidance is provided in IG 2050, *Coordination and Reliance*:

1)   The CAE should share information, coordinate activities, and consider relying upon the work of other internal and external assurance and consulting providers to ensure proper coverage and minimize duplication of efforts (Perf. Std. 2050).

a)   Whether reporting administratively to the quality audit function or to senior management, the CAE should identify appropriate liaison activities with the quality audit function to ensure coordination of audit schedules and overall audit responsibilities.

i)   The quality audit standards proposed by the quality audit manager should comply with the applicable standards for internal auditing (i.e., the *Standards*).

ii) The internal audit activity as a whole, not each auditor individually, must be proficient in all necessary competencies (Attr. Std. 1210).

2)   Internal vs. External

a)   **Internal** providers may report to senior management or be part of senior management. Their activities may address such functions as "environmental, financial control, health and safety, IT security, legal, risk management, compliance, or quality assurance. These are often considered 'second line of defense' activities, according to The IIA's Three Lines of Defense model."

b)   **External** providers may report to senior management, external parties, or the CAE.

3)   Subject to the organization's confidentiality constraints, "the parties share the objectives, scope, and timing of upcoming reviews, assessments, and audits; the results of prior audits; and the possibility of relying on one another's work."

4)   Process and Methods of Coordinating Assurance Activities

a)   The **process** varies by organization. Smaller entities may have informal coordination. Large or regulated entities may have formal and complex coordination.

b)   **Methods** of Coordinating Assurance Coverage

i)   **Assurance mapping** (a) connects significant risk categories and sources of assurance and (b) assesses each category. The CAE then can determine whether assurance services sharing the results with other providers facilitates agreement on coordinating services to avoid duplication and maximize efficiency and effectiveness of coverage.

ii) In the **combined assurance model**, the internal audit activity coordinates activities with second line of defense activities, e.g., compliance, to minimize "the nature, frequency and redundancy of internal audit engagements."

5)   **Coordinating activities** include the following:

a)   Simultaneity of the nature, extent, and timing of scheduled work

b)   Mutual understanding of methods and vocabulary

c)   The parties' access to each other's programs, workpapers, and communications of results

d)   Reliance on others' work to avoid overlap

e)   Meeting to adjust the timing of scheduled work given results to date

6) Reliance on another service provider does not excuse the CAE from final responsibility for conclusions and opinions.

7) **Criteria** the CAE may consider in determining whether to rely on the work of another service provider include the following:

a) The objectivity, independence, competency, and due professional care of the provider relating to the relevant assurance or consulting service

b) The scope, objectives, and results of the service provider's work to evaluate the degree of reliance

c) Assessing the service provider's findings to determine whether they are reasonable and meet the information criteria in the *Standards*

d) The incremental effort required to obtain sufficient, reliable, relevant, and useful information as a basis for the degree of planned reliance

3. **Coordinating with Regulatory Oversight Bodies**

a. Businesses and not-for-profit organizations are subject to governmental regulation in many countries.

1) Below is a sample of typical subjects of regulation:

a) Labor relations
b) Occupational safety and health
c) Environmental protection
d) Consumer product safety
e) Business mergers and acquisitions
f) Securities issuance and trading
g) Trading of commodities

2) Local and regional governments may have their own regulatory bodies.

b. Particularly in larger organizations, entire departments or functions are established to monitor compliance with the regulations issued by these governmental bodies.

1) For example, broker-dealers in securities establish compliance departments to ensure that trades are executed according to the requirements of securities laws. Moreover, manufacturers have departments to monitor wage-and-hour compliance, workplace safety issues, and discharge of toxic wastes.

c. Among the responsibilities of the internal audit activity is the evaluation of the organization's compliance with applicable laws and regulations.

1) The internal audit activity coordinates its work with that of inspectors and other personnel from the appropriate governmental bodies and with personnel from internal assurance functions.

Stop and review! You have completed the outline for this subunit. Study multiple-choice questions 17 through 21 beginning on page 25.

QUESTIONS

1.1 Introduction to Internal Auditing

1. Internal auditing is an assurance and consulting activity. An example of an assurance service is a(n)

A. Advisory engagement.

B. Facilitation engagement.

C. Training engagement.

D. Compliance engagement.

Answer (D) is correct.
REQUIRED: The example of an assurance service.
DISCUSSION: According to The IIA Glossary, an assurance service is "an objective examination of evidence for the purpose of providing an independent assessment of governance, risk management, and control processes for the organization. Examples may include financial, performance, compliance, system security, and due diligence engagements."
Answer (A) is incorrect. An advisory engagement is a consulting service. Answer (B) is incorrect. A facilitation engagement is a consulting service. Answer (C) is incorrect. A training engagement is a consulting service.

2. Which of the following potentially are subject to the internal auditors' evaluations?

1. The human resources function.

2. The purchasing process.

3. The manufacturing and production database system.

A. 1 only.

B. 2 only.

C. 1, 2, and 3.

D. None of the answers are correct.

Answer (C) is correct.
REQUIRED: The scope of internal auditing's evaluations.
DISCUSSION: Internal auditing is an organizationally independent and individually objective assurance and consulting activity that adds value and improves operations. It evaluates and contributes to the improvement of the organization's governance, risk management, and control processes. When performing the assurance function, internal auditing evaluates the adequacy and effectiveness of controls. For example, it evaluates the effectiveness and efficiency of operations and programs.
Answer (A) is incorrect. Items 2 and 3 are subject to internal auditor evaluation. Answer (B) is incorrect. Items 1 and 3 are subject to internal auditor evaluation. Answer (D) is incorrect. All of the listed items are subject to internal auditor evaluation.

3. What is the most accurate term for the procedures used by the board to oversee activities performed to achieve organizational objectives?

A. Governance.

B. Control.

C. Risk management.

D. Monitoring.

Answer (A) is correct.
REQUIRED: The most accurate term for the means of providing oversight of processes administered by management.
DISCUSSION: Governance is the "combination of processes and structures implemented by the board to inform, direct, manage, and monitor the activities of the organization toward the achievement of its objectives" (The IIA Glossary).
Answer (B) is incorrect. Control is "any action taken by management, the board, and other parties to manage risk and increase the likelihood that established objectives and goals will be achieved. Management plans, organizes, and directs the performance of sufficient actions to provide reasonable assurance that objectives and goals will be achieved" (The IIA Glossary). Answer (C) is incorrect. Risk management is "a process to identify, assess, manage, and control potential events or situations to provide reasonable assurance regarding the achievement of the organization's objectives" (The IIA Glossary). Answer (D) is incorrect. Monitoring consists of actions taken by management and others to assess the quality of internal control performance over time. It is not currently defined in the *Standards* or The IIA Glossary.

4. A basic principle of governance is

A. Assessment of the governance process by an independent internal audit activity.

B. Holding the board, senior management, and the internal audit activity accountable for its effectiveness.

C. Exclusive use of external auditors to provide assurance about the governance process.

D. Separation of the governance process from promoting an ethical culture in the organization.

Answer (A) is correct.
REQUIRED: The basic principle of governance.
DISCUSSION: The internal audit activity must assess and make appropriate recommendations for improving the governance process (Perf. Std. 2110).
Answer (B) is incorrect. The internal audit activity is an assessor of the governance process. It is not accountable for that process. Answer (C) is incorrect. External parties and internal auditors may provide assurance about the governance process. Answer (D) is incorrect. The internal audit activity must assess and make appropriate recommendations for improving the governance process in its promotion of appropriate ethics and values within the organization.

1.2 Internal Audit Administrative Activities

5. Which of the following is most essential for guiding the internal audit staff?

A. Quality program assessments.

B. Position descriptions.

C. Performance appraisals.

D. Policies and procedures.

Answer (D) is correct.
REQUIRED: The item most essential for guiding the internal audit staff.
DISCUSSION: The chief audit executive must establish policies and procedures to guide the internal audit activity (Perf. Std. 2040).

6. The key factor in the success of an internal audit activity's human resources program is

A. An informal program for developing and counseling staff.

B. A compensation plan based on years of experience.

C. A well-developed set of selection criteria.

D. A program for recognizing the special interests of individual staff members.

Answer (C) is correct.
REQUIRED: The key factor in the success of an internal audit activity's human resources program.
DISCUSSION: Internal auditors should be qualified and competent. Because the selection of a superior staff is dependent on the ability to evaluate applicants, selection criteria must be well-developed. Appropriate questions and forms should be prepared in advance to evaluate, among other things, the applicant's technical qualifications, educational background, personal appearance, ability to communicate, maturity, persuasiveness, self-confidence, intelligence, motivation, and potential to contribute to the organization.
Answer (A) is incorrect. The human resources program should be formal. Answer (B) is incorrect. The quality of the human resources is more significant than compensation. Answer (D) is incorrect. The quality of the human resources is more significant than special interests of the staff.

7. Written policies and procedures relative to managing the internal audit activity should

A. Ensure compliance with its performance standards.

B. Give consideration to its structure and the complexity of the work performed.

C. Result in consistent job performance.

D. Prescribe the format and distribution of engagement communications and the classification of observations.

Answer (B) is correct.
REQUIRED: The correct statement about written policies and procedures relative to the internal audit department.
DISCUSSION: The form and content of policies and procedures are dependent upon the size and structure of the internal audit activity and the complexity of its work (Inter. Std. 2040).
Answer (A) is incorrect. No written policy or procedure can ensure compliance with standards. Answer (C) is incorrect. Consistent performance depends on various factors, especially adequate training and supervision. Answer (D) is incorrect. The format and distribution of engagement communications and the classification of observations may vary from engagement to engagement.

1.3 Stakeholder Relationships

8. An audit committee should be designed to enhance the independence of both the internal and external auditing functions and to insulate these functions from undue management pressures. Using this criterion, audit committees should be composed of

A. A rotating subcommittee of the board of directors or its equivalent.

B. Only members from the relevant outside regulatory agencies.

C. Members from all important constituencies, specifically including representatives from banking, labor, regulatory agencies, shareholders, and officers.

D. Only external members of the board of directors or its equivalent.

Answer (D) is correct.
REQUIRED: The most effective composition of an audit committee.
DISCUSSION: The audit committee of the board of directors should be composed entirely of outside directors. Outside directors are members of the board who are independent of internal management. Because the primary purpose of the audit committee is to promote the independence of the internal and external auditors from management, an audit committee composed of inside directors would be ineffective.
Answer (A) is incorrect. The audit committee is not required to be rotated periodically. Answer (B) is incorrect. Regulators ordinarily do not serve as directors. Answer (C) is incorrect. Officers are not outside directors.

9. Audit committees have been identified as a major factor in promoting the independence of both internal and external auditors. Which of the following is the most important limitation on the effectiveness of audit committees?

    A. Audit committees may be composed of independent directors. However, those directors may have close personal and professional friendships with management.

    B. Audit committee members are compensated by the organization and thus favor an owner's view.

    C. Audit committees devote most of their efforts to external audit concerns and do not pay much attention to the internal audit activity and the overall control environment.

    D. Audit committee members do not normally have degrees in the accounting or auditing fields.

Answer (A) is correct.
    REQUIRED: The most important limitation on the effectiveness of audit committees.
    DISCUSSION: The audit committee is a subcommittee made up of outside directors who are independent of management. Its purpose is to help keep external and internal auditors independent of management and to ensure that the directors are exercising due care. However, if independence is impaired by personal and professional friendships, the effectiveness of the audit committee may be limited.
    Answer (B) is incorrect. The compensation audit committee members receive is usually minimal. They should be independent and therefore not limited to an owner's perspective. Answer (C) is incorrect. Although audit committees are concerned with external audits, they also devote attention to the internal audit activity. Answer (D) is incorrect. Audit committee members do not need degrees in accounting or auditing to understand engagement communications.

10. The audit committee strengthens the control processes of an organization by

    A. Assigning the internal audit activity responsibility for interaction with governmental agencies.

    B. Using the chief audit executive as a major resource in selecting the external auditors.

    C. Following up on recommendations made by the chief audit executive.

    D. Approving internal audit activity policies.

Answer (C) is correct.
    REQUIRED: The way in which the audit committee strengthens control processes.
    DISCUSSION: Among the audit committee's functions are ensuring that engagement results are given due consideration and overseeing appropriate corrective action for deficiencies noted by the internal audit activity, which includes following up on recommendations by the CAE.

1.4 Internal Audit Resource Requirements

11. Johnny Hagert, Chief Audit Executive, is determining the sufficiency of his resource allocation. Mr. Hagert must consider all of the following **except**

    A. Communication received from management and the board.

    B. The audit universe.

    C. Knowledge of the internal audit staff.

    D. Consequences of not completing the engagement on time.

Answer (B) is correct.
    REQUIRED: The factor the CAE must consider when determining how to allocate resources.
    DISCUSSION: Sufficiency relates to the quantity of resources needed to accomplish the audit plan. The audit universe includes all possible audits within an organization. The audit plan only includes a portion of those audits.
    Answer (A) is incorrect. To determine the sufficiency of resource allocation, the CAE must consider all relevant factors, including (1) communications received from management and the board; (2) information about ongoing and new engagements; (3) consequences of not completing an engagement on time; and (4) knowledge, skills, and competencies of the internal audit staff. Answer (C) is incorrect. To determine the sufficiency of resource allocation, the CAE must consider all relevant factors, including (1) communications received from management and the board; (2) information about ongoing and new engagements; (3) consequences of not completing an engagement on time; and (4) knowledge, skills, and competencies of the internal audit staff. Answer (D) is incorrect. To determine the sufficiency of resource allocation, the CAE must consider all relevant factors, including (1) communications received from management and the board; (2) information about ongoing and new engagements; (3) consequences of not completing an engagement on time; and (4) knowledge, skills, and competencies of the internal audit staff.

12. Gator Financial Service is considering outsourcing its internal audit activity. Gator Financial Service

    A. Cannot outsource the activity because it will impair the effectiveness of the engagement.

    B. Can outsource the services as long as it places responsibility for maintaining effective internal controls in the hands of the external auditor.

    C. Must outsource all internal audit activity to maintain independence.

    D. Can outsource the services as long as Gator Financial Service continues to have the responsibility for maintaining effective internal controls.

Answer (D) is correct.
    REQUIRED: The true statement about outsourcing the internal audit activity.
    DISCUSSION: An organization's governing body may decide that an external service provider is the most effective means of obtaining internal audit services. In these cases, Performance Standard 2070 requires that the external audit service provider remind the organization that the responsibility for maintaining effective internal controls lies with the organization.
    Answer (A) is incorrect. An organization's governing body may decide that an external service provider is the most effective means of obtaining internal audit services. Answer (B) is incorrect. An organization's governing body may decide that an external service provider is the most effective means of obtaining internal audit services. In these cases, the external audit service provider must remind the organization that the responsibility for maintaining effective internal controls lies with the organization. Answer (C) is incorrect. The internal audit function is most often performed through internal sources and does not impair the independence of the engagement.

13. Which of the following parties is (are) primarily responsible for resource management in an internal auditing engagement?

1.   The chief audit executive
2.   Senior management
3.   The board of directors

    A. 1 and 2.

    B. 2 and 3.

    C. 1 only.

    D. 1 and 3.

Answer (C) is correct.
    REQUIRED: The party(ies) primarily responsible for resource management.
    DISCUSSION: The CAE is primarily responsible for the sufficiency and management of resources of the internal audit activity, including communication of needs and status to senior management and the board. These parties must ensure the adequacy of resources.
    Answer (A) is incorrect. Senior management is not primarily responsible for the sufficiency and management of resources of the internal audit activity. Senior management and the board must ensure the adequacy of resources. Answer (B) is incorrect. Senior management and the board of directors are not primarily responsible for the sufficiency and management of resources of the internal audit activity. These parties must ensure the adequacy of resources. Answer (D) is incorrect. The board of directors is not primarily responsible for the sufficiency and management of resources of the internal audit activity. Senior management and the board must ensure the adequacy of resources.

14. Which of the following statements about the chief audit executive's responsibilities for internal audit resources is most accurate?

    A. The CAE is responsible for ensuring that audit coverage is based on the skills of the internal audit activity.

    B. The CAE is responsible for presenting a detailed summary of audit resources to management.

    C. The CAE is responsible for the effective deployment of resources to achieve the approved audit plan.

    D. The CAE is responsible for administering the organization's compensation program.

Answer (C) is correct.
    REQUIRED: The true statement about the chief audit executive's responsibilities for internal audit resources.
    DISCUSSION: The CAE must ensure that internal audit resources are appropriate, sufficient, and effectively deployed to achieve the approved audit plan. This responsibility includes the effective communication of resource needs and reporting of status to senior management and the board.
    Answer (A) is incorrect. The CAE has responsibility for ensuring that the skills assessment is driven by the needs of the audit coverage, not by the capabilities already present in the internal audit activity. Answer (B) is incorrect. The CAE has responsibility for presenting a detailed summary of the status and adequacy of internal audit resources to the board. Answer (D) is incorrect. The human resources (personnel) department ordinarily is responsible for administering the organization's compensation program.

15. Internal audit resources should be appropriate, sufficient, and effectively deployed. Consequently,

    A. Resource planning should be limited to expected activities.

    B. The chief audit executive should perform a periodic skills assessment.

    C. Only members of the internal audit staff should perform internal audit activities.

    D. The chief audit executive ultimately must ensure the adequacy of resources.

Answer (B) is correct.
    REQUIRED: The true statement about internal audit resources.
    DISCUSSION: The skills, technical knowledge, and capabilities of the internal audit staff should be appropriate for the planned work. Thus, the chief audit executive should perform a periodic skills assessment based on the needs identified in the risk assessment and the audit plan.
    Answer (A) is incorrect. Resource planning considers (1) the audit universe, (2) relevant risks, (3) the internal audit plan, (4) coverage expectations, and (5) an estimate of unexpected activities. Answer (C) is incorrect. The CAE's consideration of resourcing needs and available resources should address whether needed skills are present. If not, other appropriate ways to meet needs include (1) external service providers, (2) specialized consultants, or (3) other employees of the organization. Answer (D) is incorrect. The CAE is primarily responsible for the sufficiency and management of internal audit resources, including communication of needs and status, to senior management and the board. These parties ultimately must ensure the adequacy of internal audit resources.

16. When determining the number and experience level of an internal audit staff to be assigned to an engagement, the chief audit executive should consider which of the following?

1. Complexity of the engagement.
2. Length of the engagement.
3. Available internal audit activity resources.
4. Lapsed time since the last engagement.

    A. 1 and 2 only.

    B. 2 and 3 only.

    C. 1 and 3 only.

    D. 1, 2, 3, and 4.

Answer (C) is correct.
    REQUIRED: The consideration in determining the number and experience level of an internal audit staff to be assigned to an engagement.
    DISCUSSION: The complexity of the engagement determines the experience and skills required of the assigned staff. Available resources also are a factor in a staffing decision.
    Answer (A) is incorrect. Length of the engagement is not a factor affecting engagement staffing. Answer (B) is incorrect. Length of the engagement is not a factor affecting engagement staffing. Answer (D) is incorrect. Length of the engagement is not a factor affecting engagement staffing. Lapsed time since the last engagement is a factor affecting engagement scheduling, not staffing.

1.5 Coordination

17. Exchange of engagement communications and management letters by internal and external auditors is

    A. Consistent with the coordination responsibilities of the chief audit executive.

    B. Not consistent with the independence guidelines of the *Standards*.

    C. A violation of the Code of Ethics.

    D. Not addressed by the *Standards*.

Answer (A) is correct.
    REQUIRED: The reason internal and external auditors exchange audit reports and management letters.
    DISCUSSION: Exchange of engagement communications and management letters is properly a component of coordination between internal and external audit.
    Answer (B) is incorrect. The standard independence guidelines are not relevant to this exchange between internal and external auditors. Answer (C) is incorrect. The exchange does not violate the Code of Ethics. Answer (D) is incorrect. The *Standards* address the coordination of internal and external auditing work.

18. Coordination of internal and external auditing can reduce the overall costs. Who is responsible for actual coordination of internal and external auditing efforts?

    A. The chief audit executive.

    B. The external auditor.

    C. The board.

    D. Management.

Answer (A) is correct.
    REQUIRED: The person responsible for coordinating internal and external audit efforts.
    DISCUSSION: Coordination of internal and external audit work is the responsibility of the CAE. The CAE obtains the support of the board to coordinate audit work effectively.
    Answer (B) is incorrect. The external auditor is an interested party but not one that has direct responsibility for coordinating internal and external auditing efforts. Answer (C) is incorrect. The board has oversight responsibility, but the CAE is responsible for the actual coordination of internal and external auditing work. Answer (D) is incorrect. Management is an interested party but not one that has direct responsibility for coordinating internal and external auditing efforts.

19. Which of the following are responsibilities of the chief audit executive (CAE)?

1. Coordinating activities with other providers of assurance and consulting services.
2. Understanding the work of external auditors.
3. Providing sufficient information to the external auditors to permit them to understand the internal auditors' work.

    A. 1 and 2 only.

    B. 2 and 3 only.

    C. 1 and 3 only.

    D. 1, 2, and 3.

Answer (D) is correct.
    REQUIRED: The responsibilities of the CAE.
    DISCUSSION: Organizations may use the work of external auditors to provide assurance related to activities within the scope of internal auditing. In these cases, the CAE takes the steps necessary to understand the work performed by the external auditors. Moreover, the external auditor may rely on the work of the internal audit activity in performing their work. In this case, the CAE needs to provide sufficient information to enable external auditors to understand the internal auditor's techniques, methods, and terminology to facilitate reliance by external auditors on work performed.
    Answer (A) is incorrect. Providing sufficient information to the external auditors to permit them to understand the internal auditors' work is a responsibility of the CAE when external auditors rely on the internal audit activity's work. Answer (B) is incorrect. Coordinating activities with other providers of assurance and consulting services is a responsibility of the CAE. Answer (C) is incorrect. Understanding the work of external auditors is necessary whenever external auditors provide assurance about matters within the scope of the internal audit activity.

20. Which of the following is responsible for coordination of internal and external audit work?

    A. The board.

    B. The chief audit executive.

    C. Internal auditors.

    D. External auditors.

Answer (B) is correct.
    REQUIRED: The individual(s) responsible for coordination of internal and external audit work.
    DISCUSSION: Oversight of the work of external auditors, including coordination with the internal audit activity, is the responsibility of the board. Coordination of internal and external audit work is the responsibility of the chief audit executive (CAE). The CAE obtains the support of the board to coordinate audit work effectively.
    Answer (A) is incorrect. The board oversees but is not actually responsible for the coordination. Answer (C) is incorrect. Internal auditors carry out the coordinated directions from the CAE. Answer (D) is incorrect. External auditors perform their work in coordination with information provided by the CAE.

21. Coordinating internal and external audit activity can increase efficiency by using which of the following?

1. Similar techniques
2. Similar methods
3. Similar terminology

    A. 1 only.

    B. 1 and 3 only.

    C. 1 and 2 only.

    D. 1, 2, and 3.

Answer (D) is correct.
    REQUIRED: The item(s) that will increase efficiency of audit activity.
    DISCUSSION: It may be efficient for internal and external auditors to use similar techniques, methods, and terminology to coordinate their work effectively and to rely on the work of one another.
    Answer (A) is incorrect. Similar methods and terminology also increase efficiency. Answer (B) is incorrect. Similar methods also increase efficiency. Answer (C) is incorrect. Similar terminology also increases efficiency.

Access the **Gleim CIA Premium Review System** featuring our SmartAdapt technology from your Gleim Personal Classroom to continue your studies. You will experience a personalized study environment with exam-emulating multiple-choice questions.

STUDY UNIT TWO
ASSURANCE AND COMPLIANCE ENGAGEMENTS

(22 pages of outline)

This study unit is the second of four covering **Domain I: Managing the Internal Audit Activity** from The IIA's CIA Exam Syllabus. This domain makes up 20% of Part 2 of the CIA exam and is tested at the **basic** and **proficient** cognitive levels. The relevant portion of the syllabus is highlighted below. (The complete syllabus is in Appendix B.)

		Managing the Internal Audit Activity (20%)	
		1. Internal Audit Operations	
	A	Describe policies and procedures for the planning, organizing, directing, and monitoring of internal audit operations	Basic
	B	Interpret administrative activities (budgeting, resourcing, recruiting, staffing, etc.) of the internal audit activity	Basic
		2. Establishing a Risk-based Internal Audit Plan	
	A	Identify sources of potential engagements (audit universe, audit cycle requirements, management requests, regulatory mandates, relevant market and industry trends, emerging issues, etc.)	Basic
	B	Identify a risk management framework to assess risks and prioritize audit engagements based on the results of a risk assessment	Basic
I	**C**	**Interpret the types of assurance engagements (risk and control assessments, audits of third parties and contract compliance, security and privacy, performance and quality audits, key performance indicators, operational audits, financial and regulatory compliance audits)**	**Proficient**
	D	Interpret the types of consulting engagements (training, system design, system development, due diligence, privacy, benchmarking, internal control assessment, process mapping, etc.) designed to provide advice and insight	Proficient
	E	Describe coordination of internal audit efforts with the external auditor, regulatory oversight bodies, and other internal assurance functions, and potential reliance on other assurance providers	Basic
		3. Communicating and Reporting to Senior Management and the Board	
	A	Recognize that the chief audit executive communicates the annual audit plan to senior management and the board and seeks the board's approval	Basic
	B	Identify significant risk exposures and control and governance issues for the chief audit executive to report to the board	Basic
	C	Recognize that the chief audit executive reports on the overall effectiveness of the organization's internal control and risk management processes to senior management and the board	Basic
	D	Recognize internal audit key performance indicators that the chief audit executive communicates to senior management and the board periodically	Basic

2.1 ASSURANCE ENGAGEMENTS

> The professional standards for internal auditors and external auditors differ significantly in the scope of their treatment of consulting services. For example, the AICPA's standards for financial statement auditing in the United States are extremely detailed, but its standards for consulting are limited. However, The IIA recognizes that consulting is a way for internal auditors to add significant value to the organization. Candidates for the CIA exam must be able to distinguish the requirements for consulting engagements from those for assurance engagements.

1. **Financial, Compliance, Operational, and IT Auditing**

   a. According to the Introduction to the *Standards*, "Assurance services involve the internal auditor's objective assessment of evidence to provide opinions or conclusions regarding an entity, operation, function, process, system, or other subject matters."

   b. **Assurance services** are "[a]n objective examination of evidence for the purpose of providing an independent assessment on governance, risk management, and control processes for the organization.

      1) Examples may include financial, performance, compliance, system security, and due diligence engagements" (The IIA Glossary).

      2) The nature and scope of the assurance engagement are determined by the internal auditor.

   c. The following overview of assurance services is based on various publications of The IIA:

      1) **Financial** assurance provides analysis of the economic activity of an entity as measured and reported by accounting methods.

         a) **Financial auditing** looks at the past to determine whether financial information was properly recorded and adequately supported. It also assesses whether the financial statement assertions about past performance are fair, accurate, and reliable.

      2) **Compliance** assurance is the review of financial and operating controls to assess conformance with established laws, standards, regulations, policies, plans, procedures, contracts, and other requirements.

         a) **Compliance auditing** looks at the past and examines the present to ask such questions as the following:

            i) Have we adhered to laws and regulations?

            ii) Are we currently complying with legal and regulatory requirements?

            iii) What are our organization's corporate standards of business conduct?

            iv) Do all members of our staff and management team consistently comply with internal policies and procedures?

      3) **Operational** assurance is the review of a function or process to appraise the efficiency and economy of operations and the effectiveness with which those functions achieve their objectives.

         a) **Operational auditing** focuses on the present and future. It is closely aligned with the organization's mission, vision, and objectives. It also evaluates the effectiveness (ensuring the right things are done), efficiency (ensuring things are done the right way), and economy (ensuring cost-effectiveness) of operations. This mindset includes such areas as (1) product quality, (2) customer service, (3) revenue maximization, (4) expense minimization, (5) fraud prevention, (6) asset safeguarding, (7) corporate social responsibility and citizenship, (8) streamlined workflows, (9) safety, and (10) planning. It concentrates on what is working and what is not as well as the opportunities for future improvement.

4) **IT** assurance is the review and testing of IT (for example, computers, technology infrastructure, IT governance, mobile devices, and cloud computing) to assure the integrity of information. Traditionally, IT auditing has been done in separate projects by IT audit specialists, but increasingly it is being integrated into all audits.

d. The three distinct categories of assurance services (financial, compliance, and operational) correspond to the categories of objectives defined in the control framework adopted by the Committee of Sponsoring Organizations (COSO).

1) **Internal control** is a process effected by an entity's board, management, and other personnel that is designed to provide reasonable assurance regarding the achievement of the following objectives:

a) **Operations** objectives relate to the effectiveness and efficiency of operations, e.g., achievement of operational and financial performance goals, and the safeguarding of assets against loss.

b) **Reporting** objectives relate to internal and external financial and nonfinancial reporting and may include the reliability, timeliness, and transparency of such reporting.

c) **Compliance** objectives relate to adherence to applicable laws and regulations.

Assurance Services

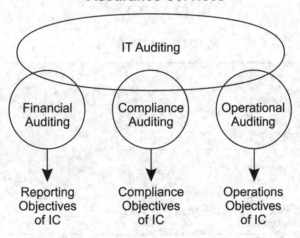

Figure 2-1

e. The services described also may be performed by external auditors, for example, in outsourcing or cosourcing engagements. Nevertheless, the traditional focus of external auditors is on the fair presentation of general purpose financial information.

1) By contrast, the traditional focus of internal auditors is on supporting management and governance authorities in performing their functions.

2. **Assurance Mapping**

a. An assurance map is a visual representation of an organization's risks and assurance activities. An assurance map may include the following:

1) Identity of the assurance providers
2) Risk
3) Level of assurance
4) Urgency or importance of the issue
5) Action to be taken

    b.   Assurance providers are internal and external stakeholders that are responsible for implementing or maintaining assurance services.

        1)   Management provides assurance through compliance with laws and regulations, quality assurance, and self-assessments.

        2)   The board of directors provides assurance through the internal audit function.

        3)   External stakeholders provide assurance through the independent external auditor, government regulators, and trade associations such as ISO.

    c.   Risk is determined by judging the inherent risk of the activity, the risk that internal controls may not prevent or detect noncompliance, and the potential consequences of noncompliance.

    d.   The level of assurance is determined by considering the quality, extent, and costs of internal controls.

    e.   The higher the risk or assurance, the more urgent or important an issue likely is.

    f.   The actions to be taken depend on the specific issue and the urgency or importance of that issue.

        1)   In general, users of an assurance map have the option to increase or decrease assurance.

        2)   If a low risk area has a high level of assurance, the entity may want to consider shifting those assurance resources to a high risk area.

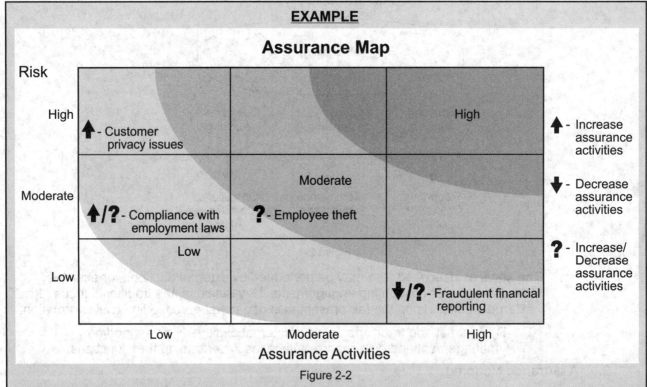

EXAMPLE

Assurance Map

Figure 2-2

Notes:

- As customer privacy concerns have become more important, the entity has determined that its assurance activities related to customer privacy need to be increased.
- Compliance with employment law has not previously been an issue. However, due to recent changes in the law, the entity is considering increasing assurance activities.
- Due to the balance between risk and assurance activities, the entity does not know whether it should increase or decrease assurance activities.
- The level of assurance activities for fraudulent financial reporting is high. The entity therefore is considering using some resources for those assurance activities elsewhere.

Stop and review! You have completed the outline for this subunit. Study multiple-choice questions 1 and 2 on page 49.

2.2 RISK AND CONTROL SELF-ASSESSMENT

1. **Control Self-Assessment (CSA)**

    a. Managers and auditors have an interest in using methods that (1) improve the assessment of risk management and control processes and (2) identify ways to improve their effectiveness.

    b. CSA increases awareness of risk and control throughout the organization.

        1) Risk assessment, business processes, and internal controls are not treated as exclusive concerns of senior management and the internal audit activity. Instead, CSA involves client personnel, asks for their input, and gives them a sense of participation.

    c. CSA's **basic philosophy** is that control is the responsibility of everyone in the organization. The people who work within the process, i.e., the employees and managers, are asked for their assessments of risks and controls in their process.

    d. CIA candidates should understand (1) the objectives of CSA, (2) its advantages to an organization, and (3) limitations.

2. **Elements of CSA**

    a. A typical CSA process has the following elements:

        1) Front-end planning and preliminary audit work.

        2) An in-person meeting, typically involving a facilitation seating arrangement (U-shaped table) and a meeting facilitator. The participants are process owners, i.e., management and staff who (a) are involved with the particular issues under examination, (b) know them best, and (c) are critical to the implementation of appropriate process controls.

        3) A structured agenda used by the facilitator to lead the group through an examination of the process's risks and controls. Frequently, the agenda is based on a well-defined framework or model so that participants can be sure to address all necessary issues. A model may focus on controls, risks, or a framework developed for that project.

        4) An option is the presence of a scribe to take an online transcription of the session and electronic voting technology to enable participants to state their perceptions of the issues anonymously.

        5) Reporting and the development of action plans.

    b. Accordingly, CSA typically employs a **workshop-facilitation approach** to self-assessment that is structured, documented, and repetitive. Thus, it should be contrasted with an approach that merely surveys employees regarding risks and controls.

3. **Responsibilities**

    a. **Senior management** should oversee the establishment, administration, and evaluation of the processes of risk management and control.

    b. **Operating managers'** responsibilities include assessment of the risks and controls in their units.

    c. **Internal and external auditors** provide varying degrees of assurance about the state of effectiveness of the risk management and control processes of the organization.

4. **How Internal Auditors Use CSA**

    a. Internal auditing's investment in CSA programs may be significant. It may (1) sponsor, design, implement, and own the process; (2) conduct the training; (3) supply the facilitators, scribes, and reporters; and (4) coordinate the participation of management and work teams.

    b. But in other organizations, internal auditing may serve only as an interested party and consultant for the whole process and as the ultimate verifier of the evaluations produced by the teams.

        1) In most programs, the investment in the organization's CSA efforts is somewhere between the two extremes described above. As the level of involvement in the CSA program and individual workshop deliberations increases, the chief audit executive (CAE) (a) monitors the objectivity of the internal audit staff, (b) takes steps to manage that objectivity (if necessary), and (c) augments internal audit testing to ensure that bias or partiality does not affect the final judgments of the staff.

    c. A CSA program augments the traditional role of the internal audit activity by assisting management in fulfilling its responsibilities to establish and maintain risk management and control processes and by evaluating the adequacy of that system. Through a CSA program, the internal audit activity and the business units and functions **collaborate** to produce better information about how well the control processes are working and how significant the residual risks are.

    d. Although it provides staff support for the CSA program as facilitator and specialist, the internal audit activity often finds that it may reduce the effort spent in gathering information about control procedures and eliminate some testing. A CSA program (1) increases the coverage of assessments of control processes across the organization, (2) improves the quality of corrective actions made by the process owners, and (3) focuses the internal audit activity's work on reviewing high-risk processes and unusual situations. A CSA also can focus on (1) validating the evaluation conclusions produced by the CSA process, (2) synthesizing the information gathered from the components of the organization, and (3) expressing its overall judgment about the effectiveness of controls to senior management and the board.

5. **Key Features**

    a. CSA includes **self-assessment surveys** and **facilitated workshops**. It is a useful and efficient approach for managers and internal auditors to collaborate in assessing and evaluating control procedures. In its purest form, CSA integrates business objectives and risks with control processes.

        1) CSA also is called control/risk self-assessment.

    b. Although CSA practitioners use different methods and formats, most implemented programs share some key features and goals. An organization that uses self-assessment will have a formal, documented process that allows management and work teams who are directly involved in a business unit, function, or process to participate in a structured manner for the purpose of

        1) Identifying risks and exposures,
        2) Assessing the control processes that mitigate or manage those risks,
        3) Developing action plans to reduce risks to acceptable levels, and
        4) Determining the likelihood of achieving the business objectives.

6. **Outcomes**

   a. People in the business units become trained and experienced in assessing risks and associating control processes with managing those risks and improving the chances of achieving business objectives.

   b. Informal, soft controls are more easily identified and evaluated.

   c. People are motivated to take ownership of the control processes in their units, and corrective actions taken by the work teams are often more effective and timely.

   d. The entire objectives-risks-controls infrastructure of an organization is subject to greater monitoring and continuous improvement.

   e. Internal auditors become involved in and knowledgeable about the self-assessment process by serving as facilitators, scribes, and reporters for the work teams and as trainers in risk and control concepts supporting the CSA program.

   f. The internal audit activity acquires more information about the control processes within the organization and can leverage that additional information in allocating its scarce resources. The result is greater effort devoted to investigating and performing tests of business units or functions that have significant control weaknesses or high residual risks.

   g. Management's responsibility for the risk management and control processes of the organization is reinforced, and managers will be less tempted to abdicate those activities to specialists, such as auditors.

   h. The primary role of the internal audit activity will continue to include validation of the evaluation process by the performance of tests and the expression of its professional judgment about the adequacy and effectiveness of the whole risk management and control system.

7. **Approaches**

   a. The three primary approaches of CSA programs are (1) facilitation, (2) survey (questionnaire), and (3) self-certification. Organizations often combine approaches.

   b. The variety of approaches used for CSA processes in organizations reflects the differences in industry, geography, structure, organizational culture, degree of employee empowerment, dominant management style, and the manner of formulating strategies and policies. Thus, the success of a particular type of CSA program in one organization might not be replicated in another.

      1) The CSA process should be customized to fit the unique characteristics of each organization. Also, a CSA approach needs to be dynamic and change with the continual development of the organization.

8.   **Facilitation Approach**

a.   The facilitation approach has four possible formats:

1)   The **objective-based format** focuses on the best way to accomplish a business objective. The workshop begins by identifying the controls presently in place to support the objective and then determines the residual risks remaining.

a)   The aim of the workshop is to decide whether the control procedures are working effectively and are resulting in residual risks within an acceptable level.

2)   The **risk-based format** focuses on listing the risks to achieving an objective. The workshop begins by listing all possible barriers, obstacles, threats, and exposures that might prevent achieving an objective and then examines the control procedures to determine whether they are sufficient to manage the key risks.

a)   The workshop's aim is to determine significant residual risks. This format takes the work team through the entire objective-risks-controls formula.

3)   The **control-based format** focuses on how well the controls in place are working. This format is different from the objective-based and risk-based formats because the facilitator identifies the key risks and controls before the beginning of the workshop. During the workshop, the work team assesses how well the controls mitigate risks and promote the achievement of objectives.

a)   The aim of the workshop is to produce an analysis of the gap between how controls are working and how well management expects those controls to work.

4)   The **process-based format** focuses on selected activities that are elements of a chain of processes. The processes are usually a series of related activities that go from some beginning point to an end, such as the various steps in purchasing, product development, or revenue generation. This type of workshop usually covers the identification of the objectives of the whole process and the various intermediate steps.

a)   The workshop's aim is to evaluate, update, validate, improve, and even streamline the whole process and its component activities. This workshop format may have a greater breadth of analysis than a control-based approach by covering multiple objectives within the process and by supporting concurrent management efforts, such as reengineering, quality improvement, and continuous improvement initiatives.

9.   **Survey Approach**

a.   The survey form of CSA uses a questionnaire that tends to ask mostly simple "yes/no" or "have/have not" questions that are carefully written to be understood by the target recipients.

1)   Surveys often are used if the desired respondents are too numerous or widely dispersed to participate in a workshop. They also are preferred if the culture in the organization may limit open, candid discussions in workshop settings or if management desires to minimize the time spent and costs incurred in gathering the information.

10. **Self-Certification Approach**

    a.   This form of self-assessment is based on management-produced analyses to produce information about selected business processes, risk management activities, and control procedures. The analysis is often intended to reach an informed and timely judgment about specific characteristics of control procedures and is commonly prepared by a team in a staff or support role.

        1)   The internal auditor may synthesize this analysis with other information to enhance the understanding about controls and to share the knowledge with managers in business or functional units as part of the organization's CSA program.

11. **Understanding of Risk and Control**

    a.   All self-assessment programs assume that managers and members of the work teams understand risk and control concepts and use them in communications.

        1)   For training sessions, to facilitate the orderly flow of workshop discussions, and as a check on the completeness of the overall process, organizations often use a control framework, such as the COSO (Committee of Sponsoring Organizations) model.

12. **Workshop Reports**

    a.   In the typical CSA facilitated workshop, a report is substantially created during the deliberations. A consensus is recorded for the various segments of the discussions, and the group reviews the proposed final report before the end of the final session.

        1)   Some programs use anonymous voting to ensure the free flow of information and opinions during the workshops and to aid in negotiating differences between interest groups.

13. **Limitations**

    a.   The internal auditor may not effectively use the selected CSA approach(es), or the persons performing the self-assessment may not be skilled in risk management and control. The relevant risks and controls then may not be identified or, if identified, not properly assessed.

Stop and review! You have completed the outline for this subunit. Study multiple-choice questions 3 through 6 beginning on page 49.

2.3 AUDITS OF THIRD PARTIES AND CONTRACT AUDITING

1. **External Business Relationships**

    a.   Organizations have multiple external (extended) business relationships (EBRs). The IIA's Practice Guide, *Auditing External Business Relationships*, contains extensive guidance.

        1)   Each EBR has risks, and management is responsible for managing and monitoring the risks and achieving the benefits.

        2)   Internal auditing assists management and validates its efforts.

    b.   EBRs may involve the following:

        1)   Service providers (e.g., for providing internal audit services, processing of payroll, sharing of services, or use of IT services)

        2)   Supply-side partners (e.g., outsourcing of production or R&D)

        3)   Demand-side partners (e.g., licensees or distributors)

        4)   Strategic alliances and joint ventures (e.g., cost-, revenue-, and profit-sharing in media production and development)

        5)   Intellectual property (IP) partners (e.g., licensing of software)

    c.   Among other things, EBR partners may offer lower costs, better operational efficiency, special expertise, new technology, a known brand, or economies of scale.

    d.   The internal audit activity helps management and the board identify, assess, and manage risks, including reputation risks as well as economic risks. The following are examples of significant risks of EBRs:

        1)   They may not be identified and therefore may not be (a) managed in accordance with relevant policies, (b) assessed, or (c) monitored.

        2)   EBRs may adversely affect the organization's reputation, e.g., by violating laws, committing fraud, or not complying with contracts.

        3)   EBRs may have inadequate insurance coverage.

        4)   Service levels or products may be unsatisfactory, e.g., because of inadequate definition in the contract.

        5)   Conflicts of interest may arise, e.g., when the work is affected by the EBR's contractual obligations to others.

        6)   Licensing of intellectual property may result in misuse, theft, or loss of revenue.

        7)   The organization may be overcharged for services.

        8)   The EBR partner may become insolvent.

        9)   The organization's confidential information (e.g., personally identifiable information) may be lost.

2.   Auditing EBRs

    a.   Before auditing an EBR, the internal auditors first must determine whether the EBR partner has agreed to the audit.

        1)   This right ordinarily is granted in an audit clause in the contract creating the EBR.

    b.   Internal auditors need to understand all elements of an EBR:

        1)   Initiating the EBR

        2)   Contracting for and defining the EBR

        3)   Procurement

        4)   Managing and monitoring the EBR (including control environment considerations of objectivity and independence of managers)

        5)   Discontinuing the EBR

    c.   The internal auditors need to understand the expectations of the parties and the processes for managing and monitoring the EBR.

        1)   They then develop an appropriate audit program with relevant objectives.

            a)   Internal audit procedures may include evaluating compliance with the contract to determine whether monetary and nonmonetary obligations are met.

            b)   Audit procedures may discover missed revenue or cost savings, improve reporting, and add value to the EBR through the following:

                i)   Limiting fraud

                ii)   Increasing trust

                iii)   Fostering feedback

                iv)   Improving relationships

                v)   Helping management improve internal and external controls

d. The CAE decides whether to audit (1) each EBR separately, (2) certain EBRs, or (3) the total EBR process. The following is the cycle for an EBR audit:

1) **Understanding the organization, its environment, its processes, and the nature of each EBR**

a) The internal auditors need to understand (1) the reasons for, and the importance of, EBRs; (2) whether they have been identified; and (3) the risks of noncompliance by EBR partners.

2) **Assessing risks and controls**

a) The internal auditors need to (1) understand the EBR's inherent risks and the design of relevant controls; (2) determine the key controls; and (3) understand the EBR partner's environment, processes, and controls (including the work done by its auditors).

3) **Performing the audit**

a) The internal auditors need to determine whether to (1) do on-site work at the EBR, (2) evaluate results, (3) identify findings and their application (to one EBR, certain EBRs, or the total EBR process), and (4) reach conclusions.

4) **Reporting**

a) The internal auditors need to determine the frequency and content of reports to the board and senior management.

5) **Monitoring progress**

a) The internal auditors may determine whether findings (especially deficiencies) have been addressed. They also may assist in determining whether EBRs are well managed.

3. **Third-Party Audits**

a. The organization may be audited. This is routine for organizations that issue general-use financial statements and for many EBRs.

1) For example, if the organization is a service provider, the external and internal auditors of the organization's clients must obtain assurance about the security of the organization's operations and the fulfillment of contractual obligations. Such audits are also common for joint ventures.

2) Another typical third-party audit is the audit performed by a qualified registrar as part of the ISO 9000 certification process.

b. In these cases, the internal auditors should coordinate their activities with those of the third-party auditor to share information and to prevent duplication of effort.

4. **Contract Auditing**

a. Internal auditors often perform engagements to monitor and evaluate significant construction contracts and operating contracts that involve the provision of services. The usual types of arrangements for such contracts are lump-sum (fixed-price), cost-plus, and unit-price.

b. **Lump-sum contracts.** The internal auditor may have little to evaluate when the work is performed in accordance with the contract. However, reviewing such an agreement may call for consideration of the following:

1) Progress payments
2) Incentives (e.g., for early completion)
3) An escalator clause (e.g., one causing the entire price to be due in the event of some breach of the contract)
4) Adjustments for labor costs (e.g., premiums paid to obtain necessary labor)
5) Change orders

c. **Cost-plus contracts** are ways to cope with uncertainties about costs by setting a price equal to (1) cost plus a fixed amount or (2) cost plus a fixed percentage of cost. A problem is that the contractor may have little incentive for economy and efficiency, a reason for careful review by the internal auditors. These contracts may have provisions for

1) Maximum costs, with any savings shared by the parties, or
2) Incentives for early completion.

d. **Unit-price contracts** are often used when a convenient measure of work is available, such as acres of land cleared, cubic yards of earth moved, or square footage patrolled by a security service.

1) The key issue is the accurate measurement of the work performed.

e. To protect the organization, internal auditors should be involved throughout the contracting process, not merely in the performance phase. They should review the terms of the contract and the following:

1) Procedures for bidding (e.g., competitive bidding)
2) Procedures for cost estimation and control
3) Budgets and financial forecasts
4) The contractor's information and control systems
5) The contractor's financial position
6) Funding and tax matters
7) Progress of the project and costs incurred

f. When reviewing a contract for the purchase of a business application systems, the internal auditor should recommend that the contract contain a **source code escrow clause**.

1) A source code escrow clause requires the application source code to be held in escrow by a trusted third party. The third party releases the source code to the purchaser, or licensee, on the occurrence of an event, or events, specified in the clause.

Stop and review! You have completed the outline for this subunit. Study multiple-choice questions 7 and 8 beginning on page 50.

2.4 QUALITY AUDITING

1. **Quality Auditing**

a. The internal audit activity's role is to provide assurance that the approved quality structures are in place and quality processes are functioning as intended.

2. **Traditional vs. Modern Views of Quality**

a. The traditional view of quality emphasized the detection of products that do not meet standards.

1) This view involved the rejection or reworking of defective goods.

b. The modern view is that quality is a value-added activity performed throughout all processes, from product design to raw materials acquisition and final inspection.

1) It also extends to all of the organization's business processes, not just to the production of goods. This view of quality is the basis for total quality management (TQM).

3. **Total Quality Management (TQM)**

   a. TQM can increase revenues and decrease costs significantly. Thus, the internal audit activity's services with respect to the quality function may add substantial value. Indeed, the improvement of operations is part of the definition of internal auditing.

   b. Quality is best viewed from multiple perspectives:

      1) Attributes of the product (performance, serviceability, durability, etc.),

      2) Customer satisfaction,

      3) Conformity with manufacturing specifications, and

      4) Value (relation of quality and price).

   c. TQM is a comprehensive approach. It treats the pursuit of quality as a basic organizational function that is as important as production or marketing. It is also a strategic weapon because its cumulative effects cannot be easily duplicated by competitors.

      1) TQM is the **continuous pursuit of quality** in every aspect of organizational activities through

         a) A philosophy of doing it right the first time,

         b) Employee training and empowerment,

         c) Promotion of teamwork,

         d) Improvement of processes, and

         e) Attention to satisfaction of internal and external customers.

   d. TQM emphasizes the supplier's relationship with the customer and identifies customer needs. It also recognizes that everyone in a process is at some time a customer or supplier of someone else, either within or outside the organization.

      1) Thus, TQM begins with external customer requirements, identifies internal customer-supplier relationships and requirements, and establishes requirements for external suppliers.

   e. The management of quality is not limited to quality management staff, engineers, production personnel, etc.

      1) Given the organization-wide scope of TQM and of the internal audit activity, the role of the internal auditors is to evaluate the entire quality function.

         a) The internal audit activity is well qualified to perform risk assessments and promote continuous improvement of controls.

            i) The personnel involved in the technical improvements of processes may be unqualified with regard to risk management and control issues.

         b) The internal audit activity performs procedures to provide assurance that the basic objectives of TQM are reached: customer satisfaction, continuous improvement, and promotion of teamwork.

         c) TQM concepts also apply to the operations of the internal audit activity itself. For example, periodic internal assessments of those operations may include benchmarking its practices and performance metrics against relevant best practices of the profession.

Stop and review! You have completed the outline for this subunit. Study multiple-choice questions 9 and 10 on page 51.

2.5 SECURITY AND PRIVACY AUDITS

NOTE: Physical security, such as safeguards against environmental risks and wrongful access to computers, must be audited even if software provides most of the protection for information.

1. **Information Security Auditing**

   a. Information security auditing is an expansion of the assurance services performed by auditors. The creation of organization-wide computer networks with the potential for access by numerous outside parties has greatly increased risk. Thus, risk management and control processes may be inadequate.

   b. The role of the internal audit activity in these circumstances is to assess risks, monitor the implementation of corrective action, and evaluate controls.

      1) The internal audit activity also may act in a consulting capacity by identifying security issues and by working with users of information systems and with systems security personnel to devise and implement controls.

      2) The internal audit activity works closely with senior management and the board to assist in the performance of the governance function with respect to information security.

Implementation Standard 2130.A1

The internal audit activity must evaluate the adequacy and effectiveness of controls in responding to the risks within the organization's governance, operations, and information systems regarding the:

- Achievement of the organization's strategic objectives;
- Reliability and integrity of financial and operational information;
- Effectiveness and efficiency of operations and programs;
- Safeguarding of assets; and
- Compliance with laws, regulations, policies, procedures, and contracts.

---

   c. **Information Reliability and Integrity**

      1) Information reliability and integrity includes accuracy, completeness, and security. The internal audit activity determines whether senior management and the board clearly understand that it is a management responsibility for all critical information regardless of its form.

      2) The CAE determines whether the internal audit activity has competent audit resources for evaluating internal and external risks to information reliability and integrity.

      3) The CAE determines whether senior management, the board, and the internal audit activity will be promptly notified about breaches and conditions that might represent a threat.

      4) Internal auditors assess the effectiveness of preventive, detective, and mitigative measures against past and future attacks. They also determine whether the board has been appropriately informed.

      5) Internal auditors periodically assess reliability and integrity practices and recommend new or improved controls. Such assessments can be made as separate engagements or as multiple engagements integrated with other elements of the audit plan.

   d. Internal auditors also evaluate compliance with privacy laws and regulations. Thus, they assess the adequacy of the identification of risks and the controls that reduce those risks.

2. **Security Auditing**

    a. The most common use of the term **security** in an organizational setting is in connection with information technology (IT).

        1) However, the organization must take a more comprehensive view of security.

        2) One example is the protection of employees and visitors from workplace violence. Thus, security is an appropriate governance and risk management issue even in the absence of IT.

    b. The internal audit activity evaluates the adequacy and effectiveness of controls designed and implemented by management in all areas of security.

3. **Privacy Auditing**

    a. The amount of personal information stored on computers has greatly increased. The security risks involved also have increased because of the interconnections among computers permitted by the Internet.

    b. **Evaluation of a Privacy Framework**

        1) Protection of personal information prevents such negative organizational consequences as legal liability and loss of reputation.

        2) The following are various definitions of privacy:

            a) Personal privacy (physical and psychological)

            b) Privacy of space (freedom from surveillance)

            c) Privacy of communication (freedom from monitoring)

            d) Privacy of information (collection, use, and disclosure of personal information by others)

        3) Personal information is any information that can be associated with a specific individual or that might be combined with other information to do so. The following are examples:

            a) Name, address, identification numbers, family relationships

            b) Employee files, evaluations, comments, social status, or disciplinary actions

            c) Credit records, income, financial status

            d) Medical status

        4) **The board** is ultimately accountable for identifying principal risks, implementing controls, and managing privacy risk, e.g., by establishing and monitoring a privacy framework.

        5) **The internal audit activity** assesses the adequacy of (a) management's risk identification and (b) the controls that reduce those risks.

            a) Moreover, the internal audit activity evaluates the privacy framework, identifies significant risks, and makes recommendations. The internal audit activity also considers

                i) Laws, regulations, and practices in relevant jurisdictions;

                ii) The advice of legal counsel; and

                iii) The security efforts of IT specialists.

6) The internal audit activity's role depends on the level or maturity of the organization's privacy practices.

    a) Accordingly, the internal auditors may

        i) Facilitate the development and implementation of the privacy program,

        ii) Evaluate management's privacy risk assessment, or

        iii) Perform an assurance service regarding the effectiveness of the privacy framework.

    b) However, assumption of responsibility may impair independence.

7) The internal auditor identifies

    a) Personal information gathered,

    b) Collection methods, and

    c) Whether use of the information is in accordance with its intended use and applicable law.

8) Given the difficulty of the technical and legal issues, the internal audit activity needs the knowledge and competence to assess the risks and controls of the privacy framework.

c. **Use of Personal Information in Performing Engagements**

1) Advances in IT and communications present privacy risks and threats. Thus, internal auditors need to consider the protection of personally identifiable information gathered during audits. Privacy controls are legal requirements in many jurisdictions.

2) Many jurisdictions require organizations to identify the purposes for which personal information is collected at or before collection. These laws also prohibit using and disclosing personal information for purposes other than those for which it was collected except with the individual's consent or as required by law.

3) Internal auditors must understand and comply with all laws regarding the use of personal information.

4) It may be inappropriate or illegal to access, retrieve, review, manipulate, or use personal information in conducting certain engagements. If the internal auditor accesses personal information, procedures may be necessary to safeguard this information. For example, the internal auditor may not record personal information in engagement records in some situations.

5) The internal auditor may seek advice from legal counsel before beginning audit work if questions arise about access to personal information.

d. Privacy engagements address the security of personal information, especially information stored in computer systems. An example is healthcare information in the files of insurers and providers.

1) The organization must comply with governmental statutory and regulatory mandates. Internal auditors consult the organization's legal counsel and then communicate the requirements to those responsible for designing and implementing the required safeguards.

    a) Internal auditors determine that the requirements are incorporated into the information system and that compliance is achieved in its operation.

2) Personal information needs to be protected from both unauthorized intrusion and misuse by those who have authorized access.

3) Privacy is balanced with the need to allow appropriate and prompt availability of personal information to legitimate users.

4) The organization documents compliance with privacy and other legal requirements.

       5)   Benefits of the security arrangements should exceed the costs. For example, encryption is an expensive way to address threats to the security of private information. Other methods, such as access controls, may be more appropriate relative to the assessed risk.

NOTE: The IIA's Code of Ethics requires internal auditors to maintain the confidentiality of private information.

         a)   "Internal auditors shall be prudent in the use and protection of information acquired in the course of their duties" (Rule of Conduct 3.1).

         b)   "Internal auditors shall not use information for any personal gain or in any manner that would be contrary to the law or detrimental to the legitimate and ethical objectives of the organization" (Rule of Conduct 3.2).

Stop and review! You have completed the outline for this subunit. Study multiple-choice questions 11 and 12 on page 52.

2.6 PERFORMANCE AUDITING

1. **Performance Auditing**

   a.   A performance audit may provide assurance about the organization's **key performance indicators**.

      1)   A consulting engagement may be performed to design a performance measurement system.

   b.   Internal auditors assess an organization's ability to measure its performance, recognize deficiencies, and take corrective actions.

      1)   Effective management control requires performance measurement and feedback. This process affects allocation of resources to organizational subunits. It also affects decisions about managers' compensation, advancement, and future assignments.

      2)   Furthermore, evaluating their performance serves to motivate managers to optimize the measures in the performance evaluation model. However, that model may be inconsistent with the organization's model for managerial decision making.

         a)   To achieve consistency, the models should be synchronized. For example, if senior management wishes to maximize results over the long term, subordinates should be evaluated over the long term.

   c.   A **balanced scorecard** is useful for performance measurement. It is a report that connects critical success factors determined in a strategic analysis with financial and nonfinancial measures of the elements of performance.

      1)   An organization identifies its critical success factors by means of an analysis that addresses internal factors (strengths and weaknesses) and external factors (opportunities and threats). This process is **SWOT analysis**.

         a)   The organization's greatest strengths are its core competencies. These are the basis for its ability to compete successfully and its strategy.

         b)   **Strengths** and **weaknesses** are internal resources or a lack of resources. For example, strengths include technologically advanced products, a broad product mix, capable management, leadership in R&D, modern production facilities, and a strong marketing organization. Weaknesses result from the lack of such advantages.

      c)   **Opportunities** and **threats** arise from factors external to the organization, such as government regulations, advances in technology, and demographics changes. They may be reflected in certain competitive conditions, including the following:

         i)   The number and strength of competitors in the industry

         ii)   Changes in the intensity of rivalry within the industry, for example, because of excessive production capacity

         iii) The relative availability of substitutes for the organization's products or services

         iv) Bargaining power of customers

         v)   Bargaining power of suppliers

      d)   The SWOT analysis facilitates development of a strategy by emphasizing the basic factors of cost, quality, and the speed of product development and delivery.

2)   Specific, reliable measures must be determined for each factor relevant to organizational success.

3)   Measures should be **nonfinancial** as well as financial, **long-term** as well as short-term, and **internal** as well as external. The balanced scorecard de-emphasizes short-term financial results and focuses attention on factors vital to future success.

4)   The development and implementation of a comprehensive balanced scorecard requires active participation by senior management.

      a)   The scorecard should contain detailed measures to permit everyone to understand how his or her efforts affect results.

      b)   The scorecard and the strategy it represents must be communicated to all managers and used as a basis for compensation decisions.

      c)   The scorecard should permit a determination of whether certain objectives are being achieved at the expense of others. For example, reduced spending on customer service may improve short-term financial results but cause a decline in customer satisfaction.

5)   A typical balanced scorecard includes measures in four categories:

      a)   **Financial** measures are ultimate results provided to owners, e.g., sales, fair value of the organization's stock, profits, and liquidity.

      b)   **Customer** measures reflect customer needs and satisfaction, e.g., customer retention rate, dealer and distributor relationships, marketing and selling performance, prompt delivery, quality, and market share.

      c)   **Internal** measures of key processes drive the business, e.g., quality, productivity (an input-output relationship), flexibility of response to changing conditions, operating readiness, and safety.

      d)   **Learning, growth, and innovation** measures are the basis for future success (people and infrastructure). Examples are development of new products, promptness of their introduction, human resource development, morale, and competence of the work force.

Stop and review! You have completed the outline for this subunit. Study multiple-choice questions 13 and 14 on page 52.

2.7 OPERATIONAL AUDITING

1. **Operational Audit Engagements**

    a. An operational audit assesses the efficiency and effectiveness of an organization's operations. The following are typical operational audit engagements:

    1) **Process (functional) engagements** are operational audit engagements that follow process-crossing organizational lines, service units, and geographical locations.

        a) The focus is on operations and how effectively and efficiently the organizational units affected will cooperate.

        b) These engagements tend to be challenging because of their scope and the need to deal with organizational units that may have conflicting objectives.

        c) Typical processes or functions are

            i) Purchasing and receiving
            ii) Distribution of services, materials, and supplies to users in the organization
            iii) Modification of products
            iv) Safety practices
            v) Scrap handling and disposal
            vi) Development of budgets
            vii) Marketing
            viii) Management of depreciable assets

    2) **Program-results engagements** are intended to obtain information about the costs, outputs, benefits, and effects of a program. They attempt to measure the accomplishment and relative success of the undertaking.

        a) Because benefits often cannot be quantified in financial terms, a special concern is the ability to measure effectiveness. Thus, clear definitions of objectives and standards should be provided at the outset of the program.

        b) A program is a funded activity not part of the normal, continuing operations of the organization, such as an expansion or a new information system.

    b. Measures used to assess effectiveness and efficiency include the following:

    1) The productivity ratio measures output relative to input.
    2) The productivity index measures production potential.
    3) The resource usage rate measures resource use relative to available resources.
    4) The operating ratio measures the operational efficiency of an organization.

Stop and review! You have completed the outline for this subunit. Study multiple-choice questions 15 and 16 on page 53.

2.8 COMPLIANCE AUDITING

 An internal audit activity can add value to its organization by performing many types of engagements. CIA candidates must know not only the requirements of these engagements but also when and where to perform each kind of engagement.

1. **Compliance**

    a. The IIA Glossary defines compliance as follows:

    Adherence to policies, plans, procedures, laws, regulations, contracts, or other requirements.

    b. Internal auditors assess compliance in specific areas as part of their role in organizational governance. They also follow-up and report on management's response to regulatory body reviews. Given the scope of governmental regulation, these duties of internal auditors have great importance.

    Caution: Internal auditors are encouraged to consult legal counsel in all matters involving legal issues. Requirements may vary significantly in different jurisdictions.

    c. The internal audit activity's responsibilities with regard to compliance are addressed in two Implementation Standards.

        1) The internal audit activity must evaluate risk exposures relating to governance, operations, and information systems with regard to (a) compliance (Implementation Standard 2120.A1) and (b) the adequacy and effectiveness of controls responding to these risks (Implementation Standard 2130.A1).

2. **Programs**

    a. Compliance programs assist organizations in preventing unintended employee violations, detecting illegal acts, and discouraging intentional employee violations. They also help (1) prove insurance claims, (2) determine director and officer liability, (3) create or enhance corporate identity, and (4) decide the appropriateness of punitive damages.

        1) Internal auditors need to evaluate an organization's regulatory compliance programs.

        2) The CAE should meet with regulators to provide relevant information or receive advice on necessary compliance.

3. **Organizational Standards and Procedures**

    a. The organization establishes compliance standards and procedures to be followed by its employees and other agents who are reasonably capable of reducing the probability of criminal conduct. They include the following:

        1) A clearly written, straightforward, and fair business code of conduct that provides guidance to employees on relevant issues and is user-friendly

        2) An organizational chart identifying personnel responsible for compliance programs

        3) Financial incentives that do not reward misconduct

        4) For an international organization, a compliance program on a global basis that reflects local conditions and laws

4. **Responsibility**

   a. Specific high-level personnel who are properly empowered and supplied with necessary resources should be responsible for the compliance program.

      1) Senior management also should be involved.

      2) High-level personnel should have substantial control of the organization or a substantial role in making policy.

      3) Compliance personnel should have adequate access to senior management, and the chief compliance officer should report directly to the CEO.

5. **Applicant Screening**

   a. Due care should be used to avoid delegating authority to those with a tendency to engage in illegal activities.

      1) Applications should inquire about criminal convictions or discipline by licensing boards.

      2) All applicants should be screened in a lawful manner that does not infringe upon privacy rights. The purpose is to detect evidence of past wrongdoing, especially that within the organization's industry.

6. **Communication**

   a. Standards and procedures, including readily available ethics-related documents, should be communicated effectively, preferably in an interactive format and on multiple occasions.

      1) Training programs and publications are typical methods. The best training allows employees to practice new techniques and use new information.

      2) Compliance information should be conveyed through a variety of media. Moreover, it should be targeted to the areas important to each functional employee group and its job requirements.

         a) For example, environmental compliance information should be directed to subunits, such as manufacturing, that are more likely to violate (or detect violations of) such laws and regulations.

      3) New employees should receive basic compliance training as part of their orientation, and agents of the organization should be given a presentation specifically for them.

         a) Agents should understand the organization's core values and that their actions will be monitored.

      4) Organizations also should require employees to certify periodically that they have read, understood, and complied with the code of conduct. This information is relayed annually to senior management and the board.

7. **Monitoring and Reporting**

   a. Monitoring and auditing systems for detecting illegal or unethical behavior and employee hotlines should be used. The best approach is to coordinate multiple monitoring and auditing systems.

      1) For example, the internal audit plan should be given appropriate resources and applied to all of the organization's businesses. Also, it should include a review of the compliance program.

      2) The compliance review considers (a) effectiveness of written materials, (b) employee receipt of communications, (c) handling of violations, (d) fairness of discipline, (e) observance of any protections given to informants, and (f) fulfillment of compliance unit responsibilities.

b. Attorney-client and attorney work-product privileges protect certain information disclosed to (or produced by) an attorney from being used by an adverse party in a legal proceeding. An attorney monitoring the hotline is best able to protect the privileges.

1) Employees may have little confidence in such hotlines or in write-in reports or an off-site person assigned to hear complaints. But they may have confidence in hotlines answered by an in-house representative and backed by a nonretaliation policy.

a) However, a hotline cannot ensure anonymity.

c. An on-site official may be assigned to receive and investigate complaints. This individual (an **ombudsperson**) is more effective if (s)he (1) reports directly to the chief compliance officer or the board, (2) keeps the names of informants secret, (3) provides guidance to informants, and (4) undertakes follow-up to ensure that retaliation has not occurred.

d. An ethics questionnaire should be sent to each employee asking whether the employee is aware of kickbacks, bribes, or other wrongdoing.

e. Organizational compliance standards should be consistently enforced by adequate, fair, case-specific discipline.

1) Punishment should be appropriate to the offense, such as a warning, loss of pay, suspension, transfer, or termination.

2) The program should provide for the discipline of managers and other responsible persons who knew or should have known of misconduct and did not report it. Failure to do so indicates a lack of due diligence.

a) As a result, a court may rule that (1) the program is not effective and (2) the organization is therefore legally liable for giving authority to persons with a tendency to commit crimes.

f. Termination or other discipline of employees may be limited by (1) whistleblower laws; (2) statutory exceptions to the employee-at-will doctrine (the right of an employer to fire an employee for any reason); (3) employee or union contracts; and (4) employer responsibilities with regard to discrimination, wrongful discharge, and requirements to act in good faith.

g. Employee discipline should be thoroughly documented so that the organization will be able to prove that it made its best effort to collect information and took appropriate action.

h. After detection, the response should be appropriate and designed to prevent other similar offenses.

1) In some circumstances, an appropriate response may require self-reporting of violations to the government, cooperation with investigations, and the acceptance of responsibility.

a) An effective compliance program and appropriate responses may result in more lenient punishment for committing the offense.

i. Failure to detect or prevent a serious violation may indicate that the compliance program needs to be restructured. One change that may be required is the replacement or transfer of compliance personnel.

Stop and review! You have completed the outline for this subunit. Study multiple-choice questions 17 through 20 beginning on page 53.

QUESTIONS

2.1 Assurance Engagements

1. What is the best description of information technology (IT) assurance?

- A. Review of controls that focus on an organization's ability to comply with established labor laws and policies.
- B. Review and testing of IT to assure the integrity of information.
- C. Determining that year-to-year growth in sales is measurable using accounting methods.
- D. Reviewing credit policies to determine whether only qualified customers are being granted favorable credit terms.

Answer (B) is correct.
    REQUIRED: The best description of IT assurance.
    DISCUSSION: IT assurance is the review and testing of IT (for example, computers, technology infrastructure, IT governance, mobile devices, and cloud computing) to assure the integrity of information. Traditionally, IT auditing has been done in separate projects by IT audit specialists, but increasingly it is being integrated into all audits.
    Answer (A) is incorrect. Compliance assurance is the review of financial and operating controls to assess conformance with laws, regulations, policies, plans, procedures, contracts, and other requirements. Answer (C) is incorrect. Financial assurance provides analysis of the economic activity of an entity as measured and reported by accounting methods. Answer (D) is incorrect. Operational assurance is the review of a function (credit policy) to appraise the efficiency and economy of operations and the effectiveness with which those functions achieve their objectives.

2. The primary difference between operational engagements and financial engagements is that, in the latter, the internal auditors

- A. Are not concerned with whether the client entity is generating information in compliance with financial accounting standards.
- B. Are seeking to help management use resources in the most effective manner possible.
- C. Can use analytical skills and tools that are not necessary in financial engagements.
- D. Start with the financial statements of the client entity and work backward to the basic processes involved in producing them.

Answer (D) is correct.
    REQUIRED: The primary difference between operational engagements and financial engagements.
    DISCUSSION: A financial engagement starts with financial statements to determine whether financial information was properly recorded and adequately supported. It also assesses whether the financial statement assertions about past performance are fair, accurate, and reliable.
    Answer (A) is incorrect. The reliability and integrity of financial information are important in financial engagements. Information systems provide data for decision making, control, and compliance with external requirements. Answer (B) is incorrect. Operational engagements evaluate accomplishment of established objectives and goals for operations or programs and economical and efficient use of resources. Financial engagements are primarily concerned with forming an opinion on the fairness of the financial statements. Answer (C) is incorrect. Analytical skills are necessary in all types of engagements.

2.2 Risk and Control Self-Assessment

3. Which group is charged with overseeing the establishment, administration, and evaluation of the processes of risk management and control?

- A. Operating managers.
- B. Internal auditors.
- C. External auditors.
- D. Senior management.

Answer (D) is correct.
    REQUIRED: The group charged with overseeing the establishment, administration, and evaluation of the processes of risk management and control.
    DISCUSSION: Senior management is charged with overseeing the establishment, administration, and evaluation of the processes of risk management and control. Operating managers' responsibilities include assessment of the risks and controls in their units. Internal and external auditors provide varying degrees of assurance about the state of effectiveness of the risk management and control processes of the organization.

4. Which of the following statements about control self-assessment (CSA) is **false**?

- A. CSA is usually an informal and undocumented process.
- B. In its purest form, CSA integrates business objectives and risks with control processes.
- C. CSA is also known as control/risk self-assessment.
- D. Most implemented CSA programs share some key features and goals.

Answer (A) is correct.
    REQUIRED: The false statement regarding CSA.
    DISCUSSION: A methodology encompassing self-assessment surveys and facilitated workshops called CSA is a useful and efficient approach for managers and internal auditors to collaborate in assessing and evaluating control procedures. The process is a formal and documented way of allowing participation by those who are directly involved in the business unit, function, or process.

5. Which forms of control self-assessment assume that managers and members of work teams possess an understanding of risk and control concepts and use those concepts in communications?

    A. The self-certification approach.

    B. The self-certification approach and facilitated approach.

    C. The self-certification approach and questionnaire approach.

    D. All self-assessment programs.

Answer (D) is correct.
    REQUIRED: The forms of CSA based on the assumption that managers and members of work teams possess an understanding of risk and control concepts and use them in communications.
    DISCUSSION: All self-assessment programs assume that managers and members of the work teams possess an understanding of risk and control concepts and using those concepts in communications. For training sessions, to facilitate the orderly flow of workshop discussions and as a check on the completeness of the overall process, organizations often use a control framework, such as the COSO (Committee of Sponsoring Organizations) and CoCo (Canadian Criteria of Control Board) models.

6. Why should an organization use the survey form of control self-assessment (CSA)?

    A. Few respondents are required to respond.

    B. Respondents are not widely dispersed.

    C. No time constraint is involved.

    D. The organizational culture does not encourage openness.

Answer (D) is correct.
    REQUIRED: The reason an organization should use the survey form of CSA.
    DISCUSSION: The many approaches used for CSA processes in organizations reflect differences in industry, geography, structure, organizational culture, degree of employee empowerment, dominant management style, and the manner of formulating strategies and policies. The survey form of CSA uses a questionnaire that tends to ask mostly simple "Yes or No" questions that are carefully written to be understood by the target recipients. Surveys often are used if the desired respondents are too numerous or widely dispersed to participate in a workshop. They also are preferred (1) when the culture of the organization may hinder open, candid discussions in workshop settings or (2) if management wants to minimize the time spent and costs incurred in gathering information.
    Answer (A) is incorrect. The survey form of CSA should be used when respondents are numerous. Answer (B) is incorrect. The survey form of CSA should be used when respondents are widely dispersed. Answer (C) is incorrect. The survey form of CSA should be used when management wants to minimize the time spent and costs incurred in gathering information.

2.3 Audits of Third Parties and Contract Auditing

7. In reviewing a cost-plus construction contract for a new catalog showroom, the internal auditor should be cognizant of the risk that

    A. The contractor could be charging for the use of equipment not used in the construction.

    B. Income taxes related to construction equipment depreciation may have been calculated erroneously.

    C. Contractor cash budgets could have been inappropriately compiled.

    D. Payroll taxes may have been inappropriately omitted from billings.

Answer (A) is correct.
    REQUIRED: The risk inherent in a cost-plus construction contract.
    DISCUSSION: Under a cost-plus contract, the contractor receives a sum equal to cost plus a fixed amount or a percentage of cost. The disadvantages of this arrangement are that the contractor's incentive for controlling costs is reduced and the opportunity to overstate costs is created. Consequently, internal auditors should be involved in monitoring economy and efficiency not only during the earliest phases of construction but also from the outset of the planning process.
    Answer (B) is incorrect. Income tax provisions related to depreciation charges are not a risk; only those charges incurred under the terms of the contract constitute a risk. Answer (C) is incorrect. Budgets inappropriately prepared do not affect contract costs and therefore do not constitute a risk. Answer (D) is incorrect. The omission of taxes does not involve a risk of contract overcharges or inadequacies in construction. Possible delays in payment or underpayments from the omission are of less concern.

8. Which of the following does the internal auditor of a contracting company **not** have to review as thoroughly in a lump-sum contract?

    A. Progressive payments.

    B. Adjustments to labor costs.

    C. Work completed in accordance with the contract.

    D. Incentives associated with the contract.

Answer (C) is correct.
    REQUIRED: The item the internal auditor need not review thoroughly in a lump-sum contract.
    DISCUSSION: The internal auditor usually has little to evaluate when the work is performed in accordance with the contract. Further, the internal auditor may lack the technical expertise to know if the contract is being completed according to the terms.
    Answer (A) is incorrect. The internal auditor should ensure that the contractor is receiving payment to meet expenses and complete the contract. Answer (B) is incorrect. Adjustments to labor cost may change the profitability of the contract and are of great importance to the internal auditor. Answer (D) is incorrect. Incentives such as a bonus for early completion affect the overall profitability of the contract and are frequently reviewed by the internal auditor.

2.4 Quality Auditing

9. Which of the following statements about TQM is **false**?

    A. This approach can increase revenues and decrease costs significantly.

    B. TQM is a comprehensive approach to quality.

    C. TQM begins with internal suppliers' requirements.

    D. TQM concepts are applicable to the operations of the internal audit activity itself.

Answer (C) is correct.
    REQUIRED: The false statement about TQM.
    DISCUSSION: The emergence of the total quality management (TQM) concept is one of the most significant developments in recent years because this approach can increase revenues and decrease costs significantly. TQM is a comprehensive approach to quality. It treats the pursuit of quality as a basic organizational function that is as important as production or marketing. TQM emphasizes the supplier's relationship with the customer. Thus, TQM begins with external customer requirements, identifies internal customer-supplier relationships and requirements, and establishes requirements for external suppliers. TQM concepts also are applicable to the operations of the internal audit activity itself. For example, periodic internal assessments of those operations may include benchmarking of the internal audit activity's practices and performance metrics against relevant best practices of the internal audit profession.

10. TQM is the continuous pursuit of quality in every aspect of organizational activities through a number of goals. Which of the following is **not** one of those goals?

    A. A philosophy of doing it right the first time.

    B. Promotion of individual work.

    C. Employee training and empowerment.

    D. Improvement of processes.

Answer (B) is correct.
    REQUIRED: The answer choice not included in the definition of TQM.
    DISCUSSION: TQM is the continuous pursuit of quality in every aspect of organizational activities through (1) a philosophy of doing it right the first time, (2) employee training and empowerment, (3) promotion of teamwork, (4) improvement of processes, and (5) attention to satisfaction of customers, both internal and external.

2.5 Security and Privacy Audits

11. The reliability and integrity of all critical information of an organization, regardless of the media in which the information is stored, is the responsibility of

    A. Shareholders.

    B. IT department.

    C. Management.

    D. All employees.

Answer (C) is correct.
    REQUIRED: The responsibility for information reliability and integrity.
    DISCUSSION: Internal auditors determine whether senior management and the board have a clear understanding that information reliability and integrity is a management responsibility. Information reliability and integrity includes accuracy, completeness, and security.

12. Freedom from monitoring best defines

    A. Personal privacy.

    B. Privacy of space.

    C. Privacy of communication.

    D. Privacy of information.

Answer (C) is correct.
    REQUIRED: The freedom from monitoring.
    DISCUSSION: Privacy may encompass (1) personal privacy (physical and psychological), (2) privacy of space (freedom from surveillance), (3) privacy of communication (freedom from monitoring), and (4) privacy of information (collection, use, and disclosure of personal information by others).

2.6 Performance Auditing

13. Using the balanced scorecard approach, an organization evaluates managerial performance based on

    A. A single ultimate measure of operating results, such as residual income.

    B. Multiple financial and nonfinancial measures.

    C. Multiple nonfinancial measures only.

    D. Multiple financial measures only.

Answer (B) is correct.
    REQUIRED: The nature of the balanced scorecard approach.
    DISCUSSION: The trend in managerial performance evaluation is the balanced scorecard approach. Multiple measures of performance permit a determination as to whether a manager is achieving certain objectives at the expense of others that may be equally or more important. These measures may be financial or nonfinancial and usually include items in four categories: (1) financial; (2) customer; (3) internal business processes; and (4) learning, growth, and innovation.

14. A performance audit engagement typically involves

    A. Review of financial statement information, including the appropriateness of various accounting treatments.

    B. Tests of compliance with policies, procedures, laws, and regulations.

    C. A strategic analysis of the organization's key components that are essential to the organization's success.

    D. An evaluation of the board of directors' role in the operations of the organization.

Answer (C) is correct.
    REQUIRED: The characteristics of a performance audit engagement.
    DISCUSSION: Performance audit engagements involve review of the business and control environment and key performance indicators against set criteria using balanced scorecards, SWOT analysis, and management control evaluation. A balanced scorecard is an evaluation of company performance against established criteria. SWOT analysis appraises the business and potentially the control environment.
    Answer (A) is incorrect. Financial engagements involve review of financial information. Answer (B) is incorrect. Compliance engagements involve examining control procedures and compliance with them. Answer (D) is incorrect. Operational engagements involve reviewing organizational and departmental structures.

2.7 Operational Auditing

15. Which type of engagement focuses on operations and how effectively and efficiently the organizational units affected will cooperate?

A. Program-results engagement.

B. Process engagement.

C. Privacy engagement.

D. Compliance engagement.

Answer (B) is correct.

REQUIRED: The engagement that focuses cooperation of operating subunits.

DISCUSSION: Process engagements tend to be challenging because of their scope and the need to deal with subunits that may have conflicting objectives.

Answer (A) is incorrect. A program-results engagement obtains information about the costs, outputs, benefits, and effects of a program. Answer (C) is incorrect. Privacy engagements address the security of personal information. Answer (D) is incorrect. Compliance engagements address compliance with all laws and regulations.

16. An operational assurance engagement may include an assessment of all of the following **except**

A. Accuracy of financial reporting.

B. Development and effectiveness of the budgeting process.

C. Quantity of output.

D. Disposal of scrap.

Answer (A) is correct.

REQUIRED: The item not assessed in an operational assurance engagement.

DISCUSSION: An evaluation of the accuracy of financial reporting is performed during a financial assurance engagement.

Answer (B) is incorrect. A process engagement is an operational audit engagement that follows a process crossing organizational lines. An assessment of the budgeting process is such an engagement. Answer (C) is incorrect. An assessment of the quantity of output is performed during a program-results engagement. Answer (D) is incorrect. An assessment of scrap handling and disposal methods is performed during a process engagement.

2.8 Compliance Auditing

17. Compliance programs most directly assist organizations by doing which of the following?

1. Developing a plan for business continuity management.
2. Determining director and officer liability.
3. Planning for disaster recovery.

A. 1 only.

B. 2 only.

C. 1 and 2 only.

D. 1, 2, and 3.

Answer (B) is correct.

REQUIRED: The way(s) in which compliance programs help organizations.

DISCUSSION: Compliance is "adherence to policies, plans, procedures, laws, regulations, contracts, or other requirements" (The IIA Glossary). Such programs assist organizations in preventing inadvertent employee violations, detecting illegal activities, and discouraging intentional employee violations. They also can help (1) prove insurance claims, (2) determine director and officer liability, (3) create or enhance corporate identity, and (4) decide the appropriateness of punitive damages. However, developing a plan for business continuity management and planning for disaster recovery are operational activities not performed during a compliance program.

Answer (A) is incorrect. Developing a plan for business continuity management is an operational activity, not part of a compliance program. E-commerce activities, not compliance programs, assist an organization. Answer (C) is incorrect. Determining director and officer liability is the only activity listed that is performed as part of a compliance program. Answer (D) is incorrect. Developing a plan for business continuity management and planning for disaster recovery are operational activities, not parts of a compliance program.

18. Discipline of employees may be limited by all of the following **except**

A. Whistleblower laws.

B. A requirement to report certain employee violations to a governmental entity.

C. Union contracts.

D. Exceptions to the employee-at-will doctrine.

Answer (B) is correct.

REQUIRED: The item that does not limit the termination or other discipline of employees.

DISCUSSION: Termination or other discipline of employees may be limited by (1) whistleblower laws; (2) exceptions to the employee-at-will doctrine (the right of an employer to fire an employee for any reason); (3) employee or union contracts; and (4) employer responsibilities with regard to discrimination, wrongful discharge, and requirements to act in good faith. However, a governmental requirement that an entity report certain employee violations is not itself a limitation on the employer's power to discipline employees.

19. An organization establishes compliance standards and procedures and develops a written business code of conduct to be followed by its employees. Which of the following is true concerning business codes of conduct and the compliance standards?

   A. Compliance standards should be straightforward and reasonably capable of reducing the prospect of criminal conduct.

   B. The compliance standards should be codified in the charter of the audit committee.

   C. Companies with international operations should institute various compliance programs, based on selective geographic locations, that reflect appropriate local regulations.

   D. In order to prevent future legal liability, the code should consist of legal terms and definitions.

Answer (A) is correct.
   REQUIRED: The true statement regarding the code of conduct and compliance standards.
   DISCUSSION: The code of conduct should clearly identify prohibited activities, making compliance standards reasonably capable of reducing the prospect of criminal conduct (i.e., discouraging intentional employee violations). In addition, codes that are straightforward and fair tend to decrease the risk that employees will engage in unethical or illegal behavior.
   Answer (B) is incorrect. Among the items that must be included in the audit committee's charter is reviewing the process for communicating the code of conduct to company personnel and for monitoring compliance therewith; actually codifying the compliance standards is inappropriate. Answer (C) is incorrect. Companies with international operations should institute a compliance program on a global basis, not just for selective geographic locations. Such programs should reflect appropriate local conditions, laws, and regulations. Answer (D) is incorrect. The code should be written in a language that all employees can understand, avoiding legalese.

20. Employees have the most confidence in a hotline monitored by which of the following?

   A. An expert from the legal department, backed by a nonretaliation policy.

   B. An in-house representative, backed by a retaliation policy.

   C. An on-site ombudsperson, backed by a nonretaliation policy.

   D. An off-site attorney who can better protect attorney-client privilege.

Answer (C) is correct.
   REQUIRED: The hotline monitor that employees have the most confidence in.
   DISCUSSION: Although an attorney monitoring the hotline is better able to protect attorney-client and work-product privileges, one study observed that employees have little confidence in hotlines answered by the legal department or by an outside service. The same study showed that employees have even less confidence in write-in reports or an off-site ombudsperson, but have the most confidence in hotlines answered by an in-house representative (or an on-site ombudsperson) and backed by a nonretaliation policy.
   Answer (A) is incorrect. Employees have little confidence in hotlines answered by the legal department. Answer (B) is incorrect. A retaliation policy would dissuade whistleblowers from coming forth due to concern over possible backlash. Answer (D) is incorrect. Employees have little confidence in hotlines monitored by the legal department or by an external service provider. Thus, they would have even less confidence in an outside attorney.

STUDY UNIT THREE
FINANCIAL, ENVIRONMENTAL,
AND CONSULTING ENGAGEMENTS

(26 pages of outline)

This study unit is the third of four covering **Domain I: Managing the Internal Audit Activity** from The IIA's CIA Exam Syllabus. This domain makes up 20% of Part 2 of the CIA exam and is tested at the **basic** and **proficient** cognitive levels. The relevant portion of the syllabus is highlighted below. (The complete syllabus is in Appendix B.)

	Managing the Internal Audit Activity (20%)		
	1. Internal Audit Operations		
	A	Describe policies and procedures for the planning, organizing, directing, and monitoring of internal audit operations	Basic
	B	Interpret administrative activities (budgeting, resourcing, recruiting, staffing, etc.) of the internal audit activity	Basic
	2. Establishing a Risk-based Internal Audit Plan		
	A	Identify sources of potential engagements (audit universe, audit cycle requirements, management requests, regulatory mandates, relevant market and industry trends, emerging issues, etc.)	Basic
	B	Identify a risk management framework to assess risks and prioritize audit engagements based on the results of a risk assessment	Basic
	C	**Interpret the types of assurance engagements (risk and control assessments, audits of third parties and contract compliance, security and privacy, performance and quality audits, key performance indicators, operational audits, financial and regulatory compliance audits)**	**Proficient**
I	**D**	**Interpret the types of consulting engagements (training, system design, system development, due diligence, privacy, benchmarking, internal control assessment, process mapping, etc.) designed to provide advice and insight**	**Proficient**
	E	Describe coordination of internal audit efforts with the external auditor, regulatory oversight bodies, and other internal assurance functions, and potential reliance on other assurance providers	Basic
	3. Communicating and Reporting to Senior Management and the Board		
	A	Recognize that the chief audit executive communicates the annual audit plan to senior management and the board and seeks the board's approval	Basic
	B	Identify significant risk exposures and control and governance issues for the chief audit executive to report to the board	Basic
	C	Recognize that the chief audit executive reports on the overall effectiveness of the organization's internal control and risk management processes to senior management and the board	Basic
	D	Recognize internal audit key performance indicators that the chief audit executive communicates to senior management and the board periodically	Basic

3.1 FINANCIAL ENGAGEMENTS

1. **Financial Statements and Corporate Governance**

   a. The financial reporting process encompasses the steps to create information and prepare financial statements, related notes, and other accompanying disclosures in the organization's financial reports.

   b. Internal auditors provide assurance regarding financial reporting to management and the board. For example, in many countries, laws require that management certify that the general-purpose financial statements are fairly stated in all material respects.

Implementation Standard 2120.A1

The internal audit activity must evaluate risk exposures relating to the organization's governance, operations, and information systems regarding the:

- Achievement of the organization's strategic objectives.
- Reliability and integrity of financial and operational information.
- Effectiveness and efficiency of operations and programs.
- Safeguarding of assets.
- Compliance with laws, regulations, policies, procedures, and contracts.

---

2. **Management's Assertions**

   a. Management implicitly or explicitly makes assertions about the measurement, presentation, and disclosure of information in financial statements.

      1) Part of any engagement may involve testing these assertions to determine whether they are supported by the evidence.

      2) Determining whether these assertions are supported by the evidence also can help the auditor to determine whether controls are working as designed.

   b. The following are assertions generally made by management:

      1) All transactions and events that should have been recorded were recorded.

      2) Amounts and other data were recorded appropriately.

      3) Assets, liabilities, and other interests are reported at appropriate amounts, and any valuation or allocation adjustments are appropriately recorded.

      4) Assets, liabilities, and equity interests actually exist.

      5) Transactions and events were recorded in the proper period.

      6) The entity holds or controls the rights to assets, and liabilities are its obligations.

      7) Recorded events and transactions actually occurred.

      8) Transactions and events were recorded in the proper accounts and are presented and described clearly.

3. **Key Risks**

   a. Key risks affecting the reliability and integrity of financial information include the following:

      1) Overstating revenues (e.g., improper timing of revenue recognition)

      2) Understating expenses (e.g., improperly capitalizing expenditures that should be recorded as an expense in the current period)

      3) Applying unreasonable accounting estimates (e.g., accounting estimates are neither consistent with past results nor reasonable in light of expected future events)

      4) Applying accounting principles that are no longer in effect

4. **Accounting Cycles**

   a. An audit of financial information may follow the cycle approach to internal accounting control (a cycle is a functional grouping of transactions).

   b. **Sales, Receivables, and Cash Receipts Cycle**

      1) Processing customer orders
      2) Customer acceptance and granting credit
      3) Shipping goods
      4) Recording sales and receivables (including observing a proper cutoff)
      5) Billing customers
      6) Receiving, processing, and recording cash receipts
      7) Providing for, and writing off, bad debts
      8) Receiving, processing, and recording sales returns
      9) Providing for adjustments, allowances, warranties, and other credits

   c. **Purchases, Payables, and Cash Payments Cycle**

      1) Processing purchase requests
      2) Issuing purchase orders
      3) Receiving goods and services
      4) Processing vendor invoices, receiving reports, and purchase orders
      5) Disbursing cash
      6) Accounting for and documenting receipts, liabilities, cash payments, and accrued expenses

   d. **Production or Conversion Cycle**

      1) Inventory planning
      2) Receipt and storage of goods
      3) Production or conversion of goods or provision of services
      4) Accounting for costs, deferred costs, and property
      5) Storage of produced or converted goods
      6) Shipment

   e. **Financial Capital and Payment Cycle**

      1) Issuing long-term debt and stock
      2) Paying interest and dividends
      3) Repurchase of equity and debt securities and payment at maturity
      4) Maintaining detailed records for payment of interest, dividends, and taxes
      5) Purchases and sales of investments
      6) Recording receipts of interest and dividends
      7) Recording stock options and treasury stock
      8) Accounting for investing and financing transactions

   f. **Personnel and Payroll Cycle**

      1) Personnel department's hiring of employees
      2) Personnel department's authorization of payroll rates, deductions, etc.
      3) Timekeeping
      4) Payroll preparation and payment
      5) Filing payroll tax returns and paying the taxes

   g. **External Financial Reporting Cycle**

      1) Preparation of financial statements
      2) Disclosure of related information
      3) Controls over financial reporting
      4) Selection of accounting principles
      5) Unusual or nonrecurring items
      6) Contingencies

The IIA has consistently tested candidates on the aspects of internal control in different accounting cycles. Appendix E is dedicated to reviewing the most significant accounting cycles. This review is needed for an understanding of basic internal controls. Other accounting cycles and controls may be tested. Thus, the subject of a control question on the exam may not be covered. However, an understanding of (1) basic control principles, (2) accounting cycles, and (3) how the controls help prevent or detect fraud or error should enable candidates to handle any other cycles and controls that are tested. For example, authorizations required by a health insurer before a claim is paid are not significantly different from those required for a debtor's payment of interest on a note payable. Both require the auditor to trace the payment to documentation about authorization as well as supporting documentation.

Furthermore, candidates should not necessarily be concerned about memorizing every control in every cycle. Rather, they should understand control concepts.

    h.   In Appendix E are five flowcharts and accompanying tables describing the steps in five basic accounting cycles and the controls in each step for an organization large enough to have an optimal segregation of duties.

        1)   In small- and medium-sized organizations, some duties must be combined. The internal auditor must assess whether organizational segregation of duties is adequate.

5.   **Fraud Risk**

    a.   The auditor plans and performs the audit to obtain reasonable assurance about whether the financial statements are free of material misstatement, whether caused by fraud or error.

        1)   The auditor's initial responsibility regarding errors discovered during a financial statement audit is to assess the risk of misrepresentation.

    b.   The types of fraud relevant to the financial statement auditor include misstatements arising from

        1)   Fraudulent financial reporting. These are intentional misstatements or omissions to deceive users, such as altering accounting records or documents, misrepresenting or omitting significant information, and misapplying accounting principles.

        2)   Misappropriation of assets. These result from theft, embezzlement, or an action that causes payment for items not received.

6.   **Assessment of Internal Control**

    a.   Many countries require management to provide an assessment of the organization's internal control over financial reporting. Internal auditors assist management in meeting these responsibilities.

    b.   Control is any action taken by management, the board, and other parties to manage risk and increase the likelihood that established objectives and goals will be achieved. Management plans, organizes, and directs the performance of sufficient actions to provide reasonable assurance that objectives and goals will be achieved (The IIA Glossary).

Performance Standard 2130
Control

The internal audit activity must assist the organization in maintaining effective controls by evaluating their effectiveness and efficiency and by promoting continuous improvement.

Implementation Standard 2130.A1

The internal audit activity must evaluate the adequacy and effectiveness of controls in responding to risks within the organization's governance, operations, and information systems regarding the:

- Achievement of the organization's strategic objectives.
- Reliability and integrity of financial and operational information.
- Effectiveness and efficiency of operations and programs.
- Safeguarding of assets.
- Compliance with laws, regulations, policies, procedures, and contracts.

---

c. Performance Standard 2130 and Implementation Standard 2130.A1 emphasizes the internal audit activity's responsibility regarding internal controls.

1) Thus, an internal auditor must not simply assume that controls are adequate and effective.

a) Nondiscovery is most likely to suggest a violation of the International Professional Practices Framework.

d. Further guidance on the internal audit activity's responsibilities for controls is provided in IG 2130, *Control*:

1) Controls **mitigate risks** at the entity, activity, and transaction levels.

2) The roles and responsibilities are as follows:

a) **Senior management** oversees the establishment, administration, and assessment of the system of controls.

b) **Managers** assess controls within their responsibilities.

c) The **internal auditors** provide assurance about the effectiveness of existing controls.

3) In fulfilling their responsibilities, internal auditors should

a) Clearly understand control and typical control processes

b) Consider risk appetite, risk tolerance, and risk culture

c) Understand (1) the critical risks that could prevent reaching objectives and (2) the controls that mitigate risks

d) Understand the control framework(s) used

e) Have a process for planning, auditing, and reporting control problems

4) Evaluating the **effectiveness** of controls

a) Controls should be assessed relative to risks at each level. A **risk and control matrix** may be useful to

i) Identify objectives and related risks.

ii) Determine the significance of risks (impact and likelihood).

iii) Determine responses to the significant risks (for example, accept, pursue, transfer, mitigate, or avoid).

iv) Determine key management controls.

v) Evaluate the adequacy of control design.

vi) Test adequately designed controls to ascertain whether they have been implemented and are operating effectively.

     5)   Evaluating the **efficiency** of controls

        a)   The internal auditors consider whether management monitors the **costs and benefits** of control. The issue is whether (1) resources used exceed the benefits and (2) controls create significant issues (for example, error, delay, or duplication of effort).

        b)   The level of a control should be appropriate to the relevant risk.

     6)   Promoting **continuous improvement**

        a)   The CAE may recommend a **control framework** if none exists. The internal audit activity also may recommend improvements in the **control environment** (for example, the tone at the top should promote an ethical culture and not tolerate noncompliance).

        b)   Continuous improvement of controls involves

           i)   Training and ongoing self-monitoring

           ii)   Control (or risk and control) assessment meetings with managers

           iii)   A logical structure for documentation, analysis, and assessment of design and operation

           iv)   Identification, evaluation, and correction of control weaknesses

           v)   Informing managers about new issues, laws, and regulations

           vi)   Monitoring relevant technical developments

7.   **Internal Audit Plan**

   a.   The CAE should develop a flexible internal audit plan to provide sufficient evidence to evaluate control. It should permit adjustments during the year. The plan

     1)   Covers all major operations, functions, and controls

     2)   Gives special consideration to operations most affected by recent or unexpected changes

     3)   Considers relevant work performed by others, including management's assessments of risk management, control, and quality processes and the work completed by external auditors

   b.   The CAE evaluates the plan's coverage.

     1)   If the scope of the plan is insufficient to permit expression of an opinion about risk management and control, the CAE informs senior management and the board about gaps in audit coverage.

8.   **A Framework for Internal Control**

   a.   The assessment of internal control uses a broad definition of control. One source of effective internal control guidance is *Internal Control – Integrated Framework*, published by the Committee of Sponsoring Organizations (COSO).

     1)   The COSO model is widely accepted, but it may be appropriate to use some other model recognized worldwide. Also, regulatory or legal requirements may specify a particular model or control design.

b. In the COSO framework, control has five interrelated components:

1) **Control activities** are the policies and procedures applied to ensure that management directives are executed and actions are taken to address risks affecting achievement of objectives. Whether automated or manual, they have various objectives and are applied at all levels and functions of the organization. They include

a) Performance reviews by top managers,

b) Performance reviews at the functional or activity level,

c) Analysis of performance indicators,

d) Controls over information processing (e.g., application controls and general controls),

e) Physical controls, and

f) Segregation of duties (separation of the functions of authorization, recordkeeping, and asset custody).

2) **Risk assessment** is based on a set of complementary operational, financial reporting, and compliance objectives linked across all levels of the organization. Risk assessment identifies and analyzes external or internal risks affecting achievement of the objectives at the activity level and the entity level.

3) **Information and communication.** Relevant internal and external information should be identified, captured, and communicated in a timely manner and in appropriate forms.

4) **Monitoring** assesses the quality of a system's performance over time.

5) The **control environment** reflects the attitude and actions of the board and management regarding the significance of control within the organization.

NOTE: A common memory aid is **CRIME**.

c. The following conclusions by the COSO are relevant:

1) Internal control is defined broadly. It is not limited to accounting controls or financial reporting.

2) Accounting and financial reports are important. However, other matters also are important, such as (a) resource protection; (b) operational efficiency and effectiveness; and (c) compliance with rules, regulations, and organization policies.

a) These factors affect financial reporting.

3) Internal control is management's responsibility. The participation of all persons within an organization is required if it is to be effective.

4) The control framework should relate to business objectives and be adaptable.

9.   **Reporting on the Effectiveness of Internal Control**

    a.   The CAE's report on control processes is usually presented annually to senior management and the board. It describes

        1)   The role of control processes,
        2)   The work performed, and
        3)   Any reliance on other assurance providers.

    b.   The CAE provides the board an assessment of the effectiveness of the organization's controls, including the adequacy of the control model or design. The board must rely on management to maintain adequate and effective internal control. It reinforces this reliance with independent oversight.

        1)   Controls are **effective** if management directs processes to provide reasonable assurance that objectives are achieved.

        2)   Controls are **adequate** if management has designed them to provide reasonable assurance that (a) risks are managed effectively and (b) objectives are achieved effectively (The IIA Glossary).

    c.   However, even effective internal controls cannot ensure success. Bad decisions, poor managers, or environmental factors can negate controls. Also, dishonest management may override controls and discourage, ignore, or conceal communications from subordinates.

        1)   An active and independent board needs open and truthful communications from all components of management. Moreover, the board needs to be assisted by capable financial, legal, and internal audit functions.

            a)   In these circumstances, the board can identify problems and provide effective oversight.

    d.   The board or other governance body should request evaluations of internal controls as part of its oversight function. Those evaluations by the internal audit activity depend on answers to the following questions:

        1)   Is the **ethical environment and culture** strong?

            a)   Do board members and senior executives set examples of high integrity?

            b)   Are performance and incentive targets realistic, or do they create excessive pressure for short-term results?

            c)   Is the organization's code of conduct reinforced with training and top-down communication? Does the message reach the employees in the field?

            d)   Are the organization's communication channels open? Do all levels of management get the information they need?

            e)   Does the organization have zero tolerance for fraudulent financial reporting at any level?

        2)   How does the organization **identify and manage risks**?

            a)   Does the organization have a risk management process, and is it effective?

            b)   Is risk managed throughout the organization?

            c)   Are major risks candidly discussed with the board?

3) Is the **control system** effective?

    a) Are the organization's controls over the financial reporting process comprehensive, including preparation of financial statements, related notes, and the other required and discretionary disclosures that are an integral part of the financial reports?

    b) Do senior and line management demonstrate that they accept control responsibility?

    c) Is the frequency of surprises increasing at the senior management, board, or public levels from the organization's reported financial results or in the accompanying financial disclosures?

    d) Is communication and reporting good throughout the organization?

    e) Are controls seen as enhancing the achievement of objectives or as a necessary evil?

    f) Are qualified people hired promptly, and do they receive adequate training?

    g) Are problems fixed quickly and completely?

4) Is **monitoring** strong?

    a) Is the board independent of management, free of conflicts of interest, well informed, and inquisitive?

    b) Does internal auditing have the support of senior management and the board?

    c) Do the internal and external auditors have and use open lines of communication and private access to all members of senior management and the board?

    d) Is line management monitoring the control process?

    e) Does the organization have a program to monitor outsourced processes?

10. **Roles for the Internal Auditor**

    a. Adequate internal audit resources need to be committed to helping senior management, the board, and the external auditor with their responsibilities relating to financial reporting. Furthermore, the CAE needs to review internal audit's risk assessment and audit plans for the year.

    b. The CAE's allocation of the internal audit activity's resources to the financial reporting, governance, and control processes is consistent with the organization's risk assessment.

       1) The CAE performs procedures that provide a level of assurance to senior management and the board that controls over the processes supporting the development of financial reports are adequately designed and effectively executed.

       2) Controls need to be adequate to ensure the prevention and detection of (a) significant errors; (b) fraud; (c) incorrect assumptions and estimates; and (d) other events that could result in inaccurate or misleading financial statements, related notes, or other disclosures.

c.   The following are lists of suggested topics that the CAE considers in supporting the organization's governance process and the oversight responsibilities of the board:

1) **Financial Reporting**

a)   Providing information relevant to the appointment of the independent accountants.

b)   Coordinating audit plans, coverage, and scheduling with the external auditors.

c)   Sharing audit results with the external auditors.

d)   Communicating pertinent observations to the external auditors and board about (1) accounting policies and policy decisions (including accounting decisions for discretionary items and off-balance-sheet transactions), (2) specific components of the financial reporting process, and (3) unusual or complex financial transactions and events (e.g., related party transactions, mergers and acquisitions, joint ventures, and partnership transactions).

e)   Participating in the financial reports and disclosures review process with the board, external auditors, and senior management.

f)   Evaluating the quality of financial reports, including those filed with regulatory agencies.

g)   Assessing the adequacy and effectiveness of the organization's internal controls, specifically those controls over the financial reporting process. This assessment considers the organization's susceptibility to fraud and the effectiveness of programs and controls to mitigate or eliminate those exposures.

h)   Monitoring management's compliance with the organization's code of conduct and ensuring that ethical policies and other procedures promoting ethical behavior are being followed. An important factor in establishing an effective ethical culture in the organization is that members of senior management set a good example of ethical behavior and provide open and truthful communications to employees, the board, and outside stakeholders.

2) **Governance**

a)   Reviewing the organization's policies relating to (1) compliance with laws and regulations, (2) ethics, (3) conflicts of interest, and (4) the timely and thorough investigation of misconduct and fraud allegations.

b)   Reviewing pending litigation or regulatory proceedings bearing upon organizational risk and governance.

c)   Providing information on employee conflicts of interest, misconduct, fraud, and other outcomes of the organization's ethical procedures and reporting mechanisms.

3) **Corporate Control**

a)   Reviewing the reliability and integrity of the operating and financial information compiled and reported by the organization.

b)   Performing an analysis of the controls over critical accounting policies and comparing them with preferred practices. For example, transactions that raise questions about revenue recognition or off-balance-sheet accounting treatment are reviewed for compliance with appropriate standards, such as International Financial Reporting Standards.

c)   Evaluating the reasonableness of estimates and assumptions used in preparing operating and financial reports.

      d)   Ensuring that estimates and assumptions included in disclosures or comments are consistent with underlying organizational information and practices and with similar items reported by other organizations, if appropriate.

      e)   Evaluating the process of preparing, reviewing, approving, and posting journal entries.

      f)   Evaluating the adequacy of controls in the accounting function.

Stop and review! You have completed the outline for this subunit. Study multiple-choice questions 1 through 3 on page 81.

3.2 ENVIRONMENTAL ENGAGEMENTS

1.   **Environmental Risks**

    a.   The CAE includes **environmental, health, and safety (EHS)** risks in any organization-wide risk management assessment. These activities are assessed in a balanced manner relative to other types of risk associated with an organization's operations. Among the **risk exposures** to be evaluated are the following:

      1)   Organizational reporting structures
      2)   Likelihood of causing environmental harm, fines, and penalties
      3)   Expenditures mandated by governmental agencies
      4)   History of injuries and deaths
      5)   History of losing customers
      6)   Episodes of negative publicity and loss of public image and reputation

2.   **Environmental Audit Function**

    a.   If the CAE finds that the management of these risks largely depends on an environmental audit function, the CAE needs to consider the implications of that structure and its effects on operations and reporting.

      1)   If the CAE finds that the exposures are not adequately managed and residual risks exist, changes in the internal audit activity's plan of engagements and further investigations are normal results.

      2)   The typical environmental audit function reports to the organization's environmental component or general counsel. The common models for environmental auditing are the following:

         a)   The CAE and environmental audit executive are in separate functional units and have little contact.

         b)   The CAE and environmental audit executive are in separate functional units and coordinate their activities.

         c)   The CAE has responsibility for auditing environmental issues.

3.   **Research Findings**

    a.   A research study of EHS auditing found the following risk and independence issues:

      1)   The EHS audit function is **isolated** from other auditing activities. It is (a) organized separately from internal auditing, (b) only tangentially related to external audits of financial statements, and (c) reports to an EHS executive, not to the board or senior management.

         a)   This structure suggests that management believes EHS auditing to be a technical field that is best placed within the EHS function. In this position, auditors could be unable to maintain their independence.

2) EHS audit managers usually report administratively to the executives who are responsible for the physical facilities being audited. Because poor EHS performance reflects badly on the facilities management team, these executives have an incentive to influence (a) audit findings, (b) how audits are conducted, or (c) what is included in the audit plan.

    a) This potential subordination of the auditors' professional judgment, even when only apparent, violates auditor independence and objectivity.

3) It is also common for written audit reports to be distributed no higher in the organization than to senior environmental executives.

    a) Those executives may have a potential conflict of interest, and they may prevent or limit further distribution of EHS audit results to senior management and the board.

4) Audit information is often classified as either (a) subject to the attorney-client privilege or attorney work-product doctrine (if available in the relevant jurisdiction); (b) secret and confidential; or (c) if not confidential, then closely held.

    a) The effect is severely restricted access to EHS audit information.

4. **Role of the CAE**

a. The CAE fosters a close working relationship with the chief environmental officer and coordinates activities with the plan for environmental auditing.

1) When the environmental audit function reports to someone other than the CAE, the CAE offers to review the audit plan and the performance of engagements.

2) Periodically, the CAE schedules a quality assurance review of the environmental audit function if it is organizationally independent of the internal audit activity. That review determines whether environmental risks are being adequately addressed.

3) An EHS audit program may be

    a) **Compliance-focused** (verifying compliance with laws, regulations, and the organization's own EHS policies, procedures, and performance objectives),

    b) **Management systems-focused** (providing assessments of management systems intended to ensure compliance with legal and internal requirements and the mitigation of risks), or

    c) A **combination** of both approaches.

b. The CAE evaluates whether the environmental auditors, who are not part of the CAE's organization, are conforming with recognized professional auditing standards and a recognized code of ethics.

c. The CAE evaluates the organizational placement and independence of the environmental audit function to ensure that significant matters resulting from serious risks to the organization are reported up the chain of command to the board.

1) The CAE also facilitates the reporting of significant EHS risk and control issues to the board.

NOTE: The internal audit activity has an established place in the organization and normally has a broad scope of work permitting ready assimilation of the new function. Thus, it is an advantage to conduct environmental audits under the direction of the internal audit activity because of its position within the organization.

5. **Environmental Auditing**

   a. An organization subject to environmental laws and regulations having a significant effect on its operations should establish an environmental management system.

      1) One feature of this system is environmental auditing, which includes reviewing the adequacy and effectiveness of the controls over hazardous waste. It also extends to review of the reasonableness of contingent liabilities accrued for environmental remediation.

   b. According to a research report prepared for The IIA Research Foundation,

      An **environmental management system** *is an organization's structure of responsibilities and policies, practices, procedures, processes, and resources for protecting the environment and managing environmental issues. Environmental auditing is an integral part of an environmental management system whereby management determines whether the organization's environmental control systems are adequate to ensure compliance with regulatory requirements and internal policies.*

   c. The report describes seven types of environmental audits:

      1) **Compliance audits** are the most common form for industrial organizations. Their extent depends on the degree of risk of noncompliance.

         a) They are detailed, site-specific audits of current operations, past practices, and planned future operations.

         b) They usually involve a review of all environmental media the site may contaminate, including air, water, land, and wastewater. Moreover, they have quantitative and qualitative aspects and should be repeated periodically.

         c) Compliance audits range from preliminary assessments to (1) performance of detailed tests, (2) installation of groundwater monitoring wells, and (3) laboratory analyses.

      2) **Environmental management systems audits** determine whether systems are in place and operating properly to manage future environmental risks.

         a) Environmental issues may arise from practices that were legal when they were undertaken.

      3) **Transactional audits** assess the environmental risks and liabilities of land or facilities prior to a property sale or purchase. Current landowners may be responsible for contamination whether or not they caused it.

         a) Transactional audits require due diligence (a reasonable level of research) from the auditor. What constitutes due diligence for each phase of a transactional audit and the definitions of the phases are questions for debate. These phases are often characterized as follows:

            i) Phase I – qualitative site assessments involving a review of records and site reconnaissance

            ii) Phase II – sampling for potential contamination

            iii) Phase III – confirming the rate and extent of contaminant migration and the cost of remediation

         b) A transactional audit addresses all media exposures and all hazardous substances, e.g., radon, asbestos, PCBs, operating materials, and wastes.

4) **Treatment, storage, and disposal facility (TSDF) audits.** The law may require that hazardous materials be tracked from their acquisition or creation to disposal by means of a document (a manifest). All owners in the chain of title may be liable.

   a) For example, if an organization contracts with a transporter to dispose of hazardous waste in a licensed landfill and the landfill owner contaminates the environment, all the organizations and their officers may be financially liable for cleanup.

   b) TSDF audits are conducted on facilities the organization owns, leases, or manages, or on externally owned facilities where the organization's waste is treated, stored, or disposed. Thus, when an outside vendor is used for these purposes, the audit should consist of such procedures as

      i) Reviewing the vendor's documentation on hazardous material,

      ii) Reviewing the financial solvency of the vendors,

      iii) Reviewing the vendor's emergency response planning,

      iv) Determining that the vendor is approved by the governmental organization that is responsible for environmental protection,

      v) Obtaining the vendor's permit number, and

      vi) Inspecting the vendor's facilities.

5) A **pollution prevention audit** determines how waste can be minimized and pollution can be eliminated at the source. The following is a **pollution prevention hierarchy** from most desirable (recovery) to least (release without treatment):

   a) Recovery as a usable product
   b) Elimination at the source
   c) Recycling and reuse
   d) Energy conservation
   e) Treatment
   f) Disposal
   g) Release without treatment

6) **Environmental liability accrual audits.** Recognizing, quantifying, and reporting liability accruals may require redefinition of what is probable, measurable, and estimable. When an environmental issue becomes a liability is also unclear.

   a) The internal auditors may be responsible for assessing the reasonableness of cost estimates for environmental remediation. Due diligence may require assistance from independent experts, such as engineers.

7) **Product audits** determine whether products are environmentally friendly and whether product and chemical restrictions are being met. This process may result in the development of

   a) Fully recyclable products,
   b) Changes in the use and recovery of packaging materials, and
   c) The phaseout of some chemicals.

Stop and review! You have completed the outline for this subunit. Study multiple-choice questions 4 through 8 beginning on page 82.

3.3 CONSULTING ENGAGEMENTS – OVERVIEW

1. **Definition**

   a. **Consulting services** are "advisory and related client service activities, the nature and scope of which are agreed with the client, are intended to add value and improve an organization's governance, risk management, and control processes without the internal auditor assuming management responsibility. Examples include counsel, advice, facilitation, and training" (The IIA Glossary).

Implementation Standard 1000.C1

The nature of consulting services must be defined in the internal audit charter.

---

   1) The nature and scope of the consulting engagement are subject to agreement with the engagement client.

   2) The IIA's Consulting Implementation Standards describe the requirements of consulting engagements. The related outlines are based on IIA publications.

2. **Principles Applied to Internal Auditors' Consulting Activities**

   a. **Value Proposition** – The value proposition of the internal audit activity is realized within every organization that employs internal auditors in a manner that suits the culture and resources of that organization. That value proposition is captured in the definition of internal auditing and includes assurance and consulting activities designed to add value to the organization by bringing a systematic, disciplined approach to the areas of governance, risk, and control.

   b. **Consistency with Internal Audit Definition** – A disciplined, systematic evaluation methodology is incorporated in each internal audit activity. The list of services can generally be incorporated into the broad categories of assurance and consulting. However, the services also may include evolving forms of value-adding services that are consistent with the broad definition of internal auditing.

   c. **Audit Activities beyond Assurance and Consulting** – Assurance and consulting are not mutually exclusive and do not preclude other internal audit services, such as investigations and nonaudit roles. Many audit services will have both an assurance and consultative (advising) role.

   d. **Interrelationship between Assurance and Consulting** – Internal audit consulting enriches value-adding internal auditing. While consulting is often the direct result of assurance services, assurance also could result from consulting engagements.

   e. **Empower Consulting through the Internal Audit Charter** – Internal auditors have traditionally performed many types of consulting services, including the analysis of controls built into developing systems, analysis of security products, serving on task forces to analyze operations and make recommendations, and so forth. The board empowers the internal audit activity to perform additional services if they do not represent a conflict of interest or detract from its obligations to the board. That empowerment is reflected in the internal audit charter.

   f. **Objectivity** – Consulting services may enhance the auditor's understanding of business processes or issues related to an assurance engagement and do not necessarily impair the auditor's or the internal audit activity's objectivity. Internal auditing is not a management decision-making function. Decisions to adopt or implement recommendations made as a result of an internal audit advisory service are made by management. Therefore, internal audit objectivity is not impaired by the decisions made by management.

   g. **Internal Audit Foundation for Consulting Services** – Much of consulting is a natural extension of assurance and investigative services and may represent informal or formal advice, analysis, or assessments. The internal audit activity is uniquely positioned to perform this type of consulting work based on (1) its adherence to the highest standards of objectivity and (2) its breadth of knowledge about organizational processes, risk, and strategies.

h. **Communication of Fundamental Information** – A primary internal audit value is to provide **assurance** to senior management and the board. Consulting engagements cannot be performed in a manner that masks information that, in the judgment of the chief audit executive (CAE), should be presented to senior executives and board members. All consulting is to be understood in that context.

i. **Principles of Consulting Understood by the Organization** – Organizations must have ground rules for the performance of consulting services that are understood by all members of an organization. These rules are codified in the audit charter approved by the board and issued within the organization.

j. **Formal Consulting Engagements** – Management often engages external consultants for formal consulting engagements that last a significant period of time. However, an organization may find that the internal audit activity is uniquely qualified for some formal consulting tasks. If an internal audit activity undertakes to perform a formal consulting engagement, the internal audit group brings a systematic, disciplined approach to the conduct of the engagement.

k. **CAE Responsibilities** – Consulting services permit the CAE to enter into dialogue with management to address specific managerial issues. In this dialogue, the breadth of the engagement and time frames are made responsive to management needs. However, the CAE retains the prerogative of setting the audit techniques and the right of reporting to senior executives and the board when the nature and materiality of results pose significant risks to the organization.

l. **Criteria for Resolving Conflicts or Evolving Issues** – An internal auditor is first and foremost an internal auditor. Thus, in the performance of all services, the internal auditor is guided by The IIA Code of Ethics and the Attribute and Performance Standards of the *International Standards for the Professional Practice of Internal Auditing*. The resolution of any unforeseen conflicts of activities needs to be consistent with the Code of Ethics and the *Standards*.

3. **Classification of Engagements**

Implementation Standard 2010.C1

The chief audit executive should consider accepting proposed consulting engagements based on the engagement's potential to improve management of risks, add value, and improve the organization's operations. Accepted engagements must be included in the plan.

Implementation Standard 2120.C1

During consulting engagements, internal auditors must address risk consistent with the engagement's objectives and be alert to the existence of other significant risks.

Implementation Standard 2120.C2

Internal auditors must incorporate knowledge of risks gained from consulting engagements into their evaluation of the organization's risk management processes.

Implementation Standard 2120.C3

When assisting management in establishing or improving risk management processes, internal auditors must refrain from assuming any management responsibility by actually managing risks.

Implementation Standard 2130.C1

Internal auditors must incorporate knowledge of controls gained from consulting engagements into evaluation of the organization's control processes.

    a.   The chief audit executive determines the methodology to use for classifying engagements within the organization.

        1)   In some circumstances, it may be appropriate to conduct a blended engagement that incorporates elements of both consulting and assurance activities into one consolidated approach.

        2)   In other cases, it may be appropriate to distinguish between the assurance and consulting components of the engagement.

    b.   Internal auditors may conduct consulting services as part of their normal or routine activities as well as in response to requests by management. Each organization considers the type of consulting activities to be offered and determines whether specific policies or procedures need to be developed for each type of activity. Possible categories could include the following:

        1)   **Formal consulting** engagements are planned and subject to written agreement.

        2)   **Informal consulting** engagements involve routine activities, such as (a) participation on standing committees, (b) limited-life projects, (c) ad-hoc meetings, and (d) routine information exchange.

        3)   **Special consulting** engagements include participation on a merger and acquisition team or system conversion team.

        4)   **Emergency consulting** engagements include participation on a team (a) established for recovery or maintenance of operations after a disaster or other extraordinary business event or (b) assembled to supply temporary help to meet a special request or unusual deadline.

    c.   Auditors generally should not agree to conduct a consulting engagement simply to circumvent, or to allow others to circumvent, requirements that would normally apply to an assurance engagement if the service in question is more appropriately conducted as an assurance engagement. This does not preclude adjusting methods if services once conducted as assurance engagements are deemed more suitable to being performed as a consulting engagement.

4.   **Governmental Internal Auditing**

    a.   A governmental internal audit activity's provision of consulting services may be limited by local law, audit standards, etc. The parameters of these services are defined in its charter and supported by its policies and procedures.

    b.   Assurance services help ensure management's accountability. These services include an assistance dimension when auditors recommend operational improvements. But auditors jeopardize their independence and objectivity by being responsible for implementing or authorizing improvements, even those arising from consulting.

    c.   When consulting, auditors stay within the bounds of the core elements of the audit function. These give credibility to the auditors' attestation to management assertions. **Core elements** support the principle that an objective third party is providing assurance about the assertions. The core elements that protect auditors' ability to give assurance are

        1)   Independence,

        2)   Objectivity,

        3)   Not auditing one's own work, and

        4)   Not performing functions or making decisions that are managerial.

    d.   Other threats to auditor independence include consulting work that (1) creates a mutuality of interest or (2) positions auditors as advocates for the organization.

    e.   Governing rules may restrict the internal audit activity's consulting services. These rules may apply to external auditors or all auditors. They may be based on law, regulation, a code of ethics, or audit standards. The CAE ensures that the internal audit activity's charter, policies, and procedures comply with the governing rules.

f. Even if restrictive governing rules do not apply, the quality assurance system should minimize threats to auditor independence or objectivity posed by consulting. Otherwise, the internal audit activity's assurance role and the ability of other auditors to rely on its work may be compromised. Avoiding these threats depends in part on distinguishing between (1) merely advising and (2) assuming management responsibilities.

g. The internal audit activity documents procedures for review of threats to independence and objectivity. The documentation is available to external quality control reviewers.

h. The internal audit activity implements controls to reduce the potential threats to auditor independence or objectivity posed by consulting. These controls may include the following:

  1) Charter language defining consulting service parameters
  2) Policies and procedures limiting type, nature, or level of participation in consulting
  3) Screening consulting projects, with limits on engagements threatening objectivity
  4) Segregation of consulting units from assurance units in the audit function
  5) Rotation of auditors
  6) Employing external service providers for (a) consulting or (b) assurance engagements involving activities subject to prior consulting work that impaired objectivity or independence
  7) Disclosure in audit reports when objectivity was impaired by participation in a prior consulting project

Stop and review! You have completed the outline for this subunit. Study multiple-choice questions 9 though 11 beginning on page 83.

3.4 CONSULTING ENGAGEMENTS – INTERNAL AUDITOR

1. **Independence and Objectivity**

> **Implementation Standard 1130.C1**
>
> Internal auditors may provide consulting services relating to operations for which they had previous responsibilities.
>
> **Implementation Standard 1130.C2**
>
> If internal auditors have potential impairments to independence or objectivity relating to proposed consulting services, disclosure must be made to the engagement client prior to accepting the engagement.

a. Internal auditors are sometimes requested to provide consulting services relating to operations for which they had previous responsibilities or had conducted assurance services. Prior to offering consulting services, the CAE confirms that the board understands and approves the concept of providing consulting services. Once approved, the internal audit charter is amended to include authority and responsibilities for consulting activities, and the internal audit activity develops appropriate policies and procedures for conducting such engagements.

b. Internal auditors maintain their objectivity when drawing conclusions and offering advice to management. If impairments to independence or objectivity exist prior to commencement of the consulting engagement, or subsequently develop during the engagement, disclosure is made immediately to management.

c. Independence and objectivity may be impaired if assurance services are provided within 1 year after a formal consulting engagement. Steps can be taken to minimize the effects of impairment by (1) assigning different auditors to perform each of the services, (2) establishing independent management and supervision, (3) defining separate accountability for the results of the projects, and (4) disclosing the presumed impairment. Management is responsible for accepting and implementing recommendations.

    d.   Care is taken, particularly involving consulting engagements that are ongoing or continuous in nature, so that internal auditors do not inappropriately or unintentionally assume management responsibilities that were not intended in the original objectives and scope of the engagement.

2. **Due Professional Care**

Implementation Standard 1210.C1

The chief audit executive must decline the consulting engagement or obtain competent advice and assistance if the internal auditors lack the knowledge, skills, or other competencies needed to perform all or part of the engagement.

Implementation Standard 1220.C1

Internal auditors must exercise due professional care during a consulting engagement by considering the:

- Needs and expectations of clients, including the nature, timing, and communication of engagement results;
- Relative complexity and extent of work needed to achieve the engagement's objectives; and
- Cost of the consulting engagement in relation to potential benefits.

---

    a.   The internal auditor exercises due professional care in conducting a formal consulting engagement by understanding the following:

        1)   Needs of management officials, including the nature, timing, and communication of engagement results

        2)   Possible motivations and reasons of those requesting the service

        3)   Extent of work needed to achieve the engagement's objectives

        4)   Skills and resources needed to conduct the engagement

        5)   Effect on the scope of the audit plan previously approved by the audit committee

        6)   Potential impact on future audit assignments and engagements

        7)   Potential organizational benefits to be derived from the engagement

    b.   In addition to the independence and objectivity evaluation and due professional care considerations, the internal auditor

        1)   Conducts appropriate meetings and gathers necessary information to assess the nature and extent of the service to be provided.

        2)   Confirms that those receiving the service understand and agree with (a) the relevant guidance contained in the internal audit charter, (b) internal audit activity's policies and procedures, and (c) other related guidance for consulting engagements. The internal auditor declines to perform consulting engagements that (a) are prohibited by the charter, (b) conflict with the policies and procedures of the internal audit activity, or (c) do not add value and promote the best interests of the organization.

        3)   Evaluates the consulting engagement for compatibility with the internal audit activity's overall plan of engagements. The risk-based plan of engagements may incorporate and rely on consulting engagements, to the extent deemed appropriate, to provide necessary audit coverage.

        4)   Documents general terms, understandings, deliverables, and other key factors of the formal consulting engagement in a written agreement or plan. It is essential that the internal auditor and those receiving the consulting engagement understand and agree with the reporting and communication requirements.

3.   **Scope of Work**

Implementation Standard 2201.C1

Internal auditors must establish an understanding with consulting engagement clients about objectives, scope, respective responsibilities, and other client expectations. For significant engagements, this understanding must be documented.

Implementation Standard 2210.C1

Consulting engagement objectives must address governance, risk management, and control processes to the extent agreed upon with the client.

Implementation Standard 2210.C2

Consulting engagement objectives must be consistent with the organization's values, strategies, and objectives.

Implementation Standard 2220.C1

In performing consulting engagements, internal auditors must ensure that the scope of the engagement is sufficient to address the agreed-upon objectives. If internal auditors develop reservations about the scope during the engagement, these reservations must be discussed with the client to determine whether to continue with the engagement.

---

a.   Internal auditors design the scope of work to ensure that the professionalism, integrity, credibility, and reputation of the internal audit activity will be maintained.

b.   In planning formal consulting engagements, internal auditors design objectives to meet the appropriate needs of management officials receiving these services. If management makes special requests and the internal auditor believes the objectives that need to be pursued go beyond those requested by management, the internal auditor may consider

1)   Persuading management to include the additional objectives in the consulting engagement or

2)   Documenting the failure to pursue the objectives, disclosing that observation in the final communication of consulting engagement results, and including the objectives in a separate and subsequent assurance engagement.

Implementation Standard 2240.C1

Work programs for consulting engagements may vary in form and content depending upon the nature of the engagement.

---

c.   **Work programs** for formal consulting engagements document the objectives and scope of the engagement and the methods to be used in satisfying the objectives.

1)   In establishing the scope of the engagement, internal auditors may expand or limit the scope to satisfy management. However, the internal auditor needs to be satisfied that the projected scope of work will be adequate to meet the objectives of the engagement.

2)   The objectives, scope, and terms of the engagement are periodically reassessed and adjusted during the course of the work.

Implementation Standard 2220.C2

During consulting engagements, internal auditors must address controls consistent with the engagement's objectives and be alert to significant control issues.

    d.   Internal auditors are observant of the effectiveness of risk management and control processes during formal consulting engagements. Substantial risk exposures or material control weaknesses are reported to management.

        1)   In some situations, the auditor's concerns also are communicated to senior management or the board. (According to The IIA Glossary, the board includes any "designated body of the organization, including the audit committee.")

        2)   Auditors determine (a) the significance of exposures or weaknesses and the actions taken or contemplated to mitigate or correct and (b) the expectations of senior management and the board about reporting.

4.   **Communicating Results**

Implementation Standard 2410.C1

Communication of the progress and results of consulting engagements will vary in form and content depending upon the nature of the engagement and the needs of the client.

Implementation Standard 2440.C1

The chief audit executive is responsible for communicating the final results of consulting engagements to clients.

Implementation Standard 2440.C2

During consulting engagements, governance, risk management, and control issues may be identified. Whenever these issues are significant to the organization, they must be communicated to senior management and the board.

---

    a.   Reporting requirements are generally determined by those requesting the consulting service and meet the objectives as determined and agreed to with management.

        1)   However, the format for communicating the results clearly describes the nature of the engagement and any limitations, restrictions, or other factors about which users of the information need to be made aware.

    b.   In some circumstances, the internal auditor may communicate results beyond those who received or requested the service. In such cases, the internal auditor expands the reporting so that results are communicated to the appropriate parties. The auditor therefore takes the following steps until satisfied with the resolution of the matter:

        1)   Determine what direction is provided in the agreement concerning the consulting engagement and related communications.

        2)   Attempt to persuade those receiving or requesting the service to expand the communication to the appropriate parties.

        3)   Determine what guidance is provided in the internal audit charter or the internal audit activity's policies and procedures concerning consulting communications.

        4)   Determine what guidance is provided in the organization's code of conduct, code of ethics, and other related policies, administrative directives, or procedures.

        5)   Determine what guidance is provided by The IIA's *Standards* and Code of Ethics, other standards or codes applicable to the auditor, and any legal or regulatory requirements that relate to the matter under consideration.

    c.   Internal auditors disclose to management, the board, or other governing body of the organization the nature, extent, and overall results of formal consulting engagements along with other reports of internal audit activities. Internal auditors keep management and the board informed about how audit resources are being deployed.

        1)   Neither detail reports of these consulting engagements nor the specific results and recommendations are required to be communicated. But an appropriate description of these types of engagements and their significant recommendations are communicated. This communication is essential in satisfying the CAE's responsibility to comply with Performance Standard 2060, *Reporting to Senior Management and the Board.*

5. **Documentation**

> ### Implementation Standard 2330.C1
>
> The chief audit executive must develop policies governing the custody and retention of consulting engagement records, as well as their release to internal and external parties. These policies must be consistent with the organization's guidelines and any pertinent regulatory or other requirements.

    a. Documentation requirements for assurance engagements do not necessarily apply to consulting engagements.

    b. In formal consulting engagements, auditors adopt appropriate record retention policies and address such related issues as ownership of the engagement records. Legal, regulatory, tax, and accounting matters may require special treatment in the records.

6. **Monitoring**

> ### Implementation Standard 2500.C1
>
> The internal audit activity must monitor the disposition of results of consulting engagements to the extent agreed upon with the client.

    a. Varying types of monitoring may be appropriate for differing types of consulting engagements.

    b. The monitoring effort may depend on various factors, such as management's explicit interest in the engagement or the internal auditor's assessment of the project's risks or value to the organization.

Stop and review! You have completed the outline for this subunit. Study multiple-choice questions 12 and 13 on page 84.

3.5 CONSULTING ENGAGEMENTS – BENCHMARKING

1. **Benchmarking**

    a. Benchmarking is one of the primary tools used in TQM. It is a means of helping organizations with productivity management and business process review. It is therefore a source of consulting engagements for internal auditors.

    b. Benchmarking is a continuous evaluation of the practices of the best organizations in their class and the adaptation of processes to reflect the best of these practices. It involves (1) analyzing and measuring key outputs against those of the best organizations and (2) identifying the underlying key actions and causes that contribute to the performance difference.

        1) **Best practices** are recognized by authorities in the field and by customers for generating outstanding results. They are generally innovative technically or in their management of human resources.

        2) Benchmarking is an ongoing process that involves quantitative and qualitative measurement of the difference between the organization's performance of an activity and the performance by the benchmark organization.

c. The following are kinds of benchmarking:

1) **Competitive** benchmarking studies an organization in the same industry.
2) **Process (function)** benchmarking studies operations of organizations with similar processes regardless of industry. Thus, the benchmark need not be a competitor or even a similar organization.

   a) This method may introduce new ideas that provide a significant competitive advantage.

3) **Strategic** benchmarking is a search for successful competitive strategies.
4) **Internal** benchmarking is the application of best practices in one part of the organization to its other parts.
5) **Generic** benchmarking observes a process in one operation and compares it with a process having similar characteristics but in a different industry.

d. The first phase in the benchmarking process is to select and prioritize benchmarking projects.

1) An organization must understand its critical success factors and business environment to identify key business processes and drivers and to develop parameters defining what processes to benchmark. The criteria for selecting what to benchmark are based mostly on satisfaction of customer needs.

e. The next phase is to organize benchmarking teams. A team organization is appropriate because it permits a fair division of labor, participation by those responsible for implementing changes, and inclusion of a variety of functional expertise and work experience.

1) The benchmarking team must thoroughly investigate and document the organization's internal processes.

   a) The team must develop a family of measures that are true indicators of process performance.
   b) The development of key indicators for performance measurement in a benchmarking context is an extension of the basic evaluative function of internal auditors.

f. Researching and identifying best-in-class performance is often the most difficult phase. The critical steps are

1) Setting up databases,
2) Choosing information-gathering methods (internal sources, external public domain sources, and original research),
3) Formatting questionnaires (lists of questions prepared in advance), and
4) Selecting benchmarking partners.

g. Data analysis involves identifying performance gaps, understanding the reasons, and prioritizing the key activities that will facilitate the behavioral and process changes needed to implement recommendations.

h. Leadership is most important in the implementation phase because the team must justify its recommendations. Moreover, the process improvement teams must manage the implementation of approved changes.

Stop and review! You have completed the outline for this subunit. Study multiple-choice questions 14 through 17 on page 85.

3.6 CONSULTING ENGAGEMENTS – OTHER TYPES

1. **Internal Control Training**

    a. Internal auditors may perform consulting engagements to provide internal control training to the employees of the organization.

        1) Such training may involve instruction about the organization's objectives, policies, standards, procedures, performance measurements, and feedback methods.

        2) In addition to providing courses for client personnel, the internal audit activity may offer internships to some new managers. Among other things, these managers gain experience in assessing controls.

    b. As part of their coordination with external auditors, the internal auditors may provide opportunities for joint control training and other matters.

    c. Internal auditors also should undergo internal control training, for example, with regard to control frameworks, specific controls and control objectives, standards, technological developments, and new professional literature.

    d. Control self-assessment provides training for people in business units. Participants gain experience in assessing risks and associating control processes with managing those risks and improving the chances of achieving business objectives.

    e. The ethical culture of an organization is linked to the governance process and is the most important soft control.

        1) Internal auditors have many roles in supporting the ethical culture, including those of ethics counselor and ethics expert.

2. **Due Diligence Auditing**

    a. The term "due diligence" is applied to a service in which internal auditors and others (external auditors, tax experts, finance professionals, attorneys, etc.) determine the business justification for a major transaction (business combination, joint venture, divestiture, etc.) and whether that justification is valid.

        1) Internal auditors might, for example, review operations (purchasing, shipping and receiving, inventory management, etc.), internal control over information systems, the compatibility of the organizational cultures, and finance and accounting issues.

        2) The term "due diligence" also may be used for other engagements, for example, certain environmental audits.

    b. The due diligence process establishes whether the expected benefits of the transaction (wider markets, more skilled employees, access to intellectual property, operating synergies, etc.) are likely to be realized. It also may facilitate the realization of those benefits by improving the effectiveness and efficiency of the implementation of the transaction.

    c. One of the keys to the effectiveness and efficiency of the engagement is coordination among the groups involved. For example, the same software should be used for preparation of electronic workpapers to facilitate sharing of information.

    d. The final report should be factual, not subjective, with supporting information indexed and backed up on computer disks.

        1) The report should contain an executive summary with key points highlighted.

        2) The cycle approach used by the acquiring organization to organize its business is a desirable means of structuring the report.

3. **Business Process Mapping**

   a.   One approach to business process mapping (review) is **reengineering** (also called business process reengineering). It involves process innovation and core process redesign. Instead of improving existing procedures, it finds new ways of doing things.

      1)   The emphasis is on simplification and elimination of nonvalue-adding activities. Thus, reengineering is not continuous improvement, it is not simply downsizing or modifying an existing system, and it should be reserved for the most important processes.

      2)   An organization may need to adapt quickly and radically to change. Thus, reengineering is usually a cross-departmental process of innovation requiring substantial investment in information technology and retraining. Successful reengineering may bring dramatic improvements in customer service and the speed with which new products are introduced.

   b.   One well-known tool useful in reengineering is **work measurement**, a process that involves analysis of activities. The nature and extent of a task, the procedures needed for its execution, and the efficiency with which it is carried out are determined by work measurement.

      1)   This technique is appropriate when management takes an engineered-cost approach to control. Such an approach is indicated when the workload is divisible into control-factor units, for example, accounting entries made, lines of text word processed, or number of packages shipped. The cost of a control-factor unit is treated as a variable cost for budgeting purposes.

      2)   One method used for work measurement is micromotion study, which requires videotaping the performance of a job, e.g., assembly-line activities.

      3)   Another method is work sampling, making many random observations of an activity to determine what steps it normally requires.

   c.   Reengineering and total quality management (TQM) techniques (as discussed in Study Unit 2, Subunit 4) eliminate many traditional controls. They exploit modern technology to improve productivity and decrease the number of clerical workers. Thus, the emphasis is on developing controls that are automated and self-correcting and that require minimal human intervention.

      1)   The emphasis shifts to monitoring internal control so management can determine when an operation may be out of control and corrective action is needed.

         a)   Most reengineering and TQM techniques also assume that humans will be motivated to work actively in improving operations when they are full participants in the process.

      2)   Monitoring assesses the quality of internal control over time. Management considers whether internal control is properly designed and operating as intended and modifies it to reflect changing conditions. Monitoring may be in the form of separate, periodic evaluations or of ongoing monitoring.

         a)   Ongoing monitoring occurs as part of routine operations. It includes management and supervisory review, comparisons, reconciliations, and other actions by personnel as part of their regular activities.

   d.   Internal auditors may perform the functions of determining whether the reengineering process has senior management's support, recommending areas for consideration, and developing audit plans for the new system. However, they should not become directly involved in the implementation of the process. This involvement would impair their independence and objectivity.

4. **System Development Reviews**

    a.   Internal auditor involvement throughout the systems development life cycle can ensure that the appropriate internal controls and audit trails are included in the application. According to The IIA's *GTAG Auditing IT Projects*, "Internal auditing can bring the value of their experience and methodology to review projects in the early stages to also help increase the likelihood of success." Benefits of internal audit involvement may include

        1)   Providing independent, ongoing advice throughout the project and

        2)   Identifying key risks or issues early, which enables project teams to operate proactively to mitigate risks.

    b.   The section for systems development and acquisition controls in *GTAG Information Technology Risks and Controls* is useful for understanding the role of the internal auditor. It states that "the IT auditor should assess whether the organization uses a controlled method to develop or acquire application systems and whether it delivers effective controls over and within the applications and data they process. By examining application development procedures, the auditor can gain assurance that application controls are adequate. Some basic control issues should be addressed in all systems development and acquisition work. For example,

        1)   User requirements should be documented, and their achievement should be measured.

        2)   Systems design should follow a formal process to ensure that user requirements and controls are designed into the system.

        3)   Systems development should be conducted in a structured manner to ensure that requirements and approved design features are incorporated into the finished product.

        4)   Testing should ensure that individual system elements work as required, system interfaces operate as expected, and that the system owner has confirmed that the intended functionality has been provided.

        5)   Application maintenance processes should ensure that changes in application systems follow a consistent pattern of control. Change management should be subject to structured assurance validation processes."

    c.   If "systems development is outsourced, the outsourcer or provider contracts should require similar controls. Project management techniques and controls should be part of the development process—whether developments are performed in-house or are outsourced. Management should know whether projects are on time and within budget and that resources are used efficiently. Reporting processes should ensure that management understands the current status of development projects and does not receive any surprises when the end product is delivered."

5. **Design of Performance Measurement Systems**

    a.   As an assurance engagement, internal auditors conduct performance audits to measure how well an organization is achieving its targets for its key performance indicators. As a consulting engagement, internal auditors work with clients to improve the performance measured by the key performance indicators.

Stop and review! You have completed the outline for this subunit. Study multiple-choice questions 18 through 20 on page 86.

QUESTIONS

3.1 Financial Engagements

1. Controls should be designed to ensure that

A. Operations are performed efficiently.

B. Management's plans have not been circumvented by worker collusion.

C. The internal audit activity's guidance and oversight of management's performance is accomplished economically and efficiently.

D. Management's planning, organizing, and directing processes are properly evaluated.

Answer (A) is correct.
    REQUIRED: The purpose of controls.
    DISCUSSION: The purpose of control processes is to support the organization in the management of risks and the achievement of its established and communicated objectives. The control processes are expected to ensure, among other things, that operations are performed efficiently and achieve established results.
    Answer (B) is incorrect. Collusion is an inherent limitation of internal control. Answer (C) is incorrect. The board provides oversight of risk management and control processes administered by management. Answer (D) is incorrect. Controls are actions by management, the board, and others to manage risk and increase the likelihood that established goals and objectives will be achieved (The IIA Glossary). The internal audit activity evaluates the effectiveness of control processes. Thus, controls do not directly address management's planning, organizing, and directing processes. Internal auditors evaluate management processes to determine whether reasonable assurance exists that objectives and goals will be achieved.

2. The chief audit executive's responsibility for assessing and reporting on control processes includes

A. Communicating to senior management and the board an annual judgment about internal control.

B. Overseeing the establishment of internal control processes.

C. Maintaining the organization's governance processes.

D. Arriving at a single assessment based solely on the work of the internal audit activity.

Answer (A) is correct.
    REQUIRED: The chief audit executive's responsibility for assessing and reporting on control processes.
    DISCUSSION: The CAE's report on the organization's control processes is normally presented once a year to senior management and the board.
    Answer (B) is incorrect. Senior management is responsible for overseeing the establishment of internal control processes. Answer (C) is incorrect. The board is responsible for establishing and maintaining the organization's governance processes. Answer (D) is incorrect. The challenge for the internal audit activity is to evaluate the effectiveness of the organization's system of controls based on the aggregation of many individual assessments. Those assessments are largely gained from internal auditing engagements, management's self assessments, and external assurance providers' work.

3. An internal auditor fails to discover an employee fraud during an assurance engagement. The nondiscovery is most likely to suggest a violation of the International Professional Practices Framework if it was the result of a

A. Failure to perform a detailed review of all transactions in the area.

B. Determination that any possible fraud in the area would not involve a material amount.

C. Determination that the cost of extending procedures in the area would exceed the potential benefits.

D. Presumption that the internal controls in the area were adequate and effective.

Answer (D) is correct.
    REQUIRED: The most likely reason that failure to detect fraud is a violation of the *Standards*.
    DISCUSSION: The internal audit activity evaluates the adequacy and effectiveness of controls (Impl. Std. 2130.A1). Moreover, the internal audit activity must assist the organization in maintaining effective controls by evaluating their effectiveness and efficiency and by promoting continuous improvement (Perf. Std. 2130). Thus, an internal auditor must not simply assume that controls are adequate and effective.
    Answer (A) is incorrect. Due professional care does not require detailed reviews of all transactions. Answer (B) is incorrect. The relative complexity, materiality, or significance of matters to which assurance procedures are applied should be considered. Answer (C) is incorrect. The internal auditor should consider the cost of assurance in relation to potential benefits.

3.2 Environmental Engagements

4. In any organization-wide risk management assessment, the CAE should include risks associated with which of the following activities?

    A. Environmental.

    B. Health.

    C. Safety.

    D. All of the answers are correct.

Answer (D) is correct.
    REQUIRED: The risks assessed by the CAE that should be included in any organization-wide risk assessment.
    DISCUSSION: The CAE includes environmental, health, and safety (EHS) risks in any organization-wide risk management assessment and assesses the activities in a balanced manner relative to other types of risk associated with an organization's operations.

5. Internal auditors are increasingly called on to perform audits related to an organization's environmental stewardship. Which of the following does **not** describe the objectives of a type of environmental audit?

    A. Determine whether environmental management systems are in place and operating properly to manage future environmental risks.

    B. Determine whether environmental issues are considered as part of economic decisions.

    C. Determine whether the organization's current actions are in compliance with existing laws.

    D. Determine whether the organization is focusing efforts on ensuring that its products are environmentally friendly, and confirm that product and chemical restrictions are met.

Answer (B) is correct.
    REQUIRED: The item that does not describe the objectives of an environmental audit.
    DISCUSSION: Determining whether environmental issues are considered as part of economic decisions is an audit procedure. It does not describe the objectives of an environmental audit.
    Answer (A) is incorrect. An environmental management system audit determines whether environmental management systems are in place and operating properly to manage future environmental risks. Answer (C) is incorrect. A compliance audit determines whether the organization's current actions are in compliance with existing laws. Answer (D) is incorrect. A product audit determines whether the organization focuses efforts on ensuring that its products are environmentally friendly and confirms that product and chemical restrictions are met.

6. What type of audit assesses the environmental risks and liabilities of land or facilities prior to a property transaction?

    A. Pollution prevention audit.

    B. Compliance audit.

    C. Transactional audit.

    D. Product audit.

Answer (C) is correct.
    REQUIRED: The type of audit used prior to property transactions.
    DISCUSSION: Transactional audits (also called acquisition and divestiture audits, property transfer site assessments, property transfer evaluations, and due diligence audit) assess the environmental risks and liabilities of land or facilities prior to a property transaction.
    Answer (A) is incorrect. A pollution prevention audit determines how waste can be minimized and pollution can be eliminated at the source. Answer (B) is incorrect. A compliance audit is most common for industries. They are detailed site-specific audits of current operations. Answer (D) is incorrect. A product audit determines whether products are environmentally friendly and whether product and chemical restrictions are being met.

7. Smith Ice Plant (SIP) is located on the Mississippi River. SIP has a history of leaking pollutants into the Mississippi. Among the following environmental risk exposures, which one does SIP **not** have to evaluate as part of its organization-wide environmental risk management assessment?

A. History of financial distress.

B. Likelihood of water pollution fines.

C. History of employee injuries.

D. Likelihood of loss of public reputation.

Answer (A) is correct.

REQUIRED: The environmental risk exposures that need to be evaluated during an organization-wide assessment.

DISCUSSION: As part of an environmental risk assessment, the CAE evaluates the following risk exposures: (1) organizational reporting structures; (2) likelihood of environmental harm, fines, and penalties; (3) expenditures mandated by governmental agencies; (4) history of injuries and deaths; (5) history of losing customers; and (6) episodes of negative publicity and loss of public image and reputation. The history of financial distress is not included in the list of environmental risk exposures.

Answer (B) is incorrect. The likelihood of environmental harm, fines, and penalties is included in the list of environmental risk exposures to be evaluated. Answer (C) is incorrect. The history of deaths and injuries is included in the list of environmental risk exposures to be evaluated. Answer (D) is incorrect. Episodes of negative publicity and loss of public image and reputation are included in the list of environmental risk exposures to be evaluated.

8. Which of the following is true about the interaction of the internal audit function and the environmental audit function?

A. If the environmental audit function reports to someone other than the CAE, the CAE should not offer to review the audit plan since (s)he was not consulted to do so.

B. It is not advantageous for the internal audit function to conduct environmental audits since it is too busy with its current responsibilities.

C. The CAE should evaluate whether the environmental auditors are conforming to recognized professional auditing standards and a recognized code of ethics.

D. The CAE should not evaluate the organizational placement and independence of the environmental audit function since the internal function has no control over a separate environmental audit function.

Answer (C) is correct.

REQUIRED: The role of the CAE in the environmental audit function.

DISCUSSION: This is a proper interaction between the environmental audit function and the internal audit function.

Answer (A) is incorrect. When the environmental audit function reports to someone other than the CAE, the CAE offers to review the audit plan and the performance of engagements. Answer (B) is incorrect. The internal audit activity has an established place in the organization and normally has a broad scope of work permitting ready assimilation of the new function. Thus, it is advantageous to conduct environmental audits under the direction of the internal audit activity because of its position within the organization. Answer (D) is incorrect. The CAE evaluates the organizational placement and independence of the environmental audit function to ensure that matters resulting from serious risks to the organization are reported up the chain of command to the board.

3.3 Consulting Engagements – Overview

9. Internal auditors may provide consulting services that add value and improve an organization's operations. The performance of these services

A. Impairs internal auditors' objectivity with respect to an assurance service involving the same engagement client.

B. Precludes generation of assurance from a consulting engagement.

C. Should be consistent with the internal audit activity's empowerment reflected in the charter.

D. Imposes no responsibility to communicate information other than to the engagement client.

Answer (C) is correct.

REQUIRED: The internal auditors' responsibility regarding consulting services.

DISCUSSION: According to Impl. Std. 1000.C1, the nature of consulting services must be defined in the charter.

Answer (A) is incorrect. Consulting services do not necessarily impair objectivity. Decisions to implement recommendations made as a result of a consulting service are made by management. Thus, decision making by management does not impair the internal auditors' objectivity. Answer (B) is incorrect. Assurance and consulting services are not mutually exclusive. One type of service may be generated from the other. Answer (D) is incorrect. A primary internal audit value is to provide assurance to senior management and audit committee directors. Consulting engagements cannot be rendered in a manner that masks information that in the judgment of the chief audit executive (CAE) should be presented to senior executives and board members.

10. Which of the following statements is **false**?

- A. A disciplined, systematic evaluation methodology is incorporated in each internal audit activity. The list of services can generally be incorporated into two broad categories of assurance and consulting.

- B. Assurance and consulting are mutually exclusive and do preclude other auditing services such as investigations and nonauditing roles.

- C. Many audit services will have both an assurance and consultative role.

- D. Internal audit consulting enriches value-adding internal auditing.

Answer (B) is correct.
   REQUIRED: The false statement regarding consulting and assurance services.
   DISCUSSION: Certain principles guide the performance of consulting activities of internal auditors. For example, assurance and consulting are not mutually exclusive and do not preclude other auditing services such as investigations and nonauditing roles.

11. Senior management of an entity has requested that the internal audit activity assist the purchasing function's switch from a manual entry inventory system to a fully automated inventory system. This service is best performed in a(n)

- A. Formal consulting engagement agreement.

- B. Informal consulting engagement agreement.

- C. Special consulting engagement agreement.

- D. Emergency consulting engagement agreement.

Answer (C) is correct.
   REQUIRED: The service best performed in a switch to a fully automated inventory system.
   DISCUSSION: A special consulting engagement agreement applies to occasional, one-time special arrangements. Senior management should delegate the transition from a manual system to an automated system to the internal audit function to ensure proper design and implementation of the system.
   Answer (A) is incorrect. A formal consulting engagement agreement applies to planned and continuous arrangements. Answer (B) is incorrect. An informal consulting engagement agreement applies to routine tasks. Answer (D) is incorrect. An emergency consulting engagement agreement applies to unplanned engagements.

3.4 Consulting Engagements – Internal Auditor

12. An internal auditor performed a formal consulting engagement for XYZ Corporation on June 1, Year 1. When is the earliest time the auditor can perform assurance services for XYZ Corporation and be considered independent and objective?

- A. January 1, Year 2.

- B. June 1, Year 2.

- C. July 1, Year 1.

- D. June 2, Year 1.

Answer (B) is correct.
   REQUIRED: The earliest date the internal auditor can perform assurance services and be considered independent and objective.
   DISCUSSION: Independence and objectivity may be impaired if assurance services are provided within 1 year after a formal consulting engagement. Steps can be taken to minimize the effects of impairment by assigning different auditors to perform each of the services, establishing independent management and supervision, defining separate accountability for the results of the projects, and disclosing the presumed impairment.

13. Internal auditors should design the scope of work in a consulting engagement to ensure that all of the following will be maintained **except**

- A. Independence.

- B. Integrity.

- C. Credibility.

- D. Professionalism.

Answer (A) is correct.
   REQUIRED: The attribute of the internal audit activity that need not be maintained in a consulting engagement.
   DISCUSSION: Internal auditors need to reach an understanding of the objectives and scope of the consulting engagement with those receiving the service. During a consulting engagement, the internal auditor is acting as an advocate for management, and independence is not required.

3.5 Consulting Engagements – Benchmarking

14. Which of the following is **not** a critical step in the researching and identifying best-in-class performance phase?

A. Setting up databases.

B. Choosing information-gathering methods.

C. Formatting questionnaires.

D. Employee training and empowerment.

Answer (D) is correct.

> **REQUIRED:** The step that is not critical in the researching and identifying best-in-class performance phase.
> **DISCUSSION:** The critical steps in the researching and identifying phase are setting up databases, choosing information-gathering methods, formatting questionnaires, and selecting benchmarking partners. Employee training and empowerment is part of total quality management (TQM).
> Answer (A) is incorrect. Setting up databases is a critical step in the researching and identifying phase. Answer (B) is incorrect. Choosing information-gathering methods is a critical step in the researching and identifying phase. Answer (C) is incorrect. Formatting questionnaires is a critical step in the researching and identifying phase.

15. Which of the following statements regarding benchmarking is **false**?

A. Benchmarking involves continuously evaluating the practices of best-in-class organizations and adapting company processes to incorporate the best of these practices.

B. Benchmarking, in practice, usually involves a company's formation of benchmarking teams.

C. Benchmarking is an ongoing process that entails quantitative and qualitative measurement of the difference between the company's performance of an activity and the performance by the best in the world or the best in the industry.

D. The benchmarking organization against which a firm is comparing itself must be a direct competitor.

Answer (D) is correct.

> **REQUIRED:** The false statement about benchmarking.
> **DISCUSSION:** Benchmarking is an ongoing process that entails quantitative and qualitative measurement of the difference between the company's performance of an activity and the performance by a best-in-class organization. The benchmarking organization against which a firm is comparing itself need not be a direct competitor. The important consideration is that the benchmarking organization be an outstanding performer in its industry.

16. What is the first phase in the benchmarking process?

A. Organize benchmarking teams.

B. Select and prioritize benchmarking projects.

C. Researching and identifying best-in-class performance.

D. Data analysis.

Answer (B) is correct.

> **REQUIRED:** The first phase in the benchmarking process.
> **DISCUSSION:** The first phase in the benchmarking process is to select and prioritize benchmarking projects. The next phase is to organize benchmarking teams. Researching and identifying best-in-class is the third phase in the benchmarking process. The fourth phase is data analysis, and the final phase is the implementation phase.
> Answer (A) is incorrect. Organizing benchmarking teams is a subsequent phase. Answer (C) is incorrect. Researching and identifying best-in-class performance is a subsequent phase. Answer (D) is incorrect. Data analysis is a subsequent phase.

17. Which of the following best describes process (function) benchmarking?

A. Studying an organization in the same industry.

B. Comparing a process in one operation with a similar process but in a different industry.

C. Studying operations of organizations with similar processes regardless of industry.

D. Applying best practices in one part of the organization to its other parts.

Answer (C) is correct.

> **REQUIRED:** The best description of process (function) benchmarking.
> **DISCUSSION:** Studying the operations of organizations with similar processes regardless of industry is process (function) benchmarking. Thus, the benchmark need not be a competitor or similar organization.
> Answer (A) is incorrect. Studying an organization in the same industry is competitive benchmarking. Answer (B) is incorrect. Comparing a process in one operation with a similar process but in a different industry is generic benchmarking. Answer (D) is incorrect. Applying best practices in one part of the organization to its other parts is internal benchmarking.

3.6 Consulting Engagements – Other Types

18. Monitoring is an important component of internal control. Which of the following items would **not** be an example of monitoring?

   A. Management regularly compares divisional performance with budgets for the division.

   B. Data processing management regularly generates exception reports for unusual transactions or volumes of transactions and follows up with investigation as to causes.

   C. Data processing management regularly reconciles batch control totals for items processed with batch controls for items submitted.

   D. Management has asked internal auditing to perform regular audits of the controls over cash processing.

Answer (C) is correct.
    REQUIRED: The item not an example of monitoring.
    DISCUSSION: Monitoring assesses the quality of internal control over time. Management considers whether internal control is properly designed and operating as intended and modifies it to reflect changing conditions. Reconciling batch control totals is a processing control over a single instance of accounting activity.
    Answer (A) is incorrect. Budgetary comparison is a typical example of a monitoring control. Answer (B) is incorrect. Investigation of exceptions is a monitoring control used by lower-level management to determine when their operations may be out of control. Answer (D) is incorrect. Internal auditing is a form of monitoring. It serves to evaluate management's other controls.

19. Which of the following is an example of business process reengineering?

   A. Adding a new machine to the existing production line to speed up production.

   B. Redesigning the production line to speed up production.

   C. Repairing a machine on the process line to speed up production.

   D. Updating the computer systems involved on the production line to speed up production.

Answer (B) is correct.
    REQUIRED: The example of business process reengineering.
    DISCUSSION: One approach to business process mapping is reengineering. It involves process innovation and core process redesign. Instead of improving existing procedures, it finds new ways of doing things. Redesigning the production line is an example of this.
    Answer (A) is incorrect. One approach to business process mapping is reengineering. It involves process innovation and core process redesign. Instead of improving existing procedures, it finds new ways of doing things. Adding a new machine is an example of improving existing procedures. Answer (C) is incorrect. One approach to business process mapping is reengineering. It involves process innovation and core process redesign. Instead of improving existing procedures, it finds new ways of doing things. Repairing a machine is an example of improving existing procedures. Answer (D) is incorrect. One approach to business process mapping is reengineering. It involves process innovation and core process redesign. Instead of improving existing procedures, it finds new ways of doing things. Updating the computer systems is an example of improving existing procedures.

20. Which of the following is an example of a soft control?

   A. Passwords.

   B. Ethical culture.

   C. Segregation of duties.

   D. Authorization signatures.

Answer (B) is correct.
    REQUIRED: The example of a soft control.
    DISCUSSION: The ethical culture of an organization is linked to the governance process and is the most important soft control.
    Answer (A) is incorrect. Passwords are not an example of a soft control. Answer (C) is incorrect. Segregation of duties is not an example of a soft control. Answer (D) is incorrect. Authorization signatures are not an example of a soft control.

STUDY UNIT FOUR
THE INTERNAL AUDIT PLAN

(10 pages of outline)

This study unit is the fourth of four covering **Domain I: Managing the Internal Audit Activity** from The IIA's CIA Exam Syllabus. This domain makes up 20% of Part 2 of the CIA exam and is tested at the **basic** and **proficient** cognitive levels. The relevant portion of the syllabus is highlighted below. (The complete syllabus is in Appendix B.)

	Managing the Internal Audit Activity (20%)		
I	1. Internal Audit Operations		
	A	Describe policies and procedures for the planning, organizing, directing, and monitoring of internal audit operations	Basic
	B	Interpret administrative activities (budgeting, resourcing, recruiting, staffing, etc.) of the internal audit activity	Basic
	2. Establishing a Risk-based Internal Audit Plan		
	A	**Identify sources of potential engagements (audit universe, audit cycle requirements, management requests, regulatory mandates, relevant market and industry trends, emerging issues, etc.)**	**Basic**
	B	**Identify a risk management framework to assess risks and prioritize audit engagements based on the results of a risk assessment**	**Basic**
	C	Interpret the types of assurance engagements (risk and control assessments, audits of third parties and contract compliance, security and privacy, performance and quality audits, key performance indicators, operational audits, financial and regulatory compliance audits)	Proficient
	D	Interpret the types of consulting engagements (training, system design, system development, due diligence, privacy, benchmarking, internal control assessment, process mapping, etc.) designed to provide advice and insight	Proficient
	E	Describe coordination of internal audit efforts with the external auditor, regulatory oversight bodies, and other internal assurance functions, and potential reliance on other assurance providers	Basic
	3. Communicating and Reporting to Senior Management and the Board		
	A	**Recognize that the chief audit executive communicates the annual audit plan to senior management and the board and seeks the board's approval**	**Basic**
	B	**Identify significant risk exposures and control and governance issues for the chief audit executive to report to the board**	**Basic**
	C	**Recognize that the chief audit executive reports on the overall effectiveness of the organization's internal control and risk management processes to senior management and the board**	**Basic**
	D	**Recognize internal audit key performance indicators that the chief audit executive communicates to senior management and the board periodically**	**Basic**

4.1 RISK-BASED AUDIT PLAN

1. **Risk**

    a. According to The IIA Glossary, risk is the possibility of an event occurring that will have an impact on the achievement of objectives. Risk is measured in terms of impact and likelihood.

2. **Priorities Based on the Risk Assessment**

    a. The large, complex, interconnected organizations in the modern economy require sophisticated assessment of many diverse risks. Thus, the audit plan of any internal audit activity must reflect the organization's assessment of these risks.

        1) The knowledge, skills, and other competencies of the internal auditors affect what engagements can be performed without using external service providers.

        2) However, the knowledge, skills, and other competencies of the internal auditors do not affect the risk assessment.

    b. The audit plan must be logically related to identified risks of the organization. These risks relate to the organization's strategic and operational goals. Making this connection between identified risks and how they relate to strategic and operational goals is a requirement of risk-based audit planning. This requirement is stated in the following standard:

Performance Standard 2010
Planning

The chief audit executive must establish a risk-based plan to determine the priorities of the internal audit activity, consistent with the organization's goals.

---

    c. The purpose of establishing an internal audit plan is to ensure adequate coverage of areas with greatest exposure to risks.

        1) Accordingly, the priorities of the internal audit activity are based on the results of risk assessments. The CAE should generally assign engagement priorities to activities with higher risks.

        2) The internal audit activity must prioritize to make decisions for applying resources.

    d. The importance of basing the audit work plan on a systematic assessment of risk is emphasized in the following Interpretation and Implementation Standards:

Interpretation of Standard 2010

To develop the risk-based plan, the chief audit executive consults with senior management and the board and obtains an understanding of the organization's strategies, key business objectives, associated risks, and risk management processes. The chief audit executive must review and adjust the plan, as necessary, in response to changes in the organization's business, risks, operations, programs, systems, and controls.

Implementation Standard 2010.A1

The internal audit activity's plan of engagements must be based on a documented risk assessment, undertaken at least annually. The input of senior management and the board must be considered in this process.

---

    e.   In developing the risk-based plan, the internal audit activity ordinarily reviews and corroborates the results of risk assessments performed by senior management.

        1)   The key input in the evaluation of risk is the internal auditor's judgment.

    f.   Planning also involves considering what services stakeholders want.

Implementation Standard 2010.A2

The chief audit executive must identify and consider the expectations of senior management, the board, and other stakeholders for internal audit opinions and other conclusions.

---

    g.   Planning for consulting services involves considering what benefits these engagements may offer.

Implementation Standard 2010.C1

The chief audit executive should consider accepting proposed consulting engagements based on the engagement's potential to improve management of risks, add value, and improve the organization's operations. Accepted engagements must be included in the plan.

---

    h.   The goals of the internal audit activity should be capable of accomplishment within given operating plans and budgets and should be measurable to the extent possible.

        1)   They should be accompanied by measurement criteria and targeted dates of accomplishment.

3.   **The Risk-Based Audit Plan**

    a.   Developing the internal audit activity's audit plan often follows developing or updating the audit universe.

        1)   The **audit universe** (all auditable risk areas) may include the organization's strategic plan. Thus, it may reflect

            a)   Overall business objectives,
            b)   The attitude toward risk,
            c)   The difficulty of reaching objectives,
            d)   The results of risk management, and
            e)   The operating environment.

        2)   The audit universe includes all business units, processes, or operations that can be evaluated and defined. They include accounts, divisions, functions, procedures, products, services, programs, systems, controls, and many other possibilities.

            a)   Thus, the audit plan includes audits requested by management or required by regulators, e.g., as a condition of receiving government contracts.

            b)   Moreover, many entity operations or functions are audited cyclically. Accordingly, the priority of an audit may depend on how recently a specific operation or function has been audited.

        3)   The audit universe should be assessed **at least annually** to reflect the most current strategies and direction of the organization.

            a)   But more frequent updating of audit plans may be needed to respond to changes in circumstances.

b.   The internal audit activity's **audit plan** is based on

1) The audit universe,
2) Input from senior management and the board, and
3) Assessed risks.

c.   An internal audit plan usually is prepared for an annual period. But it might be for a rolling 12-month cycle or two or more years with annual evaluation. The plan most often includes

1) A set of proposed assurance and consulting engagements.
2) The basis for inclusion of each engagement (e.g., risk or time elapsed from the most recent audit).
3) The objective and scope of each proposed engagement.
4) Projects derived from the internal audit activity's strategy.

d.   Key audit objectives are to provide assurance and information to senior management and the board.

1) Assurance includes an assessment of **risk management activities.**

e.   **Work schedules** are based on, among other factors, an assessment of risk and exposure.

1) Most **risk models** address internal and external risks using risk factors to prioritize engagements. Internal risk factors include quality of and adherence to controls, degree of change, timing and results of last engagement, impact, likelihood, materiality, asset liquidity, and management competence. External risk factors include competitor actions, suppliers, industry issues, and employee and government relations.

   a) An unexpected, significant change in an account that cannot be explained raises the assessed risk for that account.

4.   **Risk Management Process**

a.   The plan of engagements must consider the organization's risk management process.

1) The IIA Glossary defines risk management as a process to identify, assess, manage, and control potential events or situations to provide reasonable assurance regarding the achievement of the organization's objectives.

2) **Risk management (RM)** is critical to sound governance of all organizational activities. Consistent RM should be fully integrated into management at all levels.

   a) Management typically uses a framework (e.g., COSO, ERM, ISO 31000) to conduct the risk assessment and document the results.

   b) The chief audit executive takes into account the organization's risk management framework. If a framework does not exist, the chief audit executive uses his or her own judgment of risks after consultation with senior management and the board.

3) Effective RM assists in identifying key controls related to significant inherent risks.

   a) Control is often used to manage risk within the risk appetite. Internal auditors audit key controls and provide assurance on the management of significant risks.

4) Inherent risk and residual risk (also known as current risk) are fundamental risk concepts.

    a) Financial (external) auditors define **inherent risk** as the susceptibility of information or data to a material misstatement given no related mitigating controls.

    b) Current risk is the risk managed within existing controls or control systems.

5) Key controls reduce an otherwise unacceptable risk to a tolerable level. Controls are processes that address risks.

    a) Effective RM identifies key controls based on the difference between inherent and residual risk across all affected systems. Key controls are relied upon to reduce the rating of significant risks.

    b) When identifying key controls (and if RM is mature and reliable), the internal auditor looks for

        i) Individual risk factors when the reduction from inherent to residual risk is significant (particularly if inherent risk was very high).

        ii) Controls that mitigate a large number of risks.

6) Audit planning uses the organizational RM process if one exists. The internal auditor considers the significant risks of the activity and the means by which management mitigates the risks.

    a) Risk assessment methods are used to develop the audit plan and to determine priorities for allocating audit resources.

    b) Risk assessment examines auditable units and selects areas for review that have the greatest risk exposure.

7) The following factors affect the internal audit plan:

    a) Inherent and residual risks should be identified and assessed.

    b) Mitigating controls, contingency plans, and monitoring activities should be linked to events or risks.

    c) Risk registers should be systematic, complete, and accurate.

        i) A **risk register** (risk log) is used to identify and analyze risks. The register describes each risk, its impact and likelihood, and the risk score (impact × likelihood). The register also records planned responses if the event occurs, preventive measures, and a risk ranking.

    d) Risks and activities should be documented.

8) The internal auditor also coordinates with other assurance providers and considers planned reliance on their work.

9) The internal audit activity needs to identify high inherent and residual risks and key control systems, and management needs to be notified about unacceptable residual risk.

    a) Strategic audit planning identifies the following activities to include in the plan:

        i) Control reviews to provide assurance

        ii) Inquiry activities to gain a better understanding of the residual risk

        iii) Consulting activities to give advice on controls to mitigate unacceptable risks

    b) Internal auditors also identify controls with costs exceeding benefits.

10) Risk registers may document risks below the strategic level. They address (a) significant risks, (b) inherent and residual risk ratings, (c) key controls, and (d) mitigating factors.

    a)   The auditors then can identify more direct links between

        i)   Risk categories and aspects described in the risk registers and,
        ii)   If applicable, the items already in the audit universe.

11) Lower-risk audits need to be included in the audit plan to give them coverage and confirm that their risks have not changed.

    a)   Also, priorities should be set for outstanding risks not yet subject to audit.

12) An internal audit plan normally focuses on the following:

    a)   Unacceptable current risks requiring management action
    b)   Control systems on which the organization is most reliant
    c)   Areas where the difference between inherent risk and residual risk is great
    d)   Areas where inherent risk is very high

13) When planning individual audits, the internal auditor identifies and assesses risks relevant to the area under review.

14) Due professional care requires work assignments to be proportional to the complexities of the engagement and must ensure that the technical proficiency and educational background of the personnel assigned are appropriate.

    a)   A risk and skill analysis of tasks to be performed is therefore necessary.

        i)   Among the many considerations for judging an item's risk are the ease with which it can be converted to cash, its accessibility, and its monetary value.

Stop and review! You have completed the outline for this subunit. Study multiple-choice questions 1 through 15 beginning on page 97.

4.2 RISK MODELING

1.   **Rank and Validate Risk Priorities**

    a.   Risk modeling is an effective method used to rank and validate risk priorities when prioritizing engagements in the audit plan.

    b.   Risk factors (e.g., impact and likelihood) may be weighted based on professional judgments to determine their relative significance, but the weights need not be quantified.

1) This simple model and the resulting risk assessment process can be depicted as follows:

EXAMPLE

A chief audit executive is reviewing the following enterprise-wide **risk map**:

IMPACT		LIKELIHOOD		
		Remote	Possible	Likely
	Critical	Risk A	Risk C	Risk D
	Major		Risk B	
	Minor			

In establishing the appropriate priorities for the deployment of limited internal audit resources, the CAE undertakes the following analysis:

- Risk D clearly takes precedence over Risk C because D has a higher likelihood.
- Risk C also clearly has a higher priority than Risk A because C has a higher likelihood and the same impact.

Choosing the higher priority between Risk B and Risk A is a matter of professional judgment based on the organizational risk assessment and the stated priorities of senior management and the board.

- If the more likely threat is considered the greater risk, Risk B will rank higher in the internal audit work plan.
- Likewise, if the threat with the greater possible impact causes senior management and the board more concern, the internal audit activity will place a higher priority on Risk A.

---

   c. Risk modeling in a consulting service can be accomplished by ranking the engagement's potential to improve management of risks, add value, and improve the organization's operations as identified in Implementation Standard 2010.C1. Senior management assigns different weights to each of these items based on organizational objectives. The engagements with the appropriate weighted value would be included in the annual audit plan.

2. **AICPA Audit Risk Model**

   a. **Overview**

      1) Internal auditors must establish a framework for assessing risk.

      2) The American Institute of Certified Public Accountants (AICPA) is the private sector body that establishes standards for external audits of financial statements in the United States.

         a) The following is the audit risk model used by the AICPA:

$$Audit\ risk = Risk\ of\ material\ misstatement \times Detection\ risk$$
$$Audit\ risk = (Inherent\ risk \times Control\ risk) \times Detection\ risk$$

      3) This model is used by an independent auditor engaged to report on whether financial statements are fairly presented, in all material respects, in accordance with the applicable financial reporting framework.

         a) The IIA does not officially define audit risk or its components. However, internal auditors can adapt the model to other audit and assurance engagements.

b. **Audit Risk and Its Components**

1) **Audit risk** is the risk that an auditor expresses an inappropriate opinion on materially misstated financial statements.

   a) In an internal audit context, audit risk is the risk that the auditor will provide senior management and the board with flawed or incomplete information about governance, risk management, and control.

2) **Inherent risk** is the susceptibility of an assertion about a transaction class, balance, or disclosure to a material misstatement before considering relevant controls.

   a) In an internal audit context, inherent risk is the risk arising from the nature of the account or activity under review. For example, a uranium mine is inherently riskier than an accounts payable function.

3) **Control risk** is the risk that internal control will not timely prevent, or detect and correct, a material misstatement of an assertion.

   a) In an internal audit context, control risk is the risk that the system of internal control designed and implemented by management will fail to achieve management's goals and objectives for the account or activity under review.

4) **Detection risk** is the risk that the audit procedures intended to reduce audit risk to an acceptably low level will not detect a material misstatement.

   a) In an internal audit context, detection risk is the risk that the auditor will fail to discover conditions relevant to the established audit objectives for the account or activity under review.

c. **Auditor Response to Assessed Risk**

1) Of the three components, only detection risk is under the auditor's direct control.

2) The internal auditor must first determine the levels of inherent and control risk for the account or activity under review. Detection risk is then adjusted to achieve an overall acceptable level of audit risk.

   a) If inherent risk, control risk, or both are determined to be high, detection risk must be set at a low level to compensate, and the nature, timing, and extent of engagement procedures are changed.

EXAMPLE

After gathering evidence during an audit, the auditor decides to increase the assessed control risk from the level originally planned. To achieve the same overall audit risk as originally planned, the auditor should decrease the assessed detection risk.

Audit risk is a function of inherent risk, control risk, and detection risk. The only risk the auditor directly controls is detection risk. Detection risk has an inverse relationship with control risk. Accordingly, if the auditor chooses to increase the assessed control risk, the assessed detection risk should be decreased to maintain the same overall audit risk.

---

3) All three components may be assessed in quantitative (e.g., scale of 1% to 100%, with 100% being maximum risk) or nonquantitative (e.g., high, medium, low) terms.

Stop and review! You have completed the outline for this subunit. Study multiple-choice questions 16 and 17 on page 101.

4.3 COMMUNICATING AND REPORTING TO SENIOR MANAGEMENT AND THE BOARD

1. **Communication and Approval**

Performance Standard 2020
Communication and Approval

The chief audit executive must communicate the internal audit activity's plans and resource requirements, including significant interim changes, to senior management and the board for review and approval. The chief audit executive must also communicate the impact of resource limitations.

---

   a. Further guidance is provided in IG 2020, *Communication and Approval*.

    1) The **proposed internal audit plan** and the risk assessment are discussed with the board to communicate (a) the risks addressed by the plan and (b) those that cannot be because of resource limits.

    2) The proposed plan of engagement includes the following:

        a) The proposed assurance and consulting engagements

        b) The reason for selecting each engagement (e.g., risk or time elapsed since the last audit)

        c) Objectives and scope of each engagement

        d) Projects indicated by the internal audit strategy but not necessarily related to audit engagements

    3) The plan should be flexible enough to respond to changes in circumstances.

        a) Significant changes in the plan, its basis, or its effects must be approved by the board and senior management.

        b) Review of, and changes in, the plan may occur at quarterly or semiannual board meetings.

Performance Standard 2060
Reporting to Senior Management and the Board

The chief audit executive must report periodically to senior management and the board on the internal audit activity's purpose, authority, responsibility, and performance relative to its plan and on its conformance with the Code of Ethics and the *Standards*. Reporting must also include significant risk and control issues, including fraud risks, governance issues, and other matters that require the attention of senior management and/or the board.

---

2. The following excerpt from the Interpretation of Standard 2060 addresses the frequency and content of reporting:

   The frequency and content of reporting are determined collaboratively by the chief audit executive, senior management, and the board. The frequency and content of reporting depends on the importance of the information to be communicated and the urgency of the related actions to be taken by senior management and/or the board.

3. **The CAE's Duty to Report**

   a. Further guidance is provided in IG 2060, *Reporting to Senior Management and the Board*. The *Standards* require the CAE to communicate information to senior management and the board about the following:

    1) The internal audit charter

        a) The CAE periodically reviews the charter and presents it for approval.

    2)   Organizational independence of the internal audit activity

        a)   The CAE annually confirms organizational independence to the board.

        b)   Impairments of independence must be disclosed to the board.

    3)   Internal audit plans, resource requirements, and performance

        a)   Performance reporting should relate to the most recently approved plan.

        b)   "To quantify the level of performance, many CAEs use key performance indicators such as the percentage of the audit plan completed, percentage of audit recommendations that have been accepted or implemented, status of management's corrective actions, or average time taken to issue reports."

    4)   Results of audit engagements

    5)   Results of the quality assurance and improvement program

        a)   Included is a conclusion on whether the internal audit activity conforms with the Code of Ethics and *Standards*.

    6)   Significant risk and control issues and management's acceptance of risk

        a)   Significant risk exposures and control issues may result in unacceptable exposure to internal and external risks, including control weaknesses, fraud, illegal acts, errors, inefficiency, waste, ineffectiveness, conflicts of interest, and financial viability.

        b)   Senior management and the board determine the responses to significant issues.

            i)   They may assume the risk of not correcting the reported condition because of cost or other considerations.

            ii)   Senior management should inform the board of decisions about all significant issues raised by internal auditing.

        c)   When the CAE believes that senior management has accepted an unacceptable risk, the CAE must discuss the matter with senior management. The CAE should

            i)   Understand management's basis for the decision,

            ii)   Identify the cause of any disagreement,

           iii)   Determine whether management has the authority to accept the risk, and

           iv)   Preferably resolve the disagreement.

        d)   If the CAE and senior management cannot agree, the CAE must inform the board.

            i)   If possible, the CAE and management should jointly present their positions.

            ii)   The CAE should consider timely discussion of financial reporting issues with the external auditors.

  b.   The CAE may share and discuss the contents of the report with senior management before presenting it to the board.

  c.   The CAE reports on the overall effectiveness of the organization's internal control and risk management processes to senior management and the board.

Stop and review! You have completed the outline for this subunit. Study multiple-choice questions 18 through 21 beginning on page 101.

QUESTIONS

4.1 Risk-Based Audit Plan

1. A chief audit executive may use risk analysis in preparing work schedules. Which of the following is **not** considered in performing a risk analysis?

A. Issues relating to organizational governance.

B. Skills available on the internal audit staff.

C. Results of prior engagements.

D. Major operating changes.

Answer (B) is correct.
    REQUIRED: The item not considered in performing a risk analysis.
    DISCUSSION: The skills of the internal audit staff do not affect the risk associated with potential engagement clients.
    Answer (A) is incorrect. Issues relating to organizational governance are factors that should be considered. Answer (C) is incorrect. Results of prior engagements should be considered. Answer (D) is incorrect. Major operating changes should be considered.

2. The term "risk" is best defined as the possibility that

A. An internal auditor will fail to detect a material misstatement that causes financial statements or internal reports to be misstated or misleading.

B. An event could occur affecting the achievement of objectives.

C. Management will, either knowingly or unknowingly, make decisions that increase the potential liability of the organization.

D. Financial statements or internal records will contain material misstatements.

Answer (B) is correct.
    REQUIRED: The best definition of risk according to the *Standards*.
    DISCUSSION: According to The IIA Glossary, risk is "the possibility of an event occurring that will have an impact on the achievement of objectives. Risk is measured in terms of impact and likelihood."
    Answer (A) is incorrect. Detection risk is a component of audit risk. Answer (C) is incorrect. The risk of increasing the organization's liability could be termed management decision-making risk. Answer (D) is incorrect. Risk is not limited to misstated financial statements.

3. Risk modeling or risk analysis is often used in conjunction with development of long-range engagement work schedules. The key input in the evaluation of risk is

A. Previous engagement results.

B. Management concerns and preferences.

C. Specific requirements of professional standards.

D. Judgment of the internal auditors.

Answer (D) is correct.
    REQUIRED: The key input in the evaluation of risk.
    DISCUSSION: Assessing the risk of an activity entails analysis of numerous factors, estimation of probabilities and amounts of potential losses, and an appraisal of the costs and benefits of risk reduction. Consequently, in assessing the magnitude of risk associated with any factor in a risk model, informed judgment by the internal auditor is required.
    Answer (A) is incorrect. The informed judgment of the internal auditor is still required to assess the magnitude of risk indicated by previous engagement results. Answer (B) is incorrect. To assess the risk posed by management concerns, informed judgment of the internal auditor is required. Answer (C) is incorrect. Professional standards do not specify the basic inputs for a risk analysis.

4. The chief audit executive of a manufacturer is updating the long-range engagement work schedule. There are several possible assignments that can fill a given time spot. Information on potential monetary exposure and key internal controls has been gathered. Based on perceived risk, select the assignment of greatest merit.

A. Precious metals inventory -- carrying amount, US $1,000,000; separately stored, but access not restricted.

B. Branch office petty cash -- ledger amount, US $50,000; 10 branch offices, equal amounts; replenishment of accounts requires three separate approvals.

C. Sales force travel expenses -- budget, US $1,000,000; 50 sales people; all expenditures over US $25 must be receipted.

D. Expendable tools inventory -- carrying amount, US $500,000; issued by tool crib attendant upon receipt of authorization form.

Answer (A) is correct.
    REQUIRED: The item of greatest concern based on perceived audit risk.
    DISCUSSION: Among the many considerations in judging an item's risk are the ease with which it can be converted to cash, its accessibility, and its monetary value. The precious metals inventory should receive special emphasis because of its high inherent risk. The inventory can be easily converted to cash, access is not restricted, and its monetary value is relatively high.
    Answer (B) is incorrect. The monetary exposure of petty cash is much smaller than for the other proposed engagements, and the related controls are very stringent. Answer (C) is incorrect. Although the monetary value of the sales force travel expense is identical to that of the precious metal inventory, the exposure is divided among 50 people, and the receipting requirement provides substantial safety against false claims. Answer (D) is incorrect. The expendable tools inventory is subject to adequate control.

5. Risk assessment is a systematic process for assessing and integrating professional judgments about probable adverse conditions or events. Which of the following statements reflects the appropriate action for the chief audit executive to take?

    A. The CAE should generally assign engagement priorities to activities with higher risks.

    B. The CAE should restrict the number of sources of information used in the risk assessment process.

    C. Work schedule priorities should be established to lead the CAE in the risk assessment process.

    D. The risk assessment process should be conducted at least every 3 to 5 years.

Answer (A) is correct.
    REQUIRED: The appropriate action for the chief audit executive to take regarding risk assessment.
    DISCUSSION: Audit work schedules are based on, among other things, an assessment of risk and exposures. Prioritizing is needed to make decisions for applying resources. A variety of risk models exist to assist the CAE. Most risk models use risk factors, such as impact, likelihood, materiality, asset liquidity, management competence, quality of and adherence to internal controls, degree of change or stability, timing and results of last audit engagement, complexity, and employee and government relations.
    Answer (B) is incorrect. Internal auditors are expected to identify and evaluate significant risk exposures in the normal course of their duties. Thus, they not only use risk analysis to plan engagements but also to assist management and the board by examining, evaluating, reporting, and recommending improvements on the adequacy and effectiveness of the management's risk processes. For these purposes, the CAE should incorporate information from a variety of sources into the risk assessment process. The *Standards* place no limit on such sources. Answer (C) is incorrect. The risk assessment process should be used to determine work schedule priorities. Answer (D) is incorrect. The risk assessment should be undertaken at least every year.

6. When developing the internal audit plan, the chief audit executive must consider the following expectations of

1. Department managers
2. Stakeholders
3. Human resource managers

    A. 1 only.

    B. 2 only.

    C. 3 only.

    D. 2 and 3.

Answer (B) is correct.
    REQUIRED: The party/parties whose expectations the internal auditor must consider during planning.
    DISCUSSION: During planning, the chief audit executive must identify and consider the expectations of senior management, the board, and other stakeholders for internal audit opinions and other conclusions (Impl. Std. 2010.A2).
    Answer (A) is incorrect. During planning, the chief audit executive must identify and consider the expectations of senior management, the board, and other stakeholders for internal audit opinions and other conclusions. This does not include the expectations of department managers. Answer (C) is incorrect. During planning, the chief audit executive must identify and consider the expectations of senior management, the board, and other stakeholders for internal audit opinions and other conclusions. This does not include the expectations of HR managers. Answer (D) is incorrect. While the expectations of stakeholders must be considered, the expectations of HR managers are not.

7. The internal auditing activity of Rivers Financial Group is developing a plan for the current year. Which of the following should **not** be emphasized in the audit plan?

    A. All control systems.

    B. Areas where inherent risk is very high.

    C. Control systems on which the organization is most reliant.

    D. Unacceptable current risks that require management action.

Answer (A) is correct.
    REQUIRED: The items that should and should not be emphasized in the audit plan.
    DISCUSSION: An internal audit plan normally focuses on control systems for which the organization is most reliant, not all control systems.

8. The internal audit activity's audit plan is based on all of the following **except**

    A. The audit universe.

    B. The cost of the engagement.

    C. Input from senior management and the board.

    D. Assessed risk and exposures.

Answer (B) is correct.
    REQUIRED: The item the audit plan is based on.
    DISCUSSION: The cost of the engagement is not a factor to consider when developing the audit plan.
    Answer (A) is incorrect. The audit plan is based on the audit universe. Answer (C) is incorrect. The audit plan is based on input from both senior management and the board of directors. Answer (D) is incorrect. The internal audit activity's audit plan is based on the assessed risk and exposures.

9. Risk management is critical to the sound governance of which of the following?

    A. Financial activities of the organization.

    B. Manufacturing activities of the organization.

    C. All organization activities that produce more than 10% of revenue.

    D. All organizational activities, regardless of revenue.

Answer (D) is correct.
    REQUIRED: The activities to which risk management is critical.
    DISCUSSION: Risk management is crucial to sound governance of all organizational activities.
    Answer (A) is incorrect. Risk management is crucial to sound governance of all organizational activities, not just the financial activities. Answer (B) is incorrect. Risk management is crucial to sound governance of all organizational activities, not just the manufacturing activities. Answer (C) is incorrect. Risk management is crucial to sound governance of all organizational activities, not just the activities producing more than 10% of revenue.

10. An organization has no formal risk management framework. In developing a risk-based plan to determine the priorities of the internal audit activity, the chief audit executive (CAE) should

    A. Use the same risk-based plan developed for other clients.

    B. Not establish a risk-based plan because one is not necessary.

    C. Consult with senior management and the board and use the best judgment of risks.

    D. Limit the scope of the engagement.

Answer (C) is correct.
    REQUIRED: The true statement about developing a risk-based plan for the internal audit activity.
    DISCUSSION: The CAE considers the risk management framework, including the risk appetite set by management for each activity or part of the organization. If a framework does not exist, the CAE uses his or her own judgment after consulting with senior management and the board.
    Answer (A) is incorrect. The CAE should review and adjust the plan, as necessary, in response to changes in the organization's business, risks, operations, programs, systems, and controls. Answer (B) is incorrect. The CAE should establish a risk-based plan to determine the priorities of the internal audit activity, consistent with the organization's goals. Answer (D) is incorrect. The CAE should develop a risk-based plan, not limit the scope of the engagement.

11. The chief audit executive (CAE) performs a risk assessment before developing the annual audit plan. Which of the following is most likely to increase the assessment of an identified risk?

    A. An immaterial, anticipated drop in cash flow after plant closings.

    B. A request from senior management to review the strategic plan.

    C. An unexpected, significant increase in receivables not related to an increase in sales.

    D. A critical activity had not been subject to a compliance audit during the past year.

Answer (C) is correct.
    REQUIRED: The reason for increasing the assessment of an identified risk.
    DISCUSSION: Unexpected, unexplained, and significant changes in amounts, such as receivables, increase the assessed risk for that balance.
    Answer (A) is incorrect. An immaterial, expected, and explainable decrease in cash flow provides no evidence of increased risk. Answer (B) is incorrect. A request from senior management to include an engagement in the audit plan is significant, but does not provide evidence of increased risk. Answer (D) is incorrect. Compliance audits do not have to be performed annually unless evidence indicates an engagement is necessary.

12. Which internal audit planning tool is general in nature and is used to ensure adequate engagement coverage over time?

    A. The audit plan.

    B. The engagement work program.

    C. The internal audit activity's budget.

    D. The internal audit activity's charter.

Answer (A) is correct.
    REQUIRED: The internal audit planning tool used to ensure adequate engagement coverage over time.
    DISCUSSION: According to Perf. Std. 2010, the CAE must establish a risk-based audit plan to determine the priorities of the internal audit activity. Such a plan ensures adequate engagement coverage over time.
    Answer (B) is incorrect. The engagement work program is limited in scope to a particular project. Answer (C) is incorrect. The internal audit activity's budget may be used to justify a head count, but it is not used to ensure adequate engagement coverage over time. Answer (D) is incorrect. The charter is not an engagement planning tool.

13. Which of the following actions by the internal audit activity is (are) appropriate in response to a risk assessment?

1. Although input of senior management and the board should be obtained, the chief audit executive does not need to consider it when developing the internal audit activity's plan of engagements.

2. The high-risk areas should be integrated into an audit plan along with the high-priority requests of management and the audit committee.

3. The risk analysis should be used in determining an audit plan. Thus, it should be performed only on an annual basis.

    A. 1 only.

    B. 2 only.

    C. 1 and 3 only.

    D. 1 and 2 only.

Answer (B) is correct.
REQUIRED: The appropriate internal audit actions in response to a risk assessment.
DISCUSSION: The annual risk-based audit plan should integrate the risk analysis with input from senior management and the board (audit committee). It reflects consideration of the organization's risk management framework and risk appetite levels set by management.
Answer (A) is incorrect. The internal audit activity's plan of engagements must be based on a documented risk assessment. The input of senior management and the board must be considered in this process. Answer (C) is incorrect. A documented risk assessment should be undertaken at least annually. It should be updated for changes as they occur during the year, and the input of senior management and the board must be considered. Answer (D) is incorrect. Input of senior management and the board must be considered.

14. Which of the following comments is (are) true regarding the assessment of risk associated with two projects that are competing for limited internal audit resources?

1. Industry knowledge should be used to identify the project with the higher priority.

2. Activities with higher financial budgets always should be considered higher risk than those with lower financial budgets.

3. Activities that are requested by the board always should be considered higher risk than those requested by management.

4. Senior management's evaluations of the risk associated with each project must be considered.

    A. 2 and 4 only.

    B. 2 and 3 only.

    C. 1 and 4 only.

    D. 1 and 3 only.

Answer (C) is correct.
REQUIRED: The true comments regarding the assessment of risk associated with two projects that are competing for limited internal audit resources.
DISCUSSION: An understanding of the industry enables the internal auditor to identify risks of new or existing projects. The internal audit activity's plan of engagements must be based on a documented risk assessment, undertaken at least annually. The input of senior management and the board must be considered in this process.
Answer (A) is incorrect. Activities with higher financial budgets do not necessarily have greater risk. Answer (B) is incorrect. Activities with higher financial budgets do not necessarily have greater risk. Activities requested by the board do not necessarily have greater risk. Answer (D) is incorrect. A ranking based on the source of a request for performance of an engagement is unlikely to reflect a comprehensive assessment based on a sufficient number of risk factors.

15. The internal auditors of Smother Corp. are considering lower-risk audits as a part of their audit plan. They should

    A. Include the lower-risk audits to give them coverage and confirm that their risks have not changed.

    B. Not include the lower-risk audits in the audit plan since they are not risky.

    C. Include only half of the lower-risk audits to see if the risks have changed.

    D. Include the lower-risk audits only with senior management approval.

Answer (A) is correct.
REQUIRED: The treatment of lower-risk audits in the audit plan.
DISCUSSION: Lower-risk audits need to be included in the audit plan to give them coverage and confirm that their risks have not changed.
Answer (B) is incorrect. Lower-risk audits should be included in the audit plan. Answer (C) is incorrect. Including only half of the lower-risk audits is not required by any guidance of The IIA. Answer (D) is incorrect. While the internal auditor considers input from senior management when determining the audit plan, the decision to include audits in the plan is ultimately at the discretion of the internal auditor.

4.2 Risk Modeling

16. In the AICPA's audit risk model, the risk that an auditor will express an inappropriate audit opinion when the financial statements are materially misstated is

A. Audit risk.

B. Inherent risk.

C. Control risk.

D. Detection risk.

Answer (A) is correct.
　　REQUIRED: The risk that an auditor will express an inappropriate audit opinion when the financial statements are materially misstated.
　　DISCUSSION: Audit risk is "the risk that the auditor expresses an inappropriate audit opinion when the financial statements are materially misstated." In the internal audit context, audit risk is the risk that the auditor will provide senior management and the board with inaccurate or incomplete information about governance, risk management, or control.
　　Answer (B) is incorrect. Inherent risk is the susceptibility of an assertion to material misstatement in the absence of related controls. Answer (C) is incorrect. Control risk is the risk that a material misstatement will not be prevented or detected by internal control. Answer (D) is incorrect. Detection risk is the risk that the auditor will not detect a material misstatement that exists in a relevant assertion. It is affected by the auditor's procedures and can be changed at his or her discretion.

17. On the basis of audit evidence gathered and evaluated, an auditor decides to decrease the level of detection risk from that originally planned. Assuming the same planned audit risk level, the change in the planned detection risk most likely resulted from a(n)

A. Decrease in the assessed control risk.

B. Increase in materiality levels.

C. Decrease in the assessed inherent risk.

D. Increase in the assessed control risk.

Answer (D) is correct.
　　REQUIRED: The reason that an auditor decides to decrease the level of detection risk from that originally planned.
　　DISCUSSION: Audit risk is a function of inherent risk, control risk, and detection risk. The only risk the auditor directly controls is detection risk. Thus, the auditor achieves the desired level of overall audit risk by adjusting detection risk in response to the assessed levels of inherent risk and control risk. Detection risk has an inverse relationship with control risk and inherent risk. If the auditor chooses to increase his or her assessment of control risk or inherent risk, detection risk should be decreased for a given planned audit risk.
　　Answer (A) is incorrect. An increase in the assessed control risk may require a lower planned detection risk for a given planned audit risk. Answer (B) is incorrect. Materiality and risk are interrelated. However, as assessed risk increases, the auditor is likely to reduce the levels of materiality. Answer (C) is incorrect. An increase in the assessed inherent risk may require a lower planned detection risk for a given planned audit risk.

4.3 Communicating and Reporting to Senior Management and the Board

18. Who reviews and approves a summary of the internal audit plan?

A. Senior management and the board.

B. The audit committee and the board.

C. Senior management only.

D. The chief audit executive (CAE) only.

Answer (A) is correct.
　　REQUIRED: The person(s) responsible for approvals of the internal audit plan.
　　DISCUSSION: According to Perf. Std. 2020, senior management and the board review and approve the internal audit plan.
　　Answer (B) is incorrect. The CAE also submits the internal audit plan to senior management. Answer (C) is incorrect. The CAE also submits the internal audit plan to the board. Answer (D) is incorrect. The audit plan is submitted to senior management and the board.

19. As the chief audit executive, you have determined that the acquisition of some expensive, state-of-the-art software for paperless working paper files will be useful. Identify the preferred method for presenting your request to senior management.

A. The effect of not obtaining the software.

B. Statement of need.

C. Comparison with other internal audit activities.

D. Evaluation of the software's technical specifications.

Answer (A) is correct.
　　REQUIRED: The preferred method for presenting a request for resources needed by internal auditing.
　　DISCUSSION: The CAE must communicate the internal audit activity's plans and resource requirements to senior management and the board for review and approval. The CAE also must communicate the effect of resource limitations (Perf. Std. 2020).
　　Answer (B) is incorrect. The need must be weighed against the cost. Answer (C) is incorrect. Other internal audit activities may have different cost-benefit relationships. Answer (D) is incorrect. Specialists, not senior management, will perform this evaluation.

20. Bobby Fitz, CAE, believes that the internal controls over cash disbursements need major revisions. Mr. Fitz discussed this matter with senior management and was very alarmed at their acceptance of this serious risk. What action should Mr. Fitz take next?

A. Report the matter to the board immediately.

B. Understand management's basis for accepting the risk.

C. Determine whether management has the authority to accept the risk.

D. Further attempt to resolve the disagreement.

Answer (B) is correct.
    REQUIRED: The action in a situation when the CAE disagrees with senior management.
    DISCUSSION: The first thing the CAE should do is understand management's basis for the decision. It is possible that management has knowledge about the risk that the CAE does not. This knowledge may prove it suitable to accept the risk.
    Answer (A) is incorrect. While this is an action the CAE could take, the CAE should first understand and try to further resolve the disagreement before reporting it to the board. Answer (C) is incorrect. While this is an action the CAE should take, the CAE should first understand management's basis for accepting the risk. Answer (D) is incorrect. While this is an action the CAE should take, the CAE should first understand management's basis for accepting the risk. This is the last step the CAE should attempt before informing the board.

21. What should the CAE do if the scope of the internal audit plan is insufficient to permit expression of an opinion about risk management and control?

A. Design more procedures to ensure the audit plan becomes sufficient.

B. The CAE should inform senior management and the board about gaps in audit coverage.

C. Make the decision to outsource the internal audit function so the scope of the audit plan can be sufficient.

D. Hire more internal auditors to increase the scope of the engagement.

Answer (B) is correct.
    REQUIRED: The action the CAE should take if the internal audit plan is insufficient.
    DISCUSSION: In the event that the audit plan is insufficient, the CAE should inform senior management and the board about gaps in audit coverage.

Access the **Gleim CIA Premium Review System** featuring our SmartAdapt technology from your Gleim Personal Classroom to continue your studies. You will experience a personalized study environment with exam-emulating multiple-choice questions.

STUDY UNIT FIVE
ENGAGEMENT PLANNING

(15 pages of outline)

This study unit covers **Domain II: Planning the Engagement** from The IIA's CIA Exam Syllabus. This domain makes up 20% of Part 2 of the CIA exam and is tested at the **proficient** cognitive level. This study unit also is the first of four covering **Domain III: Performing the Engagement**. This domain makes up 40% of Part 2 of the CIA exam and is tested at the **basic** and **proficient** cognitive levels. The relevant portions of the syllabus are highlighted below. (The complete syllabus is in Appendix B.)

	Planning the Engagement (20%)		
	1. Engagement Planning		
II	A	**Determine engagement objectives, evaluation criteria, and the scope of the engagement**	**Proficient**
	B	**Plan the engagement to assure identification of key risks and controls**	**Proficient**
	C	**Complete a detailed risk assessment of each audit area, including evaluating and prioritizing risk and control factors**	**Proficient**
	D	**Determine engagement procedures and prepare the engagement work program**	**Proficient**
	E	**Determine the level of staff and resources for the engagement**	**Proficient**
	Performing the Engagement (40%)		
	1. Information Gathering		
III	A	**Gather and examine relevant information (review previous audit reports and data, conduct walk-throughs and interviews, perform observations, etc.) as part of a preliminary survey of the engagement area**	**Proficient**
	B	**Develop checklists and risk-and-control questionnaires as part of a preliminary survey of the engagement area**	**Proficient**
	C	Apply appropriate sampling (nonstatistical, judgmental, discovery, etc.) and statistical analysis techniques	Proficient
	2. Analysis and Evaluation		
	A	Use computerized audit tools and techniques (data mining and extraction, continuous monitoring, automated workpapers, embedded audit modules, etc.)	Proficient
	B	Evaluate the relevance, sufficiency, and reliability of potential sources of evidence	Proficient
	C	Apply appropriate analytical approaches and process mapping techniques (process identification, workflow analysis, process map generation and analysis, spaghetti maps, RACI diagrams, etc.)	Proficient
	D	Determine and apply analytical review techniques (ratio estimation, variance analysis, budget vs. actual, trend analysis, other reasonableness tests, benchmarking, etc.)	Basic
	E	Prepare workpapers and documentation of relevant information to support conclusions and engagement results	Proficient
	F	Summarize and develop engagement conclusions, including assessment of risks and controls	Proficient
	3. Engagement Supervision		
	A	Identify key activities in supervising engagements (coordinate work assignments, review workpapers, evaluate auditors' performance, etc.)	Basic

An engagement consists of planning, performing procedures, communicating results, and monitoring progress. The internal auditor's responsibility is to plan and perform the engagement, subject to review and approval by supervisors. This study unit applies to the planning phase of the engagement.

5.1 ENGAGEMENT PLANNING AND RISK ASSESSMENT

1. **Engagements**

    a. An **engagement** is a "specific internal audit assignment, task, or review activity, such as an internal audit, control self-assessment review, fraud examination, or consultancy. An engagement may include multiple tasks or activities designed to accomplish a specific set of related objectives" (The IIA Glossary).

Performance Standard 2200
Engagement Planning

Internal auditors must develop and document a plan for each engagement, including the engagement's objectives, scope, timing, and resource allocations. The plan must consider the organization's strategies, objectives, and risks relevant to the engagement.

---

    b. Internal auditors may develop a **planning memo** to document the engagement objectives, scope, risk assessment, prioritized areas for testing, and the approved audit work program.

Performance Standard 2201
Planning Considerations

In planning the engagement, internal auditors must consider:

- The strategies and objectives of the activity being reviewed and the means by which the activity controls its performance.
- The significant risks to the activity's objectives, resources, and operations and the means by which the potential impact of risk is kept to an acceptable level.
- The adequacy and effectiveness of the activity's governance, risk management, and control processes compared to a relevant framework or model.
- The opportunities for making significant improvements to the activity's governance, risk management, and control processes.

---

2. **Engagement Planning**

    a. Further guidance is provided in IG 2200, *Engagement Planning*:

    1) Planning requires internal auditors to understand the internal audit plan of engagements.

        a) The long-range schedule should adequately address essential functions at defined intervals over time.

        b) Significant changes since the engagement were included in the annual plan.

        c) How the entity's strategies, objectives, and risks affect the engagement.

2)   Setting engagement objectives is crucial to planning. Accordingly, internal auditors should consider the following matters to the extent they are relevant to the areas reviewed:

       a)   Management's current risk assessment
       b)   The risk assessment made for the plan of engagements
       c)   Prior engagement-level risk assessments
       d)   Prior audit reports

3)   Setting risk-based objectives permits definition of the scope of the engagement.

4)   The following are other considerations during the engagement planning stage:

       a)   Resources required and their most effective and efficient use.

       b)   Retention of documents and decisions about requirements and formats.

       c)   Beginning preparation of the engagement program, with attention to budgets, forms of final communications, and logistical concerns.

   b.   The CAE determines how, when, and to whom results are communicated. If appropriate, these documented determinations are communicated to management during planning.

     1)   Subsequent changes that affect the timing or reporting of engagement results also are communicated.

3.   **Preliminary Survey**

   a.   The internal auditors may perform a survey to (1) become familiar with activities, risks, and controls for the purpose of identifying areas for engagement emphasis and (2) invite comments and suggestions from stakeholders. The components of a survey include the following:

     1)   Input from stakeholders
     2)   Analytical procedures
     3)   Questionnaires (covered in Subunit 5.4 and Study Unit 6, Subunit 3)
     4)   Interviews (covered in Subunit 5.4 and Study Unit 6, Subunit 4)
     5)   Observations (covered in Subunit 5.4 and Study Unit 6, Subunit 5)
     6)   Prior audit reports and other relevant documentation
     7)   Process mapping (covered in Study Unit 8, Subunit 2)
     8)   Checklists

   b.   Input from Stakeholders

     1)   Auditee management and other stakeholders may be sources of information for the formulation of engagement objectives.

     2)   Onsite observations and interviews with users of the activity's output and other stakeholders may be part of the survey.

   c.   Prior Audit Reports and Other Relevant Documentation

     1)   Prior audit reports and workpapers may be other sources of information. The issues and the process by which they were resolved may provide insights into the client's particular circumstances.

       a)   The auditor must use such documentation for informational purposes only, not as a basis for objectives or conclusions.

d.   Checklists

1)   During the preliminary survey and throughout the engagement, checklists (reminder lists) ensure that the auditor has completed necessary tasks. For example, they include receipt of requested documentation and updates of the continuing audit file.

Sample Checklist

Add to permanent audit file:

- ☐   Amortization schedule for new bond issues
- ☐   Plan for disposal of assets of discontinued operation
- ☐   Most recent forms filed with regulators
- ☐   Most recent client-prepared process control maps

2)   Checklists increase the uniformity of data acquisition. They ensure that a standard approach is taken and minimize the possibility of omitting factors that can be anticipated.

3)   Disadvantages of checklists include the following:

a)   Providing a false sense of security that all relevant factors are addressed

b)   Inappropriately implying that equal weight is given to each item

c)   The difficulty of translating the observation represented by each item

d)   Treating a checklist as a rote exercise rather than part of a thoughtful understanding of the unique aspects of the audit

4)   Checklists may be used to control administrative details involved in performing the engagement, to prepare for opening and closing conferences, etc.

e.   Documentation and Communication of Results

1)   The results of the survey are documented and, if appropriate, communicated to management in an oral presentation.

2)   A **summary** of results is prepared that includes

a)   Significant issues;

b)   Engagement objectives and procedures;

c)   Critical control points, deficiencies, or excess controls;

d)   Methods, such as those that are technology-based; and

e)   Reasons for modifying objectives (e.g., to expand or decrease audit work) or not continuing the engagement.

4.   **Risk Identification**

a.   During planning, internal auditors must identify key business risks and controls, especially the client's inherent risks.

1)   In the context of an engagement, **risk** is an event that may impact the business objectives of the area or process under review.

2)   **Controls** are actions taken to mitigate risks.

3)   **Inherent risk** is the risk in the absence of controls.

4)   A key risk or control is determined by its significance, which is measured as a combination of risk factors (e.g., magnitude, nature, effect, relevance, impact, and likelihood).

b.   **Brainstorming.** Internal auditors may conduct brainstorming sessions to identify key risks and controls. During such sessions, internal auditors may ask the following questions to identify relevant risks:

1)   What would prevent the activity from achieving its business objectives?

2)   How would the activity be affected if no controls existed?

c. **Risk and control matrix.** Internal auditors also may create a risk and control matrix to identify key risks and controls. The risk and control matrix below is an excerpt from a relevant IIA publication.

Risk and Control Matrix for Accounts Payable

Business Objectives	Inherent Risk	Impact (L, M, H)*	Likelihood (L, M, H)*	Control
A. Personnel expenses are appropriate and authorized.	A.1 Corporate cards are issued inappropriately, resulting in fraudulent expenses.	M	M	Duties are segregated.
	A.2 Personnel are not provided guidance on corporate card usage and expense policies, resulting in inappropriate expenses.	L	M	Expense policy is communicated to personnel authorized to incur organizational expenses.
	A.3 Expense reports are not submitted/reviewed timely, resulting in inappropriate expenses.	H	H	No control is in place.
	A.4 Expense reports with receipts are not reviewed and approved by appropriate personnel, resulting in inappropriate expenses.	H	M	Approvals are based on management hierarchy. Expense reports cannot be submitted until a manager approves them. Expense team conducts monthly reviews.

*Impact and likelihood are commonly described as low (L), medium (M), or high (H).

5. **Risk Assessment**

Implementation Standard 2210.A1

Internal auditors must conduct a preliminary assessment of the risks relevant to the activity under review. Engagement objectives must reflect the results of this assessment.

---

a. After identifying risks and controls, the internal auditors perform a preliminary risk assessment.

1) Internal auditors consider

a) Management's **assessment of risks**;

b) Its reliability;

c) The process for addressing risk and control matters;

d) The reporting about, and the responses to, events exceeding the **risk appetite**; and

e) Risks in related activities.

b.   Two factors of significance commonly used to assess risks are impact and likelihood.

1)   Internal auditors may use a **heat map** to visually display assessed risks and prioritize risks according to significance. The heat map below is excerpted from the aforementioned IIA publication.

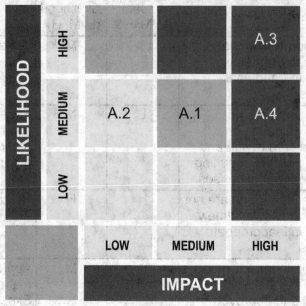

Figure 5-1

2)   Accordingly, the risks ranked from most (highest) to least (lowest) significant (priority) are A.3, A.4, A.1, and A.2.

Stop and review! You have completed the outline for this subunit. Study multiple-choice questions 1 through 3 on page 118.

5.2   ENGAGEMENT OBJECTIVES, SCOPE, AND CRITERIA

1.   **Engagement Objectives**

a.   After the preliminary survey and risk assessment are complete, internal auditors establish objectives. The objectives should explain the reasons the activity is being audited, the scope of the engagement, and the assurances to be provided.

> **Performance Standard 2210**
> **Engagement Objectives**
>
> Objectives must be established for each engagement.

b.   **Engagement objectives** are "broad statements developed by internal auditors that define intended engagement accomplishments" (The IIA Glossary).

c.   Objectives for **assurance engagements** must reflect the results of the preliminary assessment of risks relevant to the activity under review. In contrast, objectives for **consulting engagements** must address governance, risk management, and control processes to the extent agreed upon with the client (Implementation Standard 2210.C1).

d.   Further guidance is provided in IG 2210, *Engagement Objectives*:

1)   Objectives assist in determining the **procedures** to perform and the priorities for testing risks and controls.

2)   Objectives ordinarily are based on identified **key risks** relevant to the area or process under review.

3) **Preliminary objectives** of engagements may be based on (a) the plan of engagements, (b) prior results, (c) stakeholder feedback, and (d) the auditee's mission, vision, and objectives. **Risk assessment exercises** should be performed related to the auditee's governance, risk management, and controls.

Implementation Standard 2210.A2

Internal auditors must consider the probability of significant errors, fraud, noncompliance, and other exposures when developing the engagement objectives.

---

2. **Engagement Scope**

   a. After establishing risk-based objectives, internal auditors establish the engagement scope.

Performance Standard 2220
Engagement Scope

The established scope must be sufficient to achieve the objectives of the engagement.

---

   b. According to IG 2200, *Engagement Planning*, scope sets the boundaries within which the internal auditors will work.

   c. Further guidance is provided in IG 2220, *Engagement Scope*:

      1) Scope defines "what will and will not be included in the engagement."

      2) Internal auditors **generally consider** the following factors, among others, when establishing the engagement scope:

         a) The boundaries, subprocesses, and components of the area or process under review.

         b) In-scope versus out-of-scope locations.

         c) Time frame.

   d. The Implementation Standard below provides factors internal auditors **must consider** when establishing the engagement scope.

Implementation Standard 2220.A1

The scope of the engagement must include consideration of relevant systems, records, personnel, and physical properties, including those under the control of third parties.

---

3. **Engagement Criteria**

   a. Criteria are needed to evaluate the area or process under review.

Implementation Standard 2210.A3

Adequate criteria are needed to evaluate governance, risk management, and controls. Internal auditors must ascertain the extent to which management and/or the board has established adequate criteria to determine whether objectives and goals have been accomplished. If adequate, internal auditors must use such criteria in their evaluation. If inadequate, internal auditors must identify appropriate evaluation criteria through discussion with management and/or the board.

---

      1) Acceptable industry standards, standards developed by professions or associations, standards in law and government regulations, and other sound business practices are usually deemed to be appropriate criteria.

Stop and review! You have completed the outline for this subunit. Study multiple-choice questions 4 through 6 beginning on page 118.

5.3 ENGAGEMENT STAFF AND RESOURCES

> **Performance Standard 2230**
> **Engagement Resource Allocation**
>
> Internal auditors must determine appropriate and sufficient resources to achieve engagement objectives based on an evaluation of the nature and complexity of each engagement, time constraints, and available resources.

> **Interpretation of Standard 2230**
>
> Appropriate refers to the mix of knowledge, skills, and other competencies needed to perform the engagement. Sufficient refers to the quantity of resources needed to accomplish the engagement with due professional care.

1. **Resources at the Engagement Level**

    a. This standard imposes a responsibility on **internal auditors**, not on the CAE. Standards that impose responsibilities on the CAE address management of the internal audit activity, organizational independence, and certain other matters.

    b. Engagement resource allocation is based on evaluation of

    1) The number and experience of staff;
    2) The knowledge, skills, and competencies of the staff;
    3) Training needs; and
    4) Whether external resources are required.

    c. If available staff do not have the requisite skills to perform the engagement, internal auditors should consider using external resources to supplement the needed knowledge, skills, and other competencies.

2. **Audit Staff Schedules**

    a. Audit staff schedules should be prepared to achieve effective use of time.

    1) Audit teams are selected based on their knowledge, skills, and other competencies to meet engagement objectives efficiently and effectively. Any training opportunities also should be considered.

    2) All engagements should be under budgetary control. Project budgets and schedules should be developed for each engagement.

        a) Budgets are derived by carefully analyzing the time spent in the prior year on the same or a comparable engagement.

        b) Because no projects are precisely the same (even those covering the same activity), budgets are reevaluated after the preliminary survey.

            i) The CAE reduces excessive budgets, increases insufficient budgets, or changes the scope of the engagements.

            ii) Adjustments and the reasons for them are documented.

        c) Time budgets for engagements are usually prepared in employee-hours or employee-days. Time estimates are given to each internal auditor to help with time management.

       3)   Budget adjustments need to be justified and approved at a level higher than the engagement supervisor. Requests for adjustment should include the following:

          a)   The operational activities to be reviewed,
          b)   The activities actually being performed, and
          c)   The employee-days or hours attributable to the difference.

       4)   Monitoring time budgets and schedules allows the CAE to control projects and avoid overruns.

          a)   Staff auditors submit periodic time sheets that indicate time spent and the status of the job.

Stop and review! You have completed the outline for this subunit. Study multiple-choice question 7 on page 119.

5.4 ENGAGEMENT PROCEDURES

1.   **Engagement Procedures**

NOTE: Many questions on the CIA exam require the selection of engagement procedures. Few such questions are answerable based on memorization of lists. Moreover, no text can feasibly present comprehensive lists of all possible procedures. Thus, a candidate must be able to apply knowledge of auditing concepts to unfamiliar situations when choosing procedures.

    a.   Procedures are performed to obtain sufficient, reliable, relevant, and useful information to achieve the engagement objectives.

       1)   An auditor's **physical examination** provides the most persuasive form of evidence.

       2)   Direct **observation** by the auditor, e.g., of performance of work by client personnel, is the next most persuasive.

       3)   Information originating from a **third party** is less persuasive than information gathered directly by the auditor but more persuasive than information originating from the client.

       4)   Information originating with the **client** can be somewhat persuasive in documentary form, especially if it is subject to effective internal control. But client oral testimony is the least persuasive of all.

       5)   Original documents are more persuasive than copies, which can be altered.

    b.   Management implicitly or explicitly makes assertions about the area or process under review. Engagement objectives typically require internal auditors to perform procedures that test the validity of these assertions (for example, the assertions relevant to financial engagements are covered in Study Unit 3, Subunit 1).

    c.   **Sampling** procedures are frequently performed to test a population. (Sampling is covered in detail in Study Unit 7.)

    d.   Internal auditors should use available information technology (IT), such as generalized audit software (GAS), computer-assisted auditing techniques (CAAT), or integrated test facility (ITF), to assist in performing audit work (computerized audit tools are covered in Study Unit 8, Subunit 1). The benefits of using IT include

       1)   Reduced audit risk
       2)   Increased productivity, resulting in more timely audit engagements
       3)   Increased audit opportunities

2. **Audit Procedures**

    a. **Risk assessment procedures** are performed to obtain an understanding of the entity and its environment, including internal control.

    b. **Further audit procedures** include tests of controls and substantive procedures.

        1) **Tests of controls** test the operating effectiveness of controls in preventing, or detecting and correcting, instances of noncompliance, whether they take the form of a material misstatement in the financial statements, failure to comply with a law or regulation, or some other undesired outcome. They are required when

            a) The auditor's risk assessment is based on an expectation of the operating effectiveness of controls or

            b) Substantive procedures alone do not provide sufficient appropriate evidence.

        2) **Substantive procedures** are used to detect material misstatements at the relevant assertion level. They include (a) tests of details and (b) substantive analytical procedures.

            a) They should be performed for **all** relevant assertions about each material (1) transaction class, (2) account balance, and (3) disclosure.

3. **Selection of Engagement Procedures**

A necessary problem-solving skill on Part 2 of the CIA exam is the ability to determine which audit engagement procedure is appropriate in a given situation. Obtaining proficiency in this skill will increase your success on the exam.

    a. **Basic Procedures**

        1) Three basic procedures performed by internal auditors to gather information are (a) observing conditions, (b) interviewing people, and (c) examining records.

        2) **Observation** is effective for verifying whether (a) particular assets, such as inventory or equipment, exist or (b) a certain process or procedure is being performed appropriately at a moment in time. (Observation is covered in more detail in Study Unit 6, Subunit 5.)

            a) However, observation provides less persuasive information about the assertions of completeness, rights, valuation, and presentation and disclosure. For example, merely observing inventory does not determine whether the engagement client has rights in it.

3) **Interviewing** (inquiring) is especially helpful in obtaining an understanding of client operations because of the opportunity to ask questions to clarify preceding answers or to pursue additional information. (Interviewing is covered in more detail in Study Unit 6, Subunit 4.)

    a) A supplement to interviewing is the use of an **internal control questionnaire**. It consists of a series of questions about the controls designed to prevent or detect errors or fraud. (Questionnaires are covered in more detail in Study Unit 6, Subunit 3.)

        i) Answers to the questions help the internal auditor to identify specific policies and procedures relevant to specific assertions. They also help in the design of tests of controls to evaluate their effectiveness.

        ii) The questionnaire provides a means for ensuring that specific concerns are not overlooked, but it is not sufficient for an understanding of the entire system. Thus, the evidence obtained is indirect and requires corroboration by means of observation, interviews, flowcharting, examination of documents, etc.

    b) Evidence obtained by interviews should be corroborated by gathering objective data.

4) **Examining** (inspecting) records is used in many audit activities. The methods predominantly used are discussed below.

    a) **Inspection of records or documents** is the examination of records or documents, whether internal or external, in paper, electronic, or other media.

    b) **Inspection of tangible assets** is the physical examination of assets to test existence. For example, it is combined with observation of inventory counts.

    c) **Verification** is a broad term for the process of determining the validity of information.

b. Other specific procedures that are variations of the basic procedure of examining records include the following:

1) **Confirmations** obtain audit evidence as a direct, written response to the auditor from a third party.

    a) Confirmations are commonly used to verify the amounts of accounts receivable, goods on consignment, and liabilities.

    b) **Positive** confirmations are used when the amounts being confirmed are material. The recipient is asked to sign and return the letter with a positive assertion that the amount is either correct or incorrect.

        i) Because the amounts involved are material, unanswered positive confirmations require follow-up. They are thus more time-consuming than negative confirmations.

    c) **Negative** confirmations are used when the amounts being confirmed are immaterial or when controls are deemed to be functioning extremely well.

        i) The use of negative confirmations assumes that the recipients will complain only if they have a dispute with the amount. Thus, if a negative confirmation is unanswered, the auditor concludes that the amount has been confirmed.

2) **Tracing and Vouching**

    a) **Tracing** follows a transaction forward from the triggering event to a resulting event, ensuring that the transaction was accounted for properly.

        i) Tracing is used to gain assurance regarding the completeness assertion, for example, that a liability was properly accrued for all goods received.

    b) **Vouching** tracks a result backward to the originating event, ensuring that a recorded amount is properly supported.

        i) Vouching is used to gain assurance regarding the existence assertion, for example, that a receivable claimed on the statement of financial position is supported by a sale to a customer.

Source Documents   **Ledger**

Receipt

Receipt

Receipt

Tracing →

← **Vouching**

Figure 5-2

The terms "tracing" and "vouching" are defined above using classic auditing definitions. However, the CIA exam may use the word "tracing" to mean either process. Be extremely careful when encountering questions on this topic and focus on which process is relevant, not which term is used.

3) **Reperformance** (Recalculation)

    a) Reperformance consists of duplicating the client's work and comparing the results. This is most useful for checking arithmetic accuracy and the correct posting of amounts from source documents to journals to ledgers.

4) **Analytical Procedures**

    a) Analytical procedures are evaluations of financial information made by an analysis of relationships among financial and nonfinancial data. The basic premise is that plausible relationships among data may reasonably be expected to exist and continue in the absence of known conditions to the contrary.

    b) During the planning phase, analytical procedures are used by the internal auditor to determine the nature, extent, and timing of auditing procedures. The objective is to identify such things as the existence of unusual transactions and events and amounts, ratios, and trends that might indicate matters which require further investigation.

    c) Common analytical procedures performed by the internal auditor include (1) analysis of common-size financial statements, (2) ratio analysis, (3) trend analysis, (4) analysis of future-oriented information, and (5) internal and external benchmarking.

    d) **Scanning** is a use of professional judgment to review accounting data to identify significant or unusual items to test. For example, an internal auditor might scan the warehouse for damaged or obsolete inventory.

    e) Analytical procedures are covered in more detail in Study Unit 8, Subunit 3.

c. The chart below describes some of the possible engagement procedures and the information provided by these procedures.

Information Provided by Procedure	Procedures
Sales and receivables were all accounted for.	Trace shipping documents with sales invoices and journal entries. Account for the numerical sequence of sales orders, shipping documents, invoices, etc.
Sales occurred.	Vouch sample of recorded sales to customer orders and shipping documents.
Accounts receivable are valid assets.	Confirm accounts receivable.
Accounts receivable are measured appropriately.	Classify receivables by age, and compare collection rates within classifications with those of prior years (also called aging the accounts receivable). Trace cash receipts to specific accounts. Review delinquent customers' credit ratings.
Cash transactions occurred.	Vouch a sample of recorded cash receipts to accounts receivable and customer orders. Vouch a sample of recorded cash disbursements to approved vouchers.
Cash reported actually exists.	Count cash on hand. Send bank confirmations. Prepare bank reconciliations.
Inventory transactions occurred.	Vouch a sample of recorded purchases to documentation. Vouch a sample of recorded cost of sales to documentation.
Inventory actually exists.	Observe inventory and make test counts.
Inventory amounts are measured appropriately.	Determine whether some inventory is obsolete. Ensure manufactured goods are tested for reasonableness.
Inventory balance contains all inventory owned at year end.	Analytical procedures should be used. A commonly used ratio is the inventory turnover ratio.
Purchases occurred.	Vouch a sample of recorded payables to documentation, e.g., requisitions, purchase orders, receiving reports, and approved invoices.
Accounts payable are all accounted for.	Analytical procedures should be used to form expectations with which to compare management's representations. Trace subsequent payments to recorded payables. Collect supporting documentation and search for unmatched documents to determine whether relevant documents have been lost, misplaced, or misfiled.
Transactions affecting property, plant, and equipment are accounted for.	Analytical procedures should be used. Typical ratios include rate of return on plant assets and plant assets to total assets.
Transactions were recorded in the proper period.	Cutoff test. Documents are traced to the accounting records for several days prior to and after year end to determine proper recognition in the appropriate period.
Transactions and events were recorded appropriately.	Obtain management representation letter that includes assertions that transactions and events were recorded appropriately.
Amounts are appropriately described and disclosures are fairly and clearly expressed.	Inspect financial statements. Evaluate note disclosures. Inspect any other relevant documentation.

4. **Maturity Models**

   a. Audit procedures may require the internal auditor to assess the maturity of a business process (i.e., where the process currently lies on a predefined maturity scale) and compare results with management's expectations for that process. Thus, the internal auditor may use a maturity model to perform this procedure.

   b. "Maturity models establish a systematic basis of measurement for describing the 'as is' state of a process." Thus, they provide the criteria for assessing the **current state** of a business process.

   c. Generally, maturity models have five levels of maturity. The following is an example: (Terminology varies.)

      1) **Initial** level. The process is defined.
      2) **Repeatable** level. The process is established.
      3) **Defined** level. Standards that govern the process are developed.
      4) **Managed** level. Performance measures are defined.
      5) **Optimizing** level. All expectations are met and continuous improvement is enabled.

   d. The following are three steps for creating a maturity model:

      1) Determine the model's purpose and components.

         a) Considerations include

            i)   What management wants to assess
            ii) The business processes involved
            iii) How the expected outcome can be stated in terms of a metric or qualitative statement

         b) Components are the categories of attributes related to the process.

            i) For example, if a maturity model is used to assess an organization's ethics program, a component could include the organization's code of ethics.

      2) Determine the model's scale (the number of levels).
      3) Develop expectations for each component level.

Stop and review! You have completed the outline for this subunit. Study multiple-choice questions 8 through 17 beginning on page 120.

5.5 ENGAGEMENT WORK PROGRAM

> **Performance Standard 2240**
> **Engagement Work Program**
>
> Internal auditors must develop and document work programs that achieve the engagement objectives.

> **Implementation Standard 2240.A1**
>
> Work programs must include the procedures for identifying, analyzing, evaluating, and documenting information during the engagement. The work program must be approved prior to its implementation, and any adjustments approved promptly.

1. The internal auditor plans and performs the engagement, with supervisory review and approval. A primary result of engagement planning is the preparation of the work program. The **engagement work program** is a "document that lists the procedures to be followed during an engagement, designed to achieve the engagement plan" (The IIA Glossary).

2.   Further guidance is provided in IG 2240, *Engagement Work Program*:

    a.   Matters to be considered prior to preparing the work program include

        1)   Engagement scope
        2)   Means of achieving objectives
        3)   A risk and control matrix
        4)   Availability of essential resources
        5)   Sample sizes
        6)   Conclusions and judgments during planning

    b.   Work programs reflect choices of procedures needed to assess risks and test related controls in the areas reviewed. They also reflect the **nature, extent, and timing** of procedures needed to achieve objectives.

        1)   Each procedure should test a specific control over risk.
        2)   Work programs should be documented so that all team members know what remains to be done.

    c.   Work programs are **approved** by management of the internal audit activity prior to the beginning of the work.

        1)   The program is amended as necessary during the engagement to respond to findings. Amendments also should be approved by internal audit activity management.
        2)   IG 2340, *Engagement Supervision*, states that the **engagement supervisor** should approve the work program. The primary concern is that the work program is an efficient way to achieve objectives.

            a)   The work program should provide not only procedures for obtaining information but also for analysis, evaluation, and documentation of that information.

    d.   Work programs typically include a time budget used to control and evaluate the progress of the engagement.

3.   If internal auditors discover that an area was omitted from the engagement work program, they must evaluate whether completion of the engagement as planned will be adequate to achieve the engagement objectives.

4.   **Use of a Pro Forma Work Program**

    a.   A pro forma (standard) work program is used for repeated engagements related to similar operations. It is ordinarily modified over a period of years in response to problems encountered.

        1)   The pro forma work program ensures at least minimum coverage; provides comparability; and saves resources when operations at different locations have similar activities, risks, and controls.
        2)   However, a pro forma work program is not appropriate for a complex or changing operating environment. The engagement objectives and related procedures may no longer be relevant.

Stop and review! You have completed the outline for this subunit. Study multiple-choice questions 18 through 20 beginning on page 123.

QUESTIONS

5.1   Engagement Planning and Risk Assessment

1. Which of the following is **least** likely to be placed on the agenda for discussion at a pre-engagement meeting?

    A. Objectives and scope of the engagement.

    B. Client personnel needed.

    C. Sampling plan and key criteria.

    D. Expected starting and completion dates.

Answer (C) is correct.
    REQUIRED: The item least likely to be discussed at a pre-engagement meeting.
    DISCUSSION: Possible objectives and scope for the engagement, the client personnel to whom the auditors need access, and the expected start and completion dates for the engagement are all appropriate matters for discussion at a pre-engagement meeting. The sampling plan cannot be drafted until risk is assessed and the engagement objectives are set.

2. In planning an assurance engagement, a survey could assist with all of the following **except**

    A. Obtaining engagement client comments and suggestions on control problems.

    B. Obtaining preliminary information on controls.

    C. Identifying areas for engagement emphasis.

    D. Evaluating the adequacy and effectiveness of controls.

Answer (D) is correct.
    REQUIRED: The planning item not assisted by a survey.
    DISCUSSION: Internal auditors may perform a survey to (1) become familiar with activities, risks, and controls to identify areas for engagement emphasis and (2) invite comments and suggestions from stakeholders. A survey is not sufficient for evaluating the adequacy and effectiveness of controls. Evaluation requires testing.

3. Which of the following best describes a preliminary survey?

    A. A standardized questionnaire used to obtain an understanding of management objectives.

    B. A statistical sample of key employee attitudes, skills, and knowledge.

    C. A "walk-through" of the financial control system to identify risks and the controls that can address those risks.

    D. A process used to become familiar with activities and risks to identify areas for engagement emphasis.

Answer (D) is correct.
    REQUIRED: The best description of a preliminary survey.
    DISCUSSION: Internal auditors may perform a survey to (1) become familiar with the activities, risks, and controls to identify areas for engagement emphasis and (2) invite comments and suggestions from stakeholders.
    Answer (A) is incorrect. A preliminary survey covers many areas besides management objectives. Answer (B) is incorrect. A preliminary survey normally does not include statistical sampling. Answer (C) is incorrect. A walk-through of controls is only one possible component of a preliminary survey.

5.2   Engagement Objectives, Scope, and Criteria

4. The established scope of the engagement must be sufficient to satisfy the objectives of the engagement. When developing the objectives of the engagement, the internal auditor considers the

    A. Probability of significant noncompliance.

    B. Information included in the engagement work program.

    C. Results of engagement procedures.

    D. Resources required.

Answer (A) is correct.
    REQUIRED: The factor the internal auditor considers when developing the objectives of the engagement.
    DISCUSSION: Internal auditors must consider the probability of significant errors, fraud, noncompliance, and other exposures when developing assurance engagement objectives (Impl. Std. 2210.A2).
    Answer (B) is incorrect. Engagement objectives must be determined before the engagement work program is written. Answer (C) is incorrect. The objectives determine the procedures to be performed. Answer (D) is incorrect. Internal auditors determine the resources required to achieve the engagement objectives.

5. The preliminary survey phase of an engagement to evaluate recruiting activity shows that hotel and airfare expenses are approximately equal. Both hotel and airline arrangements are made by the recruiting group secretary. Based on this information, the scope of field work should include

    A. Considering competitive factors involved in the selection of hotel accommodations.

    B. Recommending that someone outside the recruiting group make hotel and airline reservations.

    C. Comparing the detail of hotel charges per candidate's expense reports with copies of hotel bills obtained directly from hotel sources.

    D. Obtaining assurance that candidates' legal rights are protected during the course of the interview experience.

Answer (A) is correct.
    REQUIRED: The scope of field work regarding travel expenses incurred for recruiting.
    DISCUSSION: Internal auditors can provide assistance to managers by determining whether underlying assumptions are appropriate, information is current and relevant, and suitable controls are incorporated into the operation in question. The scope of an engagement to evaluate recruiting expenses should include an inquiry as to whether procedures to minimize costs are in place and functioning effectively.
    Answer (B) is incorrect. Recommending that someone outside the recruiting group make hotel and airline reservations is a recommendation, not the scope of the engagement effort. Answer (C) is incorrect. Comparing the detail of hotel charges on a candidate's expense reports to copies of hotel bills obtained directly from hotel sources is an engagement procedure. It is done in the preliminary survey. Answer (D) is incorrect. The legal rights of interviewees are not relevant to an engagement to evaluate recruiting expenses.

6. Before an assurance engagement can be performed, the auditor must identify appropriate criteria. The sources of such criteria are **least** likely to include

    A. Benchmarks for the leading firms in the industry.

    B. Best practices for another industry.

    C. Historical cost information for the processes examined.

    D. Government regulations for the industry.

Answer (B) is correct.
    REQUIRED: The least likely source of criteria for an assurance engagement.
    DISCUSSION: Acceptable industry standards, standards developed by professions or associations, standards in law and government regulations, and other sound business practices are usually deemed to be appropriate criteria.
    Answer (A) is incorrect. Benchmarks for the leading firms in the industry are more likely to provide adequate criteria than those for firms in an unrelated industry. Answer (C) is incorrect. Historical cost information for the processes examined is clearly relevant if they have not changed materially. Answer (D) is incorrect. Government regulations for the industry must be followed.

5.3 Engagement Staff and Resources

7. The internal auditor-in-charge has just been informed of the next engagement, and the engagement team has been assigned. Select the appropriate phase for finalizing the engagement budget.

    A. During formulation of the long-range plan.

    B. After the preliminary survey.

    C. During the initial planning meeting.

    D. After the completion of all field work.

Answer (B) is correct.
    REQUIRED: The proper phase in which to finalize the audit budget.
    DISCUSSION: A survey permits an informed approach to planning and carrying out engagement work and is an effective tool for allocating the internal audit activity's resources where they can be used most effectively. Among other things, the results of the survey should include preliminary estimates of time and resource requirements. Thus, after the preliminary survey has been completed, the final engagement budget can be prepared.
    Answer (A) is incorrect. An initial budget is determined during the formulation of the long-range plan, but revisions based on the preliminary survey may be required. Answer (C) is incorrect. At the initial planning meeting stage, the project is not sufficiently defined to complete the final budget. Answer (D) is incorrect. After the completion of field work, the budget is no longer useful as a control and evaluation tool.

5.4 Engagement Procedures

8. Which of the following engagement objectives will be accomplished by tracing a sample of accounts receivable debit entries to customer invoices and related shipping documents?

- A. Sales are properly recorded.
- B. Sales are billed at the correct prices.
- C. Accounts receivable represent valid sales.
- D. Customer credit is approved.

Answer (C) is correct.
REQUIRED: The audit objective accomplished by tracing a sample of accounts receivable debit entries to customer invoices and related shipping documents.
DISCUSSION: The process described is vouching. It begins with amounts recorded in the ledger and tracks backwards to the source documents. The purpose is to detect fictitious sales and ensure that each claimed sale is properly supported.
Answer (A) is incorrect. The objective of determining whether sales are properly recorded is accomplished by tracing a sample of sales invoices to accounts receivable. Answer (B) is incorrect. The objective of determining whether sales are billed at the correct prices is accomplished by tracing invoice prices to the organization's approved price list. Answer (D) is incorrect. The objective of determining whether customer credit is approved is accomplished by examining sales documents for proper approvals by credit personnel.

9. Vouching entails verifying recorded amounts by examining the underlying documents from the _____ documents to the _____ documents.

- A. Final; original.
- B. Final; previous.
- C. Original; final.
- D. Original; subsequent.

Answer (A) is correct.
REQUIRED: The definition of vouching.
DISCUSSION: Vouching entails verifying recorded amounts by examining the underlying documents from the final documents to the original documents. The engagement objective of working backward is to provide information that recorded amounts reflect valid transactions. Vouching supports the existence or occurrence assertion. Vouching is irrelevant to the completeness assertion, because the existence of records of some transactions does not prove that all transactions were recorded.
Answer (B) is incorrect. Vouching entails the examination of final documents to original documents. Answer (C) is incorrect. Vouching is designed to support the engagement objective of working backward to provide information that recorded amounts reflect valid transactions. Answer (D) is incorrect. It implies the comparison of the original to the next copy. Vouching entails examination from the final document to the original.

10. An internal auditor has set an engagement objective of determining whether mail room staff is fully used. Which of the following engagement techniques will best meet this objective?

- A. Inspection of documents.
- B. Observation.
- C. Inquiry.
- D. Analytical review.

Answer (B) is correct.
REQUIRED: The engagement procedure for determining whether mail room staff is fully used.
DISCUSSION: By observing mail room operations at various times on various days of the week, the internal auditor can note whether incoming or outgoing mail backlogs exist and whether mail room staff are busy on mail room activities, idle, or working on other projects.

11. For review of an accounting department's bank reconciliation unit, which of the following is an appropriate engagement work program step for the review of canceled checks for authorized signatures?

- A. Comparing the check date with the first cancellation date.
- B. Determining that all checks are to be signed by individuals authorized by the board.
- C. Examining a representative sample of signed checks and determining that the signatures are authorized in the organizational signature book.
- D. Completing the tests of controls over check signatures in 4 hours.

Answer (C) is correct.
REQUIRED: The procedure that reviews canceled checks for authorization.
DISCUSSION: Cash disbursements must be properly authorized. The issuance of checks is performed by the treasury function after review of supporting documents, including a payment voucher prepared by the accounts payable department. Proper control procedures require that check-signing responsibility be limited to a few persons whose signatures are kept on file at the banks where the organization has accounts.
Answer (A) is incorrect. Comparing the check date with the first cancellation date has no bearing on reviewing for authorized signatures. Answer (B) is incorrect. Determining that all checks are to be signed by individuals authorized by the board is a statement of engagement objectives. Answer (D) is incorrect. Completing the tests of controls over check signatures in 4 hours is a time budget goal, not a work program step.

Question 12 is based on the following information. The legislative auditing bureau of a country is required to perform compliance engagements involving organizations that are issued defense contracts on a cost-plus basis. Contracts are clearly written to define acceptable costs, including developmental research cost and appropriate overhead rates.

During the past year, the government has engaged in extensive outsourcing of its activities. The outsourcing included contracts to run cafeterias, provide janitorial services, manage computer operations and systems development, and provide engineering of construction projects. The contracts were modeled after those used for years in the defense industry. The legislative internal auditors are being called upon to expand their efforts to include compliance engagements involving these contracts.

Upon initial investigation of these outsourced areas, the internal auditor found many areas in which the outsourced management has apparently expanded its authority and responsibility. For example, the contractor that manages computer operations has developed a highly sophisticated security program that may represent the most advanced information security in the industry. The internal auditor reviews the contract and sees reference only to providing appropriate levels of computing security. The internal auditor suspects that the governmental agency may be incurring developmental costs that the outsourcer may use for competitive advantage in marketing services to other organizations.

12. The internal auditor is concerned about whether all the debits to the computer security expense account are appropriate expenditures. The most appropriate engagement procedure is to

A. Take an attribute sample of computing invoices and determine whether all invoices are properly classified.

B. Perform an analytical review comparing the amount of expenditures incurred this year with the amounts incurred on a trend line for the past 5 years.

C. Take an attribute sample of employee wage expenses incurred by the outsourcing organization and trace to the proper account classification.

D. Take a sample of all debits to the account and investigate by examining source documents to determine the nature and authority of the expenditure.

Answer (D) is correct.
REQUIRED: The most appropriate audit procedure to determine the validity of computer security expenses.
DISCUSSION: The sample should be taken from the population of interest, that is, debits to the expense account. The proper engagement procedure is to vouch the accounting records back to the source documents.
Answer (A) is incorrect. The sample would be too broad to be efficient. The auditor is specifically interested in the debits to the account. Answer (B) is incorrect. Analytical procedures provide information as to whether the total expense is reasonable. They do not determine whether specific debits are correct. Answer (C) is incorrect. This procedure furnishes some information about the wage component of costs, but it is not relevant to other computer security costs.

13. Which of the following documents should the internal auditor examine to determine whether only authorized purchases are being accepted by the receiving department?

A. A bill of lading.

B. A copy of the purchase order.

C. An invoice.

D. Policies and procedures for the receiving function.

Answer (B) is correct.
REQUIRED: The document to examine to determine whether only authorized purchases are being accepted by the receiving department.
DISCUSSION: In determining whether the accounts accurately reflect the obligations of the firm to vendors, the three items most useful to the auditor are purchase orders, receiving reports, and vendors' invoices. The purchase order provides information as to whether the goods were actually ordered and are a voluntary obligation of the organization. The receiving report confirms that the proper amount was received and the liability recorded in the correct period. The vendor's invoice confirms that the proper amount due has been recorded. An internal auditor will also be interested in the purchase requisitions to determine whether the purchase orders were properly authorized. However, the purchase order, not the requisition, is vital to determining the engagement client's obligation.
Answer (A) is incorrect. A shipping document (bill of lading) received from the vendor cannot be used to determine whether the purchase was authorized. Answer (C) is incorrect. A billing notice (invoice) received from the vendor cannot be used to determine whether the purchase was authorized. Answer (D) is incorrect. Policies and procedures are not transaction documents.

14. Which of the following represents the most reliable information that a receivable actually exists?

A. A positive confirmation.

B. A sales invoice.

C. A receiving report.

D. A bill of lading.

Answer (A) is correct.
   REQUIRED: The most reliable evidence that a receivable actually exists.
   DISCUSSION: A confirmation is a direct communication between the internal auditor and the debtor. A positive confirmation is the most reliable kind of confirmation because it asks the debtor to respond regardless of whether (s)he agrees with the information given. The negative confirmation asks for a response only when the debtor disagrees. Positive confirmations are used when balances are large or the internal auditor believes that a substantial number of accounts are in dispute or contain errors or irregularities. The negative form is used when risk is low, balances are small, and the recipients are likely to give confirmation their consideration. Often, a combination of the two forms will be used.
   Answer (B) is incorrect. The sales invoice was internally generated. Information obtained directly from outside sources is more reliable. Answer (C) is incorrect. A receiving report provides no information of a sale and a receivable. Answer (D) is incorrect. A bill of lading is less reliable than a confirmation. It has been under the control of the engagement client.

15. Which of the following procedures provides the most relevant information to determine the adequacy of the allowance for doubtful accounts receivable?

A. Confirm the receivables.

B. Analyze the following month's payments on the accounts receivable balances outstanding.

C. Test the controls over the write-off of accounts receivable to ensure that management approves all write-offs.

D. Analyze the allowance through an aging of receivables and an analysis of current economic data.

Answer (D) is correct.
   REQUIRED: The procedure to determine the adequacy of the allowance for doubtful accounts receivable.
   DISCUSSION: The purpose of an allowance for doubtful accounts is to state accounts receivable at net realizable value. Consequently, an appropriate method of estimating collectibility of the receivables should be applied. Because the probability of collection is inversely proportional to the age of the receivables, aging the receivables provides information that is highly relevant. Current economic conditions are also relevant because collectibility varies with changes in the economic cycle.
   Answer (A) is incorrect. Accounts receivable confirmations are more likely to be effective for the existence assertion than for the valuation and completeness assertions. Answer (B) is incorrect. Although subsequent collections provide the best information about collectibility, they do not indicate the value of uncollected receivables. Answer (C) is incorrect. Testing the controls over write-offs provides no information about valuation.

16. An internal auditor has set an engagement objective of ascertaining the reasonableness of the increases in rental revenue resulting from operating costs passed on to the lessee by the landlord. The internal auditor has already inspected the lease contract to determine that such costs are allowed. Which of the following engagement procedures will best meet this objective?

A. Inspection of documents.

B. Observation.

C. Inquiry.

D. Analytical review.

Answer (D) is correct.
   REQUIRED: The last engagement procedure to determine the reasonableness of increases in rental revenue.
   DISCUSSION: Computation of the rates of increase in operating costs passed through to the lessee from period to period in relation to inflation rates provides an initial view of the reasonableness of the increases.
   Answer (A) is incorrect. The internal auditor has already inspected the documents. Answer (B) is incorrect. Analytical review is required to ascertain the reasonableness of the increases. Answer (C) is incorrect. Analytical review is required to ascertain the reasonableness of the increases.

17. An internal audit activity is planning an assurance engagement in the transportation department of a large engineering firm. The firm owns and operates a fleet of cars and trucks of various sizes. One engagement objective is to evaluate the department's vehicle maintenance procedures. Which procedures are appropriate to this engagement objective?

1. Interview service technicians to gather information about maintenance procedures.

2. Compare costs for selected procedures with industry standards.

3. Compare manufacturer maintenance guidelines with departmental procedures.

4. Analyze vehicle losses.

   A. 1 and 2 only.

   B. 1, 2, and 3 only.

   C. 4 only.

   D. 1, 2, 3, and 4.

Answer (D) is correct.
   REQUIRED: The procedure(s) appropriate to the evaluation of vehicle maintenance.
   DISCUSSION: All the listed procedures are relevant to the engagement objective. Comparing department costs for selected procedures with industry standards provides information about cost control. Comparing manufacturer maintenance guidelines with department procedures provides information about the competence of the workforce. Analyzing vehicle losses determines whether improper maintenance was a cause. Interviewing service technicians to gather information about department maintenance procedures is part of obtaining an understanding of the transportation department's procedures and whether they are being implemented correctly.
   Answer (A) is incorrect. The internal auditors also should analyze vehicle losses and compare manufacturer maintenance guidelines with industry standards. Answer (B) is incorrect. The internal auditors also should analyze vehicle losses. Answer (C) is incorrect. Comparing costs for selected procedures with industry standards, comparing manufacturer maintenance guidelines with departmental procedures, and interviewing service technicians are relevant procedures.

5.5 Engagement Work Program

18. The purpose of including a time budget in an engagement work program is to

   A. Provide an objective means of evaluating the internal auditor's competence.

   B. Ensure timely completion of the engagement.

   C. Provide a means of controlling and evaluating the progress of the engagement.

   D. Restrict the scope of the engagement.

Answer (C) is correct.
   REQUIRED: The purpose of a time budget in an engagement work program.
   DISCUSSION: Supervision includes, among other things, ensuring the approved engagement program is completed unless changes are justified and authorized. For this purpose, a time budget is necessary to evaluate and control the progress of the engagement. It permits comparison of the actual time spent on a procedure with its allotted time.
   Answer (A) is incorrect. Whether an internal auditor remains within the time budget is affected by many factors other than professional competence. Answer (B) is incorrect. The establishment of a budget cannot ensure that work will be completed on a timely basis. Answer (D) is incorrect. A time budget is not intended to limit the scope of the engagement.

19. One of the primary roles of an engagement work program is to

   A. Serve as a tool for planning and conducting engagement work.

   B. Document an internal auditor's evaluations of controls.

   C. Provide for a standardized approach to the engagement.

   D. Assess the risks associated with the activity under review.

Answer (A) is correct.
   REQUIRED: The item that states one of the primary roles of an engagement work program.
   DISCUSSION: Among other things, work programs state the objectives of the engagement, identify technical requirements, and state the nature, extent, and timing of testing required.
   Answer (B) is incorrect. Engagement workpapers include results of control evaluations. Answer (C) is incorrect. The work program may not be consistent from year to year given the changing conditions to which the engagement client must adapt. Since the work program must reflect the current year's situation, standardization may not be appropriate. Answer (D) is incorrect. The risk assessment in the planning phase helps to identify objectives, a step that must be taken before the work program can be developed.

20. Engagement work programs testing controls ordinarily must

   A. Be specifically designed for each operation evaluated.

   B. Be generalized to fit all situations without regard to departmental lines.

   C. Be generalized so as to be usable at all locations of a particular department.

   D. Reduce costly duplication of effort by ensuring that every aspect of an operation is examined.

Answer (A) is correct.

REQUIRED: The true statement about work programs.

DISCUSSION: A work program must be adapted to the specific needs of the engagement after the internal auditor establishes the engagement objectives and scope and determines the resources required. A pro forma (standard) work program is not appropriate for a complex or changing environment. Its stated objectives and procedures may no longer be relevant.

Answer (B) is incorrect. A work program must allow for variations resulting from changing circumstances and varied conditions. Answer (C) is incorrect. A generalized program cannot consider variations in circumstances and conditions. Answer (D) is incorrect. Every aspect of an operation need not be examined. Only those likely to conceal problems and difficulties must be considered.

STUDY UNIT SIX
INFORMATION GATHERING

(11 pages of outline)

This study unit is the second of four covering **Domain III: Performing the Engagement** from The IIA's CIA Exam Syllabus. This domain makes up 40% of Part 2 of the CIA exam and is tested at the **basic** and **proficient** cognitive levels. The relevant portion of the syllabus is highlighted below. (The complete syllabus is in Appendix B.)

	Performing the Engagement (40%)		
	1. Information Gathering		
	A	**Gather and examine relevant information (review previous audit reports and data, conduct walk-throughs and interviews, perform observations, etc.) as part of a preliminary survey of the engagement area**	**Proficient**
	B	**Develop checklists and risk-and-control questionnaires as part of a preliminary survey of the engagement area**	**Proficient**
	C	Apply appropriate sampling (nonstatistical, judgmental, discovery, etc.) and statistical analysis techniques	Proficient
	2. Analysis and Evaluation		
III	A	Use computerized audit tools and techniques (data mining and extraction, continuous monitoring, automated workpapers, embedded audit modules, etc.)	Proficient
	B	**Evaluate the relevance, sufficiency, and reliability of potential sources of evidence**	**Proficient**
	C	Apply appropriate analytical approaches and process mapping techniques (process identification, workflow analysis, process map generation and analysis, spaghetti maps, RACI diagrams, etc.)	Proficient
	D	Determine and apply analytical review techniques (ratio estimation, variance analysis, budget vs. actual, trend analysis, other reasonableness tests, benchmarking, etc.)	Basic
	E	Prepare workpapers and documentation of relevant information to support conclusions and engagement results	Proficient
	F	Summarize and develop engagement conclusions, including assessment of risks and controls	Proficient
	3. Engagement Supervision		
	A	Identify key activities in supervising engagements (coordinate work assignments, review workpapers, evaluate auditors' performance, etc.)	Basic

6.1 THE FOUR QUALITIES OF INFORMATION

> The practice of internal auditing is governed by professional standards. Thus, how an internal auditor performs an engagement is as important as the final product. Part 2 of the CIA exam contains numerous questions regarding (1) the procedures to be applied in a given situation and (2) the proper documentation. Workpapers must be formatted and cross-referenced so that a reviewer can understand how the engagement was conducted and whether the evidence gathered supports the results reported.

Performance Standard 2310
Identifying Information

Internal auditors must identify sufficient, reliable, relevant, and useful information to achieve the engagement's objectives.

Interpretation of Standard 2310

- **Sufficient** information is factual, adequate, and convincing so that a prudent, informed person would reach the same conclusions as the auditor.
- **Reliable** information is the best attainable information through the use of appropriate engagement techniques.
- **Relevant** information supports engagement observations and recommendations and is consistent with the objectives for the engagement.
- **Useful** information helps the organization meet its goals.

---

1. Determining whether information is adequate for the internal auditor's purposes is a matter of professional judgment that depends on (a) the particular situation and (b) the internal auditor's training, experience, and other personal traits.

2. **Sufficient Information**

    a. The sufficiency criterion applies an objective standard. The conclusions reached should be those of a prudent, informed person.

    1) Sufficiency is enhanced when samples are chosen using standard statistical methods.

    b. The basic issue is whether the information has the degree of persuasiveness needed.

    1) For example, persuasiveness must be greater in a fraud investigation of a senior manager than in an engagement involving petty cash. The difference in risk determines the quality and quantity of information.

3. **Reliable Information**

    a. Information is reliable when it is obtained and documented so that a prudent, informed individual can produce the same results and draw the same conclusions. Thus, the internal auditor's results should be verifiable by others. Verifiability is facilitated by systematic documentation.

    1) Reliable information is valid. It accurately represents the observed facts and is free from error and bias.

    2) A synonym for "reliable" is "competent."

    b. Information should consist of what may be collected using reasonable efforts subject to such inherent limitations as the cost-benefit constraint.

    1) Accordingly, internal auditors use different methods, e.g., statistical sampling and analytical auditing procedures.

    c.   Information is more reliable if it is

        1)   Obtained from sources independent of the engagement client, such as confirmations of receivables or expert appraisals that are timely and made by a source with no connection to the auditee

        2)   Corroborated by other information

        3)   Direct, such as the internal auditor's personal observation, rather than indirect, such as hearsay

        4)   An original document, not a copy

4.   **Relevant Information**

    a.   The definition of relevance emphasizes the need for work to be restricted to achieving objectives. However, information also should be gathered on all matters within the engagement's scope.

    b.   Relevant information has a logical relationship to what it is offered to prove.

        1)   For example, vouching journal entries to the original documents does not support the completeness assertion about reported transactions. Instead, tracing transactions to the accounting records provides relevant information.

5.   **Useful Information**

    a.   Information is useful when it helps the organization meet its objectives.

    b.   The organization's ultimate objective is to create value for its owners, other stakeholders, customers, and clients. Accordingly, this characteristic of information is consistent with the definition of internal auditing. It should add value, improve operations, and help an organization achieve its objectives.

The following is a useful memory aid for the four qualities of information:

S = Sufficient	**S**hould
R = Reliable	**R**ick
R = Relevant	**R**ecord
U = Useful	**U**niformly

Stop and review! You have completed the outline for this subunit. Study multiple-choice questions 1 through 4 beginning on page 136.

6.2 SOURCES AND NATURE OF INFORMATION

1.   **Sources of Information**

    a.   **Internal information** originates and remains with the engagement client.

        1)   Payroll records are an example. They are initially generated by the client and then are subsequently processed and retained by the client.

        2)   Lack of involvement of external parties reduces the persuasiveness of information.

            a)   The reliability of information is greater when it comes from sources that are independent of the client.

    b.   **Internal-external information** originates with the client but also is processed by an external party.

        1)   Examples are canceled checks. These documents are created by the client but circulate through the banking system. A bank's acceptance of a check is some confirmation of its validity.

        2)   Internal-external information is deemed to be more reliable than purely internal information.

c.   **External-internal information** is created by an external party but subsequently processed by the client.

    1)   Such information has greater validity than information initiated by the client, but its value is impaired because of the client's opportunity to alter or destroy it.

        a)   Suppliers' invoices are typical examples of external-internal information. Others include the canceled checks included in a cutoff bank statement received by the auditor directly from the bank.

d.   **External information** is created by an independent party and transmitted directly to the internal auditor. External information is ordinarily regarded as the most reliable because it has not been exposed to possible alteration or destruction by the client.

    1)   Common examples are confirmations of receivables sent in response to the internal auditor's requests.

e.   **Outsourcing services**, such as clerical, accounting, and internal audit services, may result in information difficult to classify in this framework.

2.   **Nature of Information**

a.   The following are forms of **legal evidence**:

    1)   **Direct evidence** establishes a particular fact or conclusion without having to make any assumptions.

        a)   Testimony by a witness to an event is a form of direct evidence.

    2)   **Circumstantial evidence** establishes a fact or conclusion that can then lead by inference to another fact.

        a)   The existence of a flat tire can lead to the conclusion that the tire was sabotaged. Obviously, such evidence must be used very carefully because the tire might have been damaged accidentally.

    3)   **Conclusive evidence** is absolute proof, by itself.

        a)   The classic example is that of a watch in the desert. The mere fact of finding the watch proves that someone put it there. It did not assemble itself spontaneously out of sand.

    4)   **Corroborative evidence** serves to confirm a fact or conclusion that can be inferred from other evidence.

        a)   An example is an employee who claims to have been working late on a certain night. A member of the building custodial staff can provide corroborating evidence that this employee was seen in the office.

b.   The following are forms of **audit evidence**:

    1)   **Physical information** consists of the internal auditor's direct observation and inspection of people, property, or activities, e.g., of the counting of inventory.

        a)   Photographs, maps, graphs, and charts may provide compelling physical information.

        b)   When physical observation is the only information about a significant condition, at least two internal auditors should view it.

    2)   **Testimonial information** consists of written or spoken statements of client personnel and others in response to inquiries or interview questions.

        a)   Such information may give important indications about the direction of engagement work.

        b)   Testimonial information may not be conclusive and should be supported by other forms of information when possible.

3) **Documentary information** exists in some permanent form, such as checks, invoices, shipping records, receiving reports, and purchase orders.

    a) Thus, it is the most common type gathered by internal auditors.

    b) Documentary information may be internal or external.

        i) Examples of external information are replies to confirmation requests, invoices from suppliers, and public information held by a governmental body, such as real estate records.

        ii) Examples of internal information include accounting records, receiving reports, purchase orders, depreciation schedules, and maintenance records.

4) **Analytical information** is drawn from the consideration of the interrelationships among data or, in the case of internal control, the particular policies and procedures of which it is composed.

    a) Analysis produces circumstantial information in the form of inferences or conclusions based on examining the components as a whole for consistencies, inconsistencies, cause-and-effect relationships, relevant and irrelevant items, etc.

3. **Levels of Persuasiveness of Evidence**

    a. An auditor's **physical examination** provides the most persuasive form of evidence.

    b. Direct **observation** by the auditor is the next most persuasive. The lack of precise measurement is a weakness. (Observation is covered in Subunit 6.5.)

    c. Information originating from a **third party** is less persuasive than information gathered by the auditor but more persuasive than information originating from the client.

    d. Information originating with the **client** can be somewhat persuasive in documentary form, especially if it is subject to effective internal control. But client oral testimony is the least persuasive of all.

4. **Incomplete Information**

    a. If the client provides the internal auditor with incomplete information that is used to conclude on the effectiveness of a function or process, the internal auditor should

        1) Perform the analysis,
        2) Assess the effects of the incomplete information, and
        3) Disclaim any assertion regarding the information's reliability.

5. **Other Issues**

    a. Engagement client feedback is valuable in the internal auditor's determination of whether the information supports observations, conclusions, and recommendations.

    b. If engagement observations are negative, the client has a reason to find flaws in the internal auditor's information and reasoning. Constructive feedback of this kind helps the internal auditor strengthen the evidential base of engagement communications.

        1) The client's tendency to be critical of negative observations means that agreement lends substantial credibility to the internal auditor's position.

        2) However, agreement with positive observations may represent client self-interest rather than useful feedback.

Stop and review! You have completed the outline for this subunit. Study multiple-choice questions 5 through 13 beginning on page 137.

6.3 QUESTIONNAIRES

1. **Internal Control Questionnaires**

    a. One use of questionnaires is to obtain an understanding of the client's controls. An internal control questionnaire is often very structured and detailed and is drafted in a yes/no or short-answer format.

    b. Appropriate uses of an internal control questionnaire include

    1) Filling out the questionnaire while interviewing the person who has responsibility for the function or subunit being reviewed,

    2) Drafting the questionnaire so that a "no" response requires attention, and

    3) Supplementing the completed questionnaire with a narrative description or flowchart.

    c. Disadvantages of these questionnaires are that

    1) They are difficult to prepare.

    2) They are time-consuming to administer.

    3) Engagement clients may anticipate the preferred responses and therefore may lie or give insufficient consideration to the task.

    4) Not all circumstances can be addressed.

    5) They are less effective than interviewing.

2. **Pre-Interview Questionnaires**

    a. Questionnaires are also an efficient way of preparing for an interview if they are properly designed and transmitted in advance. A formal questionnaire

    1) Involves the engagement client's supervisors and employees in the engagement and minimizes their anxiety.

    2) Provides an opportunity for engagement client self-evaluation.

    3) May result in a more economical engagement because the information it generates is prepared by those most familiar with it.

    a) The internal auditor must still ask clarifying questions and verify responses. However, only those answers that appear inappropriate should be pursued by asking for clarification or explanation.

    b) In this way, problems may be isolated and either compensating controls identified or extensions to the engagement procedures planned.

3. **Sequence and Format**

    a. The sequence and format of questions have many known effects on responses.

    1) For example, questions should be in a logical order, and personal questions should be asked last because of possible emotional responses.

    b. One method of reducing these effects is to use questionnaire variations that cause these biases to average out across the sample.

    1) Many types of questions may be used, e.g., multiple-choice, checklists, fill-in-the-blank, essay, or options indicating levels of agreement or disagreement.

    2) Questions must be reliably worded so that they measure what was intended to be measured.

    3) The questionnaire should be short to increase the response rate.

Stop and review! You have completed the outline for this subunit. Study multiple-choice questions 14 and 15 on page 139.

6.4 INTERVIEWING

1. **Use**

   a.   Interviewing and other data-gathering activities are usually performed during the preliminary survey phase of an audit engagement.

   1)   Interviews obtain testimonial evidence from engagement clients, other members of the organization who have contact with them, and independent parties.

   b.   An interview allows auditors to ask questions clarifying initial testimony. Thus, auditors may deepen their understanding of operations and seek reasons for unexpected results and unusual events and circumstances.

   1)   An interview is a secure and personal form of communication compared with, for example, email or paper-based documents.

   2)   People tend to be less careful in their responses if the interview is one-to-one.

   c.   The main purpose of interviews is to gather facts related to the audit engagement.

2. **Dislike of Evaluation**

   a.   One fundamental problem faced by the internal auditor-interviewer is that people dislike being evaluated.

   1)   Engagement clients may resent even the most constructive criticism and fear the possible adverse consequences of an audit report.

   b.   Consequently, the internal auditor must gain the confidence of clients by demonstrating self-assurance, persuasiveness, fairness, empathy, and competence.

   1)   The internal auditor may gain clients' willing cooperation by explaining how the engagement may be helpful and by emphasizing that all parties are members of a team with the same objectives.

   2)   Moreover, the internal auditor must avoid over-criticism.

   a)   An internal auditor who finds no major problems may be insecure about the result. (S)he may therefore resort to excessive criticism of minor matters, an approach that may alienate engagement clients and management and not be cost beneficial.

3. **Four Types of Interviews**

   a.   A **preliminary** interview is used to

   1)   Promote the value of internal auditing,
   2)   Understand the interviewee,
   3)   Gather general information, and
   4)   Serve as a basis for planning future interview strategies.

   b.   A **fact-gathering** interview is oriented to the specific details that can be provided by a particular interviewee.

   1)   Additional information can be sought in a nondirective manner, i.e., by asking open-ended questions.

   c.   A **follow-up** interview is intended to answer questions raised during the analysis of the fact-gathering interview. It also tests the interviewee's acceptance of new ideas generated by the auditor.

   d.   An **exit** interview helps to ensure the accuracy of conclusions, findings, and recommendations in the final engagement communication by discussing it with the interviewee.

4. **Planning an Interview**

   a. The auditor should prepare by reading operations manuals, organizational charts, prior engagement communications, results of questionnaires, etc.

      1) The auditor should understand not only the engagement client's functions, procedures, and terminology but also the psychological traits of auditee managers.

   b. The auditor should design basic questions.

      1) An auditor may use a directive approach emphasizing narrowly focused questions.

      2) An alternative is a nondirective approach using broad questions that are more likely to provide clarification and to result in unexpected observations.

      3) A combination of these approaches is often recommended.

5. **Scheduling Issues**

   a. Except when surprise is needed (e.g., in a review of cash or a fraud engagement), an appointment should be made well in advance for a specific time and place.

   b. The meeting should be in the engagement client's office, if feasible.

   c. The interview's duration should be set in advance.

   d. People tend to respond more freely if the interview is one-to-one.

   e. Except in fraud engagements, the purpose should be explained to the client.

   f. If possible, interviews should not be scheduled very late in the day, just before or after a vacation, or just before or after a meal.

6. **Opening the Interview**

   a. The auditor should be on time, and prompt notice should be given if delay is unavoidable.

   b. Engaging in initial, brief pleasantries may put the engagement client at ease.

   c. The purpose of the interview should be explained.

   d. The auditor should be polite, helpful, and nonthreatening.

   e. Confidentiality should be assured if feasible.

7. **Conducting the Interview**

   a. Interviewing requires an understanding of basic communications theory.

      1) A sender transmits an idea through a message.

      2) This message is encoded in a writing, in an oral statement, or in body language.

      3) The encoded message is transmitted through a channel or medium to a receiver.

         a) Barriers in the channel may interrupt or distort the message.

      4) The receiver decodes the message and interprets the message in accordance with his or her experience and knowledge.

         a) Technical jargon should be avoided so as to increase the chance that the message will be accurately decoded.

      5) The receiver may then undertake **action** or respond to the message.

      6) The words or actions of the receiver provide feedback to the sender.

         a) Feedback is vital because it tells the sender whether the message has been understood and acted upon.

7) Nonverbal communication (body language) consists of facial expressions, vocal intonations, posture, gestures, appearance, and physical distance. Thus, by its nature, nonverbal communication is much less precise than verbal communication. However, in some cases, it may convey more information than verbal communication. But it is not necessarily more truthful.

a) Nonverbal communication is heavily influenced by culture. For example, a nod of the head may have opposite meanings in different cultures.

b. The interviewer should be tactful, objective, reasonable, and interested.

1) (S)he also must avoid an accusatory tone and avoid statements not yet supported by evidence.

2) The interviewer should not react negatively if the interviewee is uncooperative. (S)he should carefully explain the situation and provide an opportunity for the interviewee to calm down and continue the interview.

3) The interviewee should not feel pressured or coerced during the interview.

c. The interview should follow the agenda developed in the planning phase.

1) Nevertheless, the interviewer should be flexible. Unexpected but worthwhile lines of inquiry may open up during the interview.

d. Active (effective) listening includes observing interviewee behavior (body language, such as eye contact), reserving judgment about what is said, asking clarifying questions, and allowing for periods of silence.

1) An effective listener also enhances the communication process by sending appropriate nonverbal signals to the speaker.

a) Thus, a listener who wishes to convey a positive and encouraging message should stop other activities and focus complete attention on the speaker.

2) Reflecting what is said, that is, summarizing or rephrasing an answer, is a means of stimulating additional comments.

3) Furthermore, the interviewee should be encouraged to ask relevant questions.

a) These questions should be respectfully heard and duly included in the record of the interview.

4) Empathy is a sensitive awareness of the speaker's feelings, thoughts, and experience. An empathic listener understands what the speaker wants to communicate rather than what the listener wants to understand.

5) Listening with intensity involves concentrating on the speaker's message and disregarding distractions.

6) Attentiveness is promoted by use of active listening techniques.

a) For example, changing the wording of the questions and the sequence in which they are asked may eliminate some of the boredom associated with a series of interviews.

i) The interviewer also may be able to refine the technique during the process.

e. Anticipation is one approach the interviewer can use to maintain focus during a far-ranging discussion. It assumes that the interviewer has done some preparation and is ready to listen intelligently.

1) Active listening permits anticipation because the mind can process information more rapidly than most people speak. Thus, the listener has time to analyze the information and determine what is most important.

f.   Leading questions (questions suggesting the answer) should be avoided.

g.   Loaded questions (questions with self-incriminating answers) also should be avoided.

h.   Questions requiring an explanatory response are usually preferable to those with binary (yes or no) responses.

i.   An interviewer should be suspicious of answers that (1) are too smoothly stated, (2) fit too neatly with the interviewer's own preconceptions, (3) consist of generalizations, or (4) contain unfamiliar technical terminology.

     1)   Thus, the interviewer must ask for greater specificity or other clarifications.

j.   Care should be taken to differentiate statements of fact from statements of opinion.

k.   The interviewer should understand what the interviewee regards as important.

l.   Debate and disagreement with the interviewee should be avoided.

8.   **Documentation**

a.   Good note taking during the interview is essential.

     1)   Notes should be sufficiently readable and thorough to permit a full reconstruction of the information gathered. This write-up step should occur as soon as possible after the interview.

     2)   The interviewee should be informed about the need for note taking.

     3)   Notes should be properly dated and labeled, and the names and positions of interviewees should be included.

     4)   The amount of time spent not looking at the interviewee should be minimized, and questions should not be asked while jotting notes.

     5)   Interviews may be recorded only with the permission of the client.

b.   The notes and the memorandum prepared with their help are part of the workpapers and therefore the documentation of the engagement used to prepare communications.

     1)   The memorandum should include significant events during the interview, such as interruptions or emotional outbursts.

     2)   The internal auditor must be careful to use information in its proper context.

9.   **Evaluation**

a.   This step is especially important if a follow-up interview is considered, but it is useful as a means of internal auditor self-improvement.

b.   The internal auditor should consider whether objectives were appropriate, whether they were attained, and, if not, why not.

c.   The internal auditor also should consider whether the planning was efficient, the interviewee was cooperative, and the interviewer made errors.

Stop and review! You have completed the outline for this subunit. Study multiple-choice questions 16 through 19 beginning on page 140.

6.5 OTHER INFORMATION-GATHERING METHODS

1. **Observation**

   a. Observation is looking at a process or procedure being performed.

   b. By watching the physical activities of employees to see how they perform their duties, the auditor can determine whether written policies have been implemented.

      1) Moreover, observing a phenomenon in its natural setting eliminates some experimental bias.

   c. Observation is limited because employees who know they are being observed may behave differently while being observed. Accordingly, unobtrusive measures may be preferable.

      1) The possibility of observing unexpected or unusual behavior makes such measures useful for exploratory investigations.

   d. Observation is most persuasive for the existence or occurrence assertion (whether assets or liabilities exist and whether transactions have occurred).

      1) It is less persuasive for the completeness assertion (whether all transactions that should be reported are reported).

   e. Lack of experimental control and measurement precision are other limitations of observational research.

      1) Another is that some things, such as private behavior, attitudes, feelings, and motives, cannot be observed.

2. **Internal Surveys**

   a. Mail questionnaires are relatively cheap, eliminate interviewer bias, and gather large amounts of data. However, they tend to be inflexible, have a slow response time, and have nonresponse bias.

      1) The sample will not be truly random if respondents as a group differ from nonrespondents. Thus, people may choose not to respond for reasons related to the purpose of the questionnaire.

   b. Telephone interviews are a flexible means of obtaining data rapidly and controlling the sample. However, they introduce interviewer bias, are more costly, and gather less data than mail surveys.

   c. Rating scales are used to allow people to rate such things as service. The scale represents a continuum of responses.

EXAMPLE of a Rating Scale

Rate the service you received on a scale of 1 to 10, 10 being the best. Circle the appropriate number.

1 2 3 4 5 6 7 8 9 10

Stop and review! You have completed the outline for this subunit. Study multiple-choice question 20 on page 141.

QUESTIONS

6.1 The Four Qualities of Information

1. In an operational audit, the internal auditors discovered an increase in absenteeism. Accordingly, the chief audit executive decided to identify information about workforce morale. To achieve this engagement objective, the internal auditors must understand that

    A. Morale cannot be reliably analyzed.

    B. Only outcomes that are directly quantifiable can be reliably analyzed.

    C. Reliable information may be obtained about morale factors such as job satisfaction.

    D. Morale is always proportional to compensation.

Answer (C) is correct.
    REQUIRED: The true statement about workforce morale.
    DISCUSSION: Reliable information is the best information attainable through the use of appropriate engagement techniques (Inter. Std. 2310). Such information need not consist only of quantifiable outcomes, such as rates of workforce turnover and absenteeism. Reliable information may be identified about such difficult-to-measure things as attitudes toward supervisors, other workers, and compensation. For example, surveys may produce statistically valid information about job satisfaction.
    Answer (A) is incorrect. Difficulty of analysis does not preclude reliability. Answer (B) is incorrect. With proper engagement tools, even emotional responses may be measured and analyzed reliably. Answer (D) is incorrect. According to research and common human experience, the availability of, for example, intrinsic awards (e.g., personal achievement) may offset a low level of extrinsic awards (e.g., compensation).

2. Which of the following evidence is the most reliable?

    A. Evidence corroborated by engagement client management.

    B. Hearsay from an independent source.

    C. Expert appraisal by audit client engineer.

    D. Original, signed contract corroborated by a bank's copies of checks.

Answer (D) is correct.
    REQUIRED: The most reliable evidence.
    DISCUSSION: Evidence is more reliable if it is (1) obtained from sources independent of the engagement client, such as confirmations of receivables or expert appraisals that are timely and made by a source with no connection to the auditee; (2) corroborated by other information; (3) direct, such as the internal auditor's personal observation, rather than indirect, such as hearsay; and (4) an original document, not a copy. The original copy of the contract with the contracted price, corroborated by a bank's (independent party's) copy of the payment checks, is more reliable than the other choices.
    Answer (A) is incorrect. Evidence is more reliable when corroborated by an independent source, not audit client management. Answer (B) is incorrect. Direct evidence is more reliable than indirect evidence, such as hearsay. Answer (C) is incorrect. Expert appraisals are more reliable when performed by independent experts, not the audit client's engineers.

3. Which of the following is a **false** statement about the reliability of audit evidence?

    A. The more effective the organization's internal control, the more assurance it provides about the accounting data.

    B. A copy of a document is as reliable as the original.

    C. Evidence obtained from independent sources outside the organization is more reliable than evidence obtained from internal sources.

    D. The auditor's direct personal knowledge is more reliable than information obtained indirectly.

Answer (B) is correct.
    REQUIRED: The false statement about the reliability of audit evidence.
    DISCUSSION: Internal auditors must identify sufficient, reliable, relevant, and useful information to achieve the engagement's objectives. Reliable information is best attainable through the use of appropriate engagement (interpretation). Several factors increase the reliability of audit evidence. Evidence is more reliable if it is (1) obtained from sources independent of the engagement client, (2) corroborated by other information, and (3) direct, such as the internal auditor's personal observation. Also, an original document is more reliable than a copy.
    Answer (A) is incorrect. The more effective the controls, the more assurance they provide about the reliability of the accounting data. Answer (C) is incorrect. Evidence obtained from independent sources outside an entity provides greater assurance of reliability than evidence obtained from within the entity. Answer (D) is incorrect. The auditor's direct personal knowledge, obtained through physical examination, observation, and inspection, is more reliable than information obtained indirectly.

4. Which of the following constitutes sufficient audit evidence for verifying air travel reimbursement?

    A. Either a pre-printed ticket or a boarding pass.

    B. Either a printout of an electronic ticket or a boarding pass.

    C. Both a printout of an electronic ticket and a boarding pass.

    D. Either a pre-printed ticket or a printout of an electronic ticket.

Answer (C) is correct.
    REQUIRED: The combination providing sufficient audit evidence.
    DISCUSSION: An electronic ticket verifies payment, and a boarding pass verifies that the employee actually took the flight instead of cashing in the ticket and using a cheaper form of transportation.
    Answer (A) is incorrect. Neither piece of evidence by itself is sufficient. Answer (B) is incorrect. Neither piece of evidence by itself is sufficient. Answer (D) is incorrect. A boarding pass is necessary to verify that the employee actually took the flight.

6.2 Sources and Nature of Information

5. The chief audit executive is reviewing the workpapers produced by an internal auditor during a fraud investigation. Among the items contained in the workpapers is a description of an item of physical information. Which of the following is the most probable source of this item of information?

    A. Observing conditions.

    B. Interviewing people.

    C. Examining records.

    D. Computing variances.

Answer (A) is correct.
    REQUIRED: The most probable source of physical information.
    DISCUSSION: Physical information results from the verification of the actual existence of things, activities, or individuals by observation, inspection, or count. It may take the form of photographs, maps, charts, or other depictions.
    Answer (B) is incorrect. Interviewing produces testimonial information. Answer (C) is incorrect. The examination of records requires documentary information and produces analytical information. Answer (D) is incorrect. Computations and verifications lead to analytical information.

6. To verify the proper value of costs charged to real property records for improvements to the property, the best source of information is

    A. Inspection by the internal auditor of real property improvements.

    B. A letter signed by the real property manager asserting the propriety of costs incurred.

    C. Original invoices supporting entries into the accounting records.

    D. Comparison of billed amounts with contract estimates.

Answer (C) is correct.
    REQUIRED: The best source of evidence to verify costs charged to real property records for improvements.
    DISCUSSION: To verify real property costs, the best method of obtaining engagement information is to examine records. Records originating outside the engagement client, such as original invoices, are much more reliable than internal documents or engagement client testimony. Also, these invoices support actual accounting record entries.
    Answer (A) is incorrect. An inspection confirms that the improvements were made, not their cost. Answer (B) is incorrect. Records or documents generated internally are less reliable than those produced externally. Answer (D) is incorrect. A comparison of billed amounts with contract estimates measures the reasonableness of costs but is less persuasive than original invoices supporting entries into the accounting records.

7. The most conclusive information to support supplier account balances is obtained by

    A. Reviewing the vendor statements obtained from the accounts payable clerk.

    B. Obtaining confirmations of balances from the suppliers.

    C. Performing analytical account analysis.

    D. Interviewing the accounts payable manager to determine the internal controls maintained over accounts payable processing.

Answer (B) is correct.
    REQUIRED: The most conclusive information to support supplier account balances.
    DISCUSSION: Confirmation has the advantage of obtaining information from sources external to the entity. Information from external sources provides greater assurances of reliability than information from sources within the entity.
    Answer (A) is incorrect. Vendor statements obtained from the accounts payable clerk may be inaccurate, purposely misstated, or prepared for nonexisting vendors. Answer (C) is incorrect. Analytical account analysis is effective for identifying circumstances that require additional consideration. Answer (D) is incorrect. Interviewing an employee provides oral, or testimonial, information, which is inherently less reliable than information obtained from independent sources.

8. A set of engagement workpapers contained a copy of a document providing information that an expensive item that had been special-ordered was actually on hand on a particular date. The most likely source of this information is a printout from a computerized

A.   Purchases journal.

B.   Cash payments journal.

C.   Perpetual inventory file.

D.   Receiving report file.

Answer (C) is correct.
REQUIRED: The most likely source of evidence that an item was actually on hand on a particular date.
DISCUSSION: In a perpetual inventory system, purchases are directly recorded in the inventory account, and cost of goods sold is determined as the goods are sold. A computerized perpetual inventory file has a record of each debit or credit transaction with its date, amount, etc., and the inventory balance for any given date could therefore be determined.
Answer (A) is incorrect. The purchases journal indicates when the item was ordered but not whether it was still on hand at a specific later date. Answer (B) is incorrect. The cash payments journal indicates when the item was paid for but not whether it was still on hand at a specific later date. Answer (D) is incorrect. The receiving report indicates when the item was received but not whether it was still on hand at a specific later date.

9. An internal auditor takes a photograph of the engagement client's workplace. The photograph is a form of what kind of information?

A.   Physical.

B.   Testimonial.

C.   Documentary.

D.   Analytical.

Answer (A) is correct.
REQUIRED: The kind of information represented by a photograph.
DISCUSSION: Physical information results from the verification of the actual existence of things, activities, or individuals by observation, inspection, or count. It may take the form of photographs, maps, charts, or other depictions.
Answer (B) is incorrect. Testimonial information consists of oral or written statements derived from inquiries or interviews. Answer (C) is incorrect. Documentary information consists of letters, memoranda, invoices, shipping and receiving reports, etc. Answer (D) is incorrect. Analytical information is derived from a study and comparison of the relationships among data.

10. Which of the following are **least** valuable in predicting the amount of uncollectible accounts for an organization?

A.   Published economic indices indicating a general business downturn.

B.   Dollar amounts of accounts actually written off by the organization for each of the past 6 months.

C.   Total monthly sales for each of the past 6 months.

D.   Written forecasts from the credit manager regarding expected future cash collections.

Answer (D) is correct.
REQUIRED: The data least valuable in predicting the amount of uncollectible accounts.
DISCUSSION: Written forecasts from the credit manager may be relevant and useful, but they cannot be considered sufficient or reliable. Opinion evidence does not have as much reliability as factual evidence. In addition, the source of the evidence may have a bias, which should be considered by the internal auditor when evaluating the reliability of this data.
Answer (A) is incorrect. Although these statistics might not be quite as relevant as some of the other data, they are reliable, having been compiled and published by an independent source. Answer (B) is incorrect. The dollar amounts of write-offs are relevant and reliable, representing the actual experience of the organization. Answer (C) is incorrect. These amounts include cash as well as credit sales. Thus, the inclusion of cash sales reduces the relevance of these data. However, prior sales also represent the actual experience of the organization and therefore have a high degree of reliability.

11. The most likely source of information indicating employee theft of inventory is

A.   Physical inspection of the condition of inventory items on hand.

B.   A warehouse employee's verbal charge of theft.

C.   Differences between an inventory count and perpetual inventory records.

D.   Accounts payable transactions vouched to inventory receiving reports.

Answer (B) is correct.
REQUIRED: The most likely source of evidence indicating employee theft of inventory.
DISCUSSION: Testimonial information may not be conclusive and should be supported by other forms of information whenever possible. However, it may provide a lead not indicated by other procedures.
Answer (A) is incorrect. Physical inspection of items on hand does not disclose shortages or indicate theft. Answer (C) is incorrect. Differences between inventory counts and perpetual records are normal and, by themselves, do not indicate theft. Answer (D) is incorrect. Vouching transactions from accounts payable to receiving reports provides no information about a shortage or theft arising after receipt of the goods.

12. Which of the following techniques is most likely to result in sufficient information with regard to an engagement to review the quantity of fixed assets on hand in a particular department?

A. Physical observation.

B. Analytical review of purchase requests and subsequent invoices.

C. Interviews with department management.

D. Examination of the account balances contained in general and subsidiary ledgers.

Answer (A) is correct.

REQUIRED: The best technique for obtaining sufficient information regarding the quantity of fixed assets.

DISCUSSION: First-hand observation by the auditor is more persuasive than analytical reviews performed, client-prepared records examined by the auditor, or interviews with client personnel.

Answer (B) is incorrect. Items purchased may no longer be present in the department being reviewed, even though they were originally purchased for that department. Answer (C) is incorrect. Interviews are useful in gaining insight into operations and understanding exceptions but are not sufficient. Answer (D) is incorrect. Ledger balances may not indicate whether assets have been moved or stolen.

13. An internal auditor at a savings and loan association concludes that a secured real estate loan is collectible. Which of the following engagement procedures provides the most persuasive information about the loan's collectibility?

A. Confirming the loan balance with the borrower.

B. Reviewing the loan file for proper authorization by the credit committee.

C. Examining documentation of a recent, independent appraisal of the real estate.

D. Examining the loan application for appropriate borrowers' signatures.

Answer (C) is correct.

REQUIRED: The most persuasive information about the loan's collectibility.

DISCUSSION: Real estate appraisals are based on estimated resale value or future cash flows. A recent, independent appraisal provides information about the borrower's ability to repay the loan. Such an appraisal tends to be reasonably reliable because it is timely and derives from an expert source independent of the engagement client.

Answer (A) is incorrect. A confirmation provides information about a loan's existence, not its collectibility. Answer (B) is incorrect. Information about the loan's authorization is not relevant to its collectibility. Answer (D) is incorrect. The validity of the loan is not relevant to the borrower's ability to repay the loan.

6.3 Questionnaires

14. A well-designed internal control questionnaire should

A. Elicit "yes" or "no" responses rather than narrative responses and be organized by department.

B. Be a sufficient source of data for assessment of control risk.

C. Help evaluate the effectiveness of internal control.

D. Be independent of the objectives of the internal auditing engagement.

Answer (C) is correct.

REQUIRED: The function of an internal control questionnaire.

DISCUSSION: An internal control questionnaire consists of a series of questions about the organization's controls designed to prevent or detect errors or fraud. Answers to the questions help the internal auditor to identify specific controls relevant to specific assertions and to design tests of controls to evaluate the effectiveness of their design and operation.

Answer (A) is incorrect. Yes/no question formats and organizing question sequence by department may facilitate administering the questionnaire, but other formats and methods of question organization are possible. Answer (B) is incorrect. The questionnaire is a tool to help understand and document internal control but is not sufficient as the sole source of information to support the assessment of control risk. Answer (D) is incorrect. The internal control questionnaire must be designed to achieve the engagement objectives.

15. A questionnaire consists of a series of questions relating to controls normally required to prevent or detect errors and fraud that may occur for each type of transaction. Which of the following is **not** an advantage of a questionnaire?

A. A questionnaire provides a framework that minimizes the possibility of overlooking aspects of internal control.

B. A questionnaire can be easily completed.

C. A questionnaire is flexible in design and application.

D. The completed questionnaire provides documentation that the internal auditor became familiar with internal control.

Answer (C) is correct.

REQUIRED: The statement not an advantage of a questionnaire.

DISCUSSION: Questionnaires are designed to be inflexible in that the responses to certain questions are expected. Questionnaires are not easily adapted to unique situations. The approach that offers the most flexibility is a narrative memorandum describing internal control. The next most flexible approach is a flowchart.

Answer (A) is incorrect. A questionnaire provides a framework to assure that control concerns are not overlooked. Answer (B) is incorrect. A questionnaire is relatively easy to complete. For the most part, only yes/no responses are elicited from management and employees. Answer (D) is incorrect. The completed questionnaire can become part of the workpapers to document the internal auditor's becoming familiar with the auditee's activities, risks, and controls.

6.4 Interviewing

16. When conducting interviews during the early stages of an internal auditing engagement, it is more effective to

    A. Ask for specific answers that can be quantified.

    B. Ask people about their jobs.

    C. Ask surprise questions about daily procedures.

    D. Take advantage of the fact that fear is an important part of the engagement.

Answer (B) is correct.
    REQUIRED: The most effective way to conduct interviews during the early stages of an engagement.
    DISCUSSION: To improve internal auditor-client cooperation, the internal auditor should, to the extent feasible, humanize the engagement process. For example, individuals feel more important being asked people-type questions, such as being asked about their jobs, rather than control-type questions.
    Answer (A) is incorrect. Later field work will cover information that can be quantified. Building rapport is more important in early interviews. Answer (C) is incorrect. Unless fraud is suspected or negotiable securities are audited, the more effective approach is to defuse the auditee anxiety that results from anticipating the engagement. Answer (D) is incorrect. Although auditee fear is a natural part of anticipating the engagement, the internal auditor should keep it from playing an important role by using good interpersonal skills to build a positive, participative relationship with the auditee.

17. The auditor conducted an interview with the supervisor. The auditor noted that the supervisor became uncomfortable and nervous, and changed the subject whenever the auditor raised questions about certain types of claims. The supervisor's answers were consistent with company policies and procedures. When documenting the interview, the auditor should

    A. Document the supervisor's answers noting the nature of the nonverbal communications.

    B. Not document the nonverbal communication because it is subjective and is not corroborated.

    C. Conclude that the nonverbal communication is persuasive and that sufficient evidence exists to charge fraud against the group.

    D. Ignore the specific answers given in the interview, because they are self-serving.

Answer (A) is correct.
    REQUIRED: The auditor action when documenting the interview with the supervisor.
    DISCUSSION: Auditors frequently encounter and act upon nonverbal communication. If the nonverbal communication affects the auditor's perception of the information gathered, it should be documented so that it can be considered as the audit proceeds.
    Answer (B) is incorrect. If the nonverbal communication affects the auditor's perception of the information gathered, it should be documented. Answer (C) is incorrect. Nonverbal communication, by itself, is not sufficient to reach a conclusion that fraud has occurred. However, along with the allegations made by the employee, it may be sufficient to justify a fraud investigation. Answer (D) is incorrect. The answers given should be documented.

18. To elicit views on broad organizational risks and objectives from the board and senior management, an internal auditor should

    A. List specific risk factors for consideration.

    B. Develop spreadsheets with quantitative data relevant to the industry.

    C. Use a nondirective approach to initiating discussion of mitigating risks.

    D. Ask each member of management about specific risks listed in an industry reference.

Answer (C) is correct.
    REQUIRED: The appropriate interview method.
    DISCUSSION: Effective interview planning includes formulating basic questions. An internal auditor may use a directive approach by asking narrowly focused questions. A preferable alternative given the interviewees and the subject matter is a nondirective approach using broad questions that are more likely to provide clarification and yield unexpected observations.
    Answer (A) is incorrect. Although such factors may be relevant, they will not necessarily create an opportunity for management to brainstorm. Answer (B) is incorrect. Facts provide more of a teaching tool than a proper means to start relevant discussion. Answer (D) is incorrect. Although an industry reference may raise many valid points, it may not address concerns specific to the organization.

19. Tolerating silence, asking open-ended questions, and paraphrasing are three aids to more effective

   A. Meetings.

   B. Listening.

   C. Interviews.

   D. Feedback.

Answer (B) is correct.

REQUIRED: The process rendered more effective by tolerating silence, asking open-ended questions, and paraphrasing.

DISCUSSION: Listening entails decoding and understanding the first message sent. The sender then becomes a listener with respect to the feedback. Thus, listening is necessary at both ends of the communication channel. Other aids to effective listening are using body language to encourage the speaker, showing appropriate emotion to signify empathy, understanding and correcting for one's biases, avoiding making premature judgments, and briefly summarizing what has been said.

Answer (A) is incorrect. Tolerating silence, asking open-ended questions, and paraphrasing may slow down a meeting. Answer (C) is incorrect. Tolerating silence, asking open-ended questions, and paraphrasing may or may not help depending on the purpose of the interview. Answer (D) is incorrect. Only paraphrasing relates to feedback.

6.5 Other Information-Gathering Methods

20. An internal auditing team developed a preliminary questionnaire with the following response choices:

1. Probably not a problem
2. Possibly a problem
3. Probably a problem

The questionnaire illustrates the use of

   A. Trend analysis.

   B. Ratio analysis.

   C. Unobtrusive measures or observations.

   D. Rating scales.

Answer (D) is correct.

REQUIRED: The method illustrated by the questionnaire.

DISCUSSION: A rating scale may be used when a range of opinions is expected. The scale represents a continuum of responses. In this case, it reflects probability statements.

Answer (A) is incorrect. Trend analysis extrapolates past and current conditions. Answer (B) is incorrect. Ratio analysis considers the internal relationships of financial data. Answer (C) is incorrect. Use of rating scales requires the participant to participate actively. Thus, it is not unobtrusive.

Access the **Gleim CIA Premium Review System** featuring our SmartAdapt technology from your Gleim Personal Classroom to continue your studies. You will experience a personalized study environment with exam-emulating multiple-choice questions.

STUDY UNIT SEVEN
SAMPLING AND STATISTICAL QUALITY CONTROL

(17 pages of outline)

This study unit is the third of four covering **Domain III: Performing the Engagement** from The IIA's CIA Exam Syllabus. This domain makes up 40% of Part 2 of the CIA exam and is tested at the **basic** and **proficient** cognitive levels. The relevant portion of the syllabus is highlighted below. (The complete syllabus is in Appendix B.)

	Performing the Engagement (40%)		
	1. Information Gathering		
III	A	Gather and examine relevant information (review previous audit reports and data, conduct walk-throughs and interviews, perform observations, etc.) as part of a preliminary survey of the engagement area	Proficient
	B	Develop checklists and risk-and-control questionnaires as part of a preliminary survey of the engagement area	Proficient
	C	**Apply appropriate sampling (nonstatistical, judgmental, discovery, etc.) and statistical analysis techniques**	**Proficient**
	2. Analysis and Evaluation		
	A	Use computerized audit tools and techniques (data mining and extraction, continuous monitoring, automated workpapers, embedded audit modules, etc.)	Proficient
	B	Evaluate the relevance, sufficiency, and reliability of potential sources of evidence	Proficient
	C	Apply appropriate analytical approaches and process mapping techniques (process identification, workflow analysis, process map generation and analysis, spaghetti maps, RACI diagrams, etc.)	Proficient
	D	Determine and apply analytical review techniques (ratio estimation, variance analysis, budget vs. actual, trend analysis, other reasonableness tests, benchmarking, etc.)	Basic
	E	Prepare workpapers and documentation of relevant information to support conclusions and engagement results	Proficient
	F	Summarize and develop engagement conclusions, including assessment of risks and controls	Proficient
	3. Engagement Supervision		
	A	Identify key activities in supervising engagements (coordinate work assignments, review workpapers, evaluate auditors' performance, etc.	Basic

7.1 STATISTICAL CONCEPTS

1. **Populations and Samples**

   a. A population is an entire group of items.

   b. Sampling involves selecting representative items from a population, examining those selected items, and drawing a conclusion about the population based on the results derived from the examination of the selected items. Other data collection methods include the following:

      1) A **case study** is a data collection method that identifies hypotheses that can be tested on a larger scale.

      2) An **evaluation synthesis** is a systematic procedure that organizes observations and results from separate engagements and combines them into a single evaluation for all of the included engagements.

      3) **Modeling** is a data collection method that simulates an existing fact, occurrence, or circumstance for further study.

   c. Auditors must draw conclusions about populations (invoices, accounts receivable, etc.) that are too numerous for every item to be tested.

      1) By applying the principles of statistics, auditors can test relatively small samples that allow them to draw conclusions about a population with measurable reliability.

      2) The main issue in sampling is choosing a sample that is representative of the population. Valid conclusions then may be stated about the population.

2. **Population Distributions**

   a. For audit purposes, each item in a population is associated with a variable of interest to the auditor.

      1) **Discrete variables**, such as the yes/no decision whether to authorize payments of invoices, are tested using **attribute sampling** (this is discussed in further detail in Subunit 7.3).

      2) **Continuous variables**, such as the monetary amounts of accounts receivable, are tested using **variables sampling** (this is discussed in further detail in Subunit 7.4).

   b. An important characteristic of a population is the distribution of the values of the variable of interest.

      1) Of the many types of distributions, the most important is the **normal distribution** (the bell curve), depicted in Figure 7-1 on the next page. Its values form a symmetrical, bell-shaped curve centered around the mean.

3. **Measures of Central Tendency**

   a. The shape, height, and width of a population's distribution curve are quantified through its measures of central tendency.

      1) The **mean** is the arithmetic average of a set of numbers.

      2) The **median** is the middle value if data are arranged in numerical order. Thus, half the values are smaller than the median, and half are larger. It is the 50th percentile.

      3) The **mode** is the most frequently occurring value. If all values are unique, no mode exists.

EXAMPLE of Mean, Median, and Mode

An investor has eight investments and calculates the measures of central tendency for returns on the portfolio.

Mean = Arithmetic average of population values
= (US $43,500 + $52,100 + $19,800 + $41,600 + $52,100 + $66,700 + $33,900 + $54,900) ÷ 8
= US $364,600 ÷ 8
= US $45,575

Median = Midpoint between two central-most population values
Values ranked: US $19,800; $33,900; $41,600; $43,500; $52,100; $52,100; $54,900; $66,700
= (US $43,500 + $52,100) ÷ 2
= US $95,600 ÷ 2
= US $47,800

Mode = Most frequent value in population
= US $52,100

---

b. In a **normal distribution**, the mean, median, and mode are the same, and the tails are identical. See Figure 7-1.

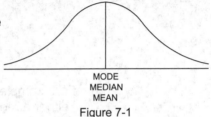

MODE
MEDIAN
MEAN

Figure 7-1

c. In some asymmetrical frequency distributions, the **mean is greater than the mode**. The right tail is longer, and the distribution is positively skewed (to the right).

1) Accounting distributions tend to be skewed to the right. For instance, accounts receivable generally include many medium- and low-value items and a few high-value items. See Figure 7-2.

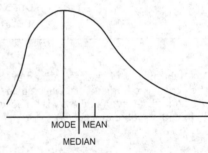

MODE | MEAN
MEDIAN

Figure 7-2

d. In some asymmetrical frequency distributions, the **median is greater than the mean**. The left tail is longer, and the distribution is negatively skewed (to the left). See Figure 7-3.

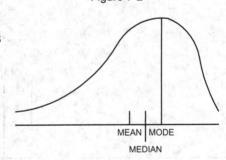

MEAN | MODE
MEDIAN

Figure 7-3

e. The median is the best estimate of central tendency for many asymmetrical distributions because the median is not biased by extremes.

4. **Standard Deviation and Confidence Level for Normal Distributions**

   a.   A population's variability is the extent to which the values of items are spread about the mean (dispersion). It is measured by the **standard deviation**.

   1)   The standard deviation is a measure of the dispersion of a set of data from its mean.

      a)   When the items have little dispersion, the standard deviation is small.

      b)   When the items are highly dispersed, the bell curve is relatively flat and the standard deviation is large.

   2)   Normal distributions may have the following fixed relationships between the area under the curve and the distance from the mean.

Distance (±) in Standard Deviations (Confidence Coefficient)	Area under the Curve (Confidence Level)
1.0	68%
1.64	90%
1.96	95%
2.0	95.5%
2.57	99%
3.0	99.7%

   3)   For example, 68% of the items are within one standard deviation of the mean in either direction.

      a)   Approximately 95% of the items are within 2 standard deviations of the mean.

EXAMPLE of a Normal Distribution

A certain species of pine tree has an average adult height of 20 feet, with each standard deviation representing 1 foot. The conclusion from the distribution below is that 68% of all trees of this species will reach a height between 19 and 21 feet (1 standard deviation), 95.5% will be between 18 and 22 feet (2 standard deviations), and 99.7% will be between 17 and 23 feet (3 standard deviations).

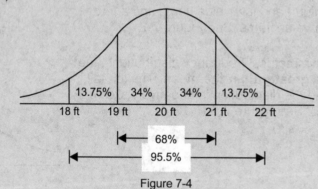

Figure 7-4

5. **Confidence Level and Confidence Interval**

    a. The area under the curve is the confidence level.

        1) The **confidence level** is the percentage of times that a sample is expected to be representative of the population; i.e., a confidence level of 95% should result in representative samples 95% of the time.

        2) A person selecting an item at random from a normally distributed population can be, for example, 95% confident that the value of the item is within 1.96 standard deviations of the mean and 99% confident that it will fall within 2.57 standard deviations of the mean.

    b. A **confidence interval** for a given confidence level is the range around a sample value that is expected to contain the true population value. It is constructed using the confidence coefficient for the number of standard deviations (based on the normal distribution) for the confidence level chosen. The confidence interval may also be referred to as precision.

        1) If repeated random samples are drawn from a normally distributed population and the auditor specifies a 95% confidence level, the probability is that 95% of the confidence intervals constructed around the sample results will contain the population value.

EXAMPLE

An auditor took a random sample of sales authorizations. Based on the sample, the sales department authorized a sale after checking the credit score of the customer 88% of the time.

- If the confidence interval (or precision) is 6%, the auditor can be confident that between 82% (88% − 6%) and 94% (88% + 6%) of all the company's sales were authorized after checking credit scores.
- The confidence level is the auditor's desired reliability of the sample. If the specified confidence level is 95% and the precision is 6%, the auditor can be 95% confident that the percentage of all the company's sales that were authorized after checking credit scores is between 82% and 94%.

---

        2) For a given confidence level, the size of the confidence interval depends on the sample size.

            a) The larger the sample size, the smaller the confidence interval can be.

            b) A smaller confidence interval means that the true population value is expected to be in the narrower range around the sample value.

        3) After the sample is drawn, the confidence interval may be widened or narrowed based on a change in the confidence level.

            a) If the confidence level is increased, then the confidence interval will be widened.

            b) If the confidence level is decreased, then the confidence interval will be narrowed.

6. **Pilot Sampling and Standard Error**

    a. The auditor can estimate the standard deviation of a population using a pilot sample.

    b. The **standard error of the mean** is the standard deviation of the distribution of sample means. The standard error is used to compute precision (the confidence interval). The larger the standard error, the wider the interval.

    c. The **coefficient of variability** measures the relative variability within the data and is calculated by dividing the standard deviation of the sample by the mean.

Stop and review! You have completed the outline for this subunit. Study multiple-choice questions 1 through 3 on page 160.

7.2 SAMPLING CONCEPTS

1. **Nonstatistical (Judgmental) Sampling**

   a. Judgmental sampling uses the auditor's **subjective** judgment to determine the sample size (number of items examined) and sample selection (which items to examine). This subjectivity is not always a weakness. The auditor, based on his or her experience, is able to select and test only the items (s)he considers to be the most important.

   b. The following are the advantages of judgmental sampling:

      1) The process can be less expensive and less time consuming. No special knowledge of statistics and no special statistics software are required.

      2) The auditor has greater discretion to use his or her judgment and expertise. Thus, if the auditor has substantial experience, no time is wasted on testing immaterial items.

   c. The following are the disadvantages of judgmental sampling:

      1) It does not provide a quantitative measure of sampling risk.
      2) It does not provide a quantitative expression of sample results.
      3) If the auditor is not proficient, the sample may not be effective.

2. **Statistical Sampling**

   a. Statistical sampling provides an objective method of determining sample size and selecting the items to be examined. Unlike judgmental sampling, it also provides a means of **quantitatively** assessing **precision** (how closely the sample represents the population) and **confidence level** (the percentage of time the sample will adequately represent the population).

   b. Statistical sampling helps the auditor design an efficient sample, measure the sufficiency of evidence obtained, and evaluate the sample results based on quantified data.

   c. The following are the advantages of statistical sampling:

      1) It provides a quantitative measure of sampling risk, confidence level, and precision.
      2) It provides a quantitative expression of sample results.
      3) It helps the auditor to design an efficient sample.

   d. The following are the disadvantages of statistical sampling:

      1) It can be more expensive and time consuming than nonstatistical sampling.
      2) It requires special statistical knowledge and training.
      3) It requires statistical software.

   e. In some instances, internal auditors may need to evaluate whether the use of historical data or drawing a new sample is optimal.

3. **Nonsampling vs. Sampling Risk**

   a. **Nonsampling risk** is audit risk not related to sampling. A common audit risk is the auditor's failure to detect an error in a sample.

      1) Nondetection of an error in a sample can be caused by auditor inattention or fatigue. It also can be caused by application of an inappropriate audit procedure, such as looking for the wrong approvals in a sample of documents.

   b. **Sampling risk** is the risk that a sample is not representative of the population. An unrepresentative sample may result in an incorrect conclusion.

      1) Statistical sampling allows the auditor to quantify sampling risk. An auditor should never attempt to quantify the sampling risk of a nonstatistically drawn sample.

      2) Sampling risk is **inversely related** to sample size. As the sample increases, sampling risk decreases.

4. **Selecting the Sampling Approach**

   a. In a **random sample**, every item in the population has an equal and nonzero chance of being selected.

      1) If enough large random samples are drawn, the mean of their means will approximate the population mean closely enough that they are considered to be representative of the population.

      2) For very large populations, the absolute size of the sample affects the precision of its results more than its size relative to the population. Thus, above a certain population size, the sample size generally does not increase.

      3) The traditional means of ensuring randomness is to assign a random number to each item in the population. Random number tables are often used for this purpose.

         a) Random number tables contain collections of digits grouped randomly into columns and clusters. After assigning numbers to the members of the population, the tables can be used to select the sample items.

   b. An **interval (systematic) sampling** plan assumes that items are arranged randomly in the population. If they are not, a random selection method should be used.

      1) Interval sampling divides the population by the sample size and selects every nth item after a random start in the first interval. For example, if the population has 1,000 items and the sample size is 35, every 28th item ($1,000 \div 35 = 28.57$) is selected.

         a) Interval sampling is appropriate when, for instance, an auditor wants to test whether controls were operating throughout an entire year. (A random sample might result in all items being selected from a single month.)

         b) Because interval sampling requires only counting in the population, no correspondence between random numbers and the items in the population is necessary as in random number sampling.

EXAMPLE

If the population contains 8,200 items and a sample of 50 is required, every 164th item is selected ($8,200 \div 50$). After a random start in the first interval (1 to 164), every additional 164th item is selected. For example, if the 35th item is the first selected randomly, the next is the 199th ($35 + 164$). The third item is the 363rd ($199 + 164$). The process is continued until the 50 items are identified.

---

   c. **Block (cluster) sampling** randomly selects groups of items as the sampling units rather than individual items. An example is the inclusion in the sample of all cash payments for May and September.

      1) One possible disadvantage is that the variability of items within the clusters may not be representative of the variability within the population.

5. **Basic Steps in a Statistical Plan**

   a. **Determine the objectives of the plan.**

      1) For a test of controls, an example is to conclude that control is reasonably effective.

      2) For a test of details, an example is to conclude that a balance is not misstated by more than an immaterial amount.

   b. **Define the population.** This step includes defining the sampling unit (an individual item in the population) and considering the completeness of the population.

      1) For tests of controls, the period covered is defined.
      2) For tests of details, individually significant items may be defined.

    c.   **Determine acceptable levels of sampling risk** (e.g., 5% or 10%).

    d.   **Calculate the sample size** using tables or sample-size formulas.

        1)   In some cases, it is efficient to divide the population into subpopulations or strata. The primary objective of **stratification** is to minimize variability.

        2)   Stratification also allows the auditor to apply more audit effort to larger elements or more risky parts of the population.

        3)   For example, when auditing sales revenue, an auditor could divide the population into strata of dollar increments. The auditor could test transactions under US $500, between US $501 and US $2,000, and US $2,001 and above.

    e.   **Select the sampling approach**, e.g., random, interval, or block.

    f.   **Take the sample.** The auditor selects the items to be evaluated.

    g.   **Evaluate the sample results.** The auditor draws conclusions about the population.

    h.   **Document the sampling procedures.** The auditor prepares appropriate workpapers.

Stop and review! You have completed the outline for this subunit. Study multiple-choice questions 4 through 8 beginning on page 161.

7.3 ATTRIBUTE SAMPLING

1.   **Uses**

    a.   In attribute sampling, each item in the population has an attribute of interest to the auditor, e.g., evidence of proper authorization. Thus, attribute sampling is appropriate for **discrete variables**.

        1)   Attribute sampling is used for tests of controls, i.e., when two outcomes are possible (compliance or noncompliance).

2.   **Sample Size**

    a.   The sample size for an attribute test depends on the following four factors:

        1)   The **confidence level** is the percentage of times that a sample is expected to be representative of the population. The **greater** the desired confidence level, the **larger** the sample size should be.

            a)   For a test of the controls, the confidence level is the complement of the allowable risk of **overreliance** on the control. For example, if this risk is 5%, the confidence level is 95% (100% − 5%).

        2)   The **population size** is the sum of the items to be considered for testing. The larger the population size, the larger the sample size should be.

            a)   However, for a very large population, the population size has a small effect on the sample size. Above a certain population size, the sample size generally does not increase.

        3)   The **expected deviation rate** (expected rate of occurrence) is an estimate of the deviation rate in the current population.

            a)   The **greater** the population deviation (variability in the population), the **larger** the sample size should be.

        4)   The **tolerable deviation rate** (desired precision) is the highest allowable percentage of the population that can be in error (noncompliance rate) and still allow the auditor to rely on the tested control.

            a)   The **lower** the tolerable deviation rate, the **larger** the sample size should be.

Factors Affecting Attribute Sample Size			
As the confidence level	increases,	the sample size must	increase.
As the expected deviation rate	increases,	the sample size must	increase.
As the tolerable deviation rate	increases,	the sample size can	decrease.
As the confidence level	decreases,	the sample size must	decrease.
As the expected deviation rate	decreases,	the sample size must	decrease.
As the tolerable deviation rate	decreases,	the sample size can	increase.

3. **Evaluation of Sample Results**

   a. The evaluation includes calculating the sample deviation rate and the achieved upper deviation limit.

   b. The **sample deviation rate** is the number of deviations observed in a sample divided by the sample size.

      1) This rate is the best estimate of the population deviation rate.

   c. The **achieved upper deviation limit (UDL)** is based on the sample size and the number of deviations discovered. Auditors use standard tables to calculate the UDL. In Table 1 below (adapted from an Audit Practice Release of the AICPA), the intersection of the sample size and the number of deviations indicates the achieved upper deviation limit.

   d. The **allowance for sampling risk** (achieved precision) is the difference between the achieved UDL determined from a standard table and the sample deviation rate.

      1) When the sample deviation rate exceeds the expected population deviation rate, the achieved UDL exceeds the tolerable rate at the given risk of overreliance. In that case, the sample does not support the planned reliance on the control.

      2) When the sample deviation rate does not exceed the expected population deviation rate, the achieved UDL does not exceed the tolerable rate at the given risk level. Thus, the sample supports the planned reliance on the control.

EXAMPLE

Assume the risk of overreliance is 5%, the tolerable rate is 6%, the expected population deviation rate is 2.5%, and the population size is over 5,000. Given these data, the sample size is 150.

During the engagement, the auditor discovered 3 deviations in the sample of 150. Using Table 1, the auditor can state at a 95% confidence level (the complement of a 5% risk of overreliance) that the true error occurrence rate is not greater than 5.1%.

The sample deviation rate equals 2% (3 deviations ÷ 150 sample size). Thus, the allowance for sampling risk equals 3.1% (5.1% – 2%).

The sample deviation rate (2%) does not exceed the expected population deviation rate (2.5%), and the sample supports the planned reliance on the control.

Table 1 -- Results Evaluation for Tests of Controls -- Upper % Limits at 5% Risk of Overreliance											
Sample Size	Actual Number of Deviations Found										
	0	1	2	3	4	5	6	7	8	9	10
100	3.0	4.7	6.2	7.6	9.0	10.3	11.5	12.8	14.0	15.2	16.4
125	2.4	3.8	5.0	6.1	7.2	8.3	9.3	10.3	11.3	12.3	13.2
150	2.0	3.2	4.2	5.1	6.0	6.9	7.8	8.6	9.5	10.3	11.1
200	1.5	2.4	3.2	3.9	4.6	5.2	5.9	6.5	7.2	7.8	8.4

e. Each deviation should be analyzed to determine its nature, importance, and probable cause. Obviously, some are much more significant than others. Sampling provides a means of forming a conclusion about the overall population but should not be used as a substitute for good judgment.

1) The table below is based on a method for testing sampling concepts related to tests of controls. It is used to explain how to analyze the information. Many questions can be answered based on the analysis. The table depicts the possible combinations of the sample results and the true state of the population.

Auditor's Estimate Based on Sample Results	True State of Population	
	Deviation rate is less than tolerable rate.	Deviation rate exceeds tolerable rate.
Deviation rate is less than tolerable rate.	I. Correct	III. Incorrect
Deviation rate exceeds tolerable rate.	II. Incorrect	IV. Correct

a) Cell II represents potential underreliance on internal control. It affects the efficiency but not the effectiveness of the audit.

b) Cell III represents potential overreliance on internal control. It may result in audit failure.

4. **Other Attribute Sampling Methods**

a. **Discovery sampling** is appropriate when even a single deviation (noncompliance) is critical.

1) The occurrence rate is assumed to be at or near 0%, and the method cannot be used to evaluate results statistically if deviations are found in the sample.

2) The sample size is calculated so that it will include **at least one** instance of a deviation if deviations occur in the population at a given rate.

b. The objective of **stop-or-go sampling**, also called sequential sampling, is to reduce the sample size when the auditor believes the deviation rate in the population is low.

1) The auditor examines only enough sample items to be able to state that the deviation rate is below a specified rate at a specified level of confidence. If the auditor needs to expand the sample to obtain the desired level of confidence, (s)he can do so in stages.

2) Because the sample size is not fixed, the internal auditor can achieve the desired result, even if deviations are found, by enlarging the sample sufficiently. In contrast, discovery sampling uses a fixed sample size.

Stop and review! You have completed the outline for this subunit. Study multiple-choice questions 9 through 12 beginning on page 162.

7.4 VARIABLES SAMPLING

1. **Uses**

   a.   Variables sampling is used for **continuous variables**, such as weights or monetary amounts. Variables sampling provides information about whether a stated amount (e.g., the balance of accounts receivable) is materially misstated.

   1)   Thus, variables sampling is useful for substantive tests. The auditor can determine, at a specified confidence level, a range that includes the true value.

   b.   In variables sampling, both the upper and lower limits are relevant (a balance, such as accounts receivable, can be either under- or overstated).

   c.   Auditors may employ the following variables sampling techniques:

   1)   Unstratified mean-per-unit
   2)   Stratified mean-per-unit
   3)   Difference estimation
   4)   Ratio estimation
   5)   Monetary unit sampling

   NOTE: Each method is covered in this subunit, following a discussion of sample selection and interpretation.

2. **Sample Size**

   a.   The sample size for a variables test depends on the following four factors:

   1)   **Confidence level.** The **greater** the desired confidence level, the **greater** the sample size should be. For a variables sampling application, the confidence level is the complement of the allowable risk of **incorrect rejection**. For example, if this risk is 5%, the confidence level is 95% (100% − 5%).

   a)   If the auditor needs a more precise estimate of the tested amount, (s)he must increase the confidence level and the sample size.

   b)   The confidence coefficient serves the same function as in attribute sampling. But, in variables sampling, it corresponds to a range around the calculated amount rather than an estimate of the maximum error rate.

   2)   **Population size.** The **larger** the population, the **larger** the sample. However, for a very large population, the population size has a small effect on sample size. Above a certain population size, the sample size generally does not increase.

   3)   **Tolerable misstatement** (precision) is an interval around the sample statistic that is expected to include the true balance of the population at the specific confidence level.

   a)   For example, an auditor has tested a variables sample with precision of ±4% and a confidence level of 90%. The conclusion is that the true balance of the account is US $1,000,000. The precision of ±4% gives the boundaries of the computed range. Thus, 4% of US $1,000,000 equals US $40,000, resulting in a range of US $960,000 to US $1,040,000. The auditor can conclude that the probability is only 10% that the true balance lies outside this range.

   b)   The **narrower** the precision, the **larger** the sample should be.

   4)   **Standard deviation** (variability) of the population is a measure of the variability of the amounts in the population. An **increase** in the estimated standard deviation **increases** the sample size. The estimate can be based on pilot sample.

Factors Affecting Variables Sample Size			
As the confidence level	*increases,*	*the sample size must*	*increase.*
As the estimated standard deviation	*increases,*	*the sample size must*	*increase.*
As the population size	*increases,*	*the sample size must*	*increase.*
As the tolerable misstatement	*increases,*	*the sample size can*	*decrease.*
As the confidence level	*decreases,*	*the sample size must*	*decrease.*
As the estimated standard deviation	*decreases,*	*the sample size must*	*decrease.*
As the population size	*decreases,*	*the sample size must*	*decrease.*
As the tolerable misstatement	*decreases,*	*the sample size can*	*increase.*

3. **Primary Methods of Variables Sampling**

   a. **Mean-per-unit (MPU) estimation** (also called unstratified MPU) averages the audited amounts of the sample items. It multiplies the average by the number of items in the population to estimate the population amount. An achieved precision at the desired level of confidence is then calculated.

      1) **Stratified** MPU is a means of increasing audit efficiency by separating the population into logical groups, usually by various ranges of the tested amounts. By creating multiple populations, the variability within each is reduced, allowing for a smaller overall sample size.

   b. **Difference estimation** estimates the misstatement of an amount by calculating the difference between the observed and recorded amounts for items in the sample. This method is appropriate only when per-item recorded amounts and their total are known. Difference estimation

      1) Determines differences between the audited and recorded amounts of items in the sample,
      2) Adds the differences,
      3) Calculates the mean difference,
      4) Multiplies the mean by the number of items in the population, and
      5) Calculates an achieved precision at the desired level of confidence.

   c. **Ratio estimation** is similar to difference estimation. However, it estimates the population misstatement by multiplying the recorded amount of the population by the ratio of the total audited amount of the sample items to their total recorded amount.

      1) Ratio estimation is preferable to MPU estimation when the standard deviation of the sample item amounts is greater than the standard deviation of the distribution of the ratios of the audited amounts of sample items compared to their recorded amounts.

      2) Ratio estimation is preferable to difference estimation when differences between the audited amounts of sample items and their recorded amounts are expected to vary in proportion to the size of the sample items.

         a) For example, a sample of two items consists of an account with a US $1,000 recorded balance and a misstatement of US $100 and an account with a recorded balance of US $100 and a misstatement of US $10. The misstatements of US $900 and US $90 are quite different but vary in proportion to the size of the account since each misstatement is 10% of the account value. In situations like this, ratio estimation is preferable to difference estimation.

EXAMPLE

An auditor examines a sample of 150 accounts receivable with a total recorded amount of US $172,500. The total population of 3,400 accounts receivable has a total recorded amount of US $3,500,000. Based on the audit, the total amount of the 150 sampled accounts is US $168,000.

MPU Estimation

- The average amount per sampled item is US $1,120 ($168,000 ÷ 150).
- The estimated correct balance of the population (accounts receivable) is **US $3,808,000** ($1,120 mean per unit value × 3,400 number of items in the population).

Difference Estimation

- The difference between the audited and recorded amounts of items in the sample is US $4,500 ($172,500 – $168,000).
- The mean difference is US $30 ($4,500 ÷ 150 number sample items).
- The estimated total population error is determined by multiplying the mean by the number of items in the population. It equals US $102,000 (3,400 × $30).
- The estimated correct balance of the population (accounts receivable) is **US $3,398,000** ($3,500,000 recorded amount of the population – $102,000 estimated error).

Ratio Estimation

- The ratio of the total audited amount of the sample items to their total recorded amount is 0.974 (US $168,000 audited amount ÷ $172,500 recorded amount).
- The estimated correct balance of the population (accounts receivable) is **US $3,409,000** ($3,500,000 recorded amount of the population × 0.974 ratio).

NOTE: An achieved precision at the desired level of confidence is then calculated. For example, assume the sample of 150 accounts with a total amount of US $168,000 was based on precision of ±3% and a confidence level of 95%. **Using ratio estimation**, the precision interval equals ±US $102,270 ($3,409,000 × 3%). The auditor can conclude that the **probability** is only 5% that the true balance lies outside the range of US $3,306,730 to US $3,511,270.

d.   **Monetary-unit sampling (MUS)**, also known as probability-proportional-to-size (PPS) sampling, uses a monetary unit as the sampling unit. It applies **attribute sampling** methods to reach a conclusion about the probability of overstating monetary amounts.

   1)   Under MUS, the sampling unit is a unit of money rather than, for example, an invoice or an account balance. The item (invoice, account, etc.) containing the sampled monetary unit is selected for testing.

   2)   MUS is appropriate for testing account balances for overstatement when some items may be far larger than others in the population. In effect, it stratifies the population because the larger account balances have a greater chance of being selected.

   3)   MUS is most useful if few misstatements are expected.

   4)   MUS does not require the use of a measure of variability (e.g., standard deviation) to determine the sample size or interpret the results.

   5)   Thus, in the example above, the objective of MUS may be to determine that the total recorded amount of accounts receivable (US $3,500,000) is not overstated by more than 3%, with a confidence level of 95%.

Stop and review! You have completed the outline for this subunit. Study multiple-choice questions 13 through 18 beginning on page 163.

7.5 STATISTICAL QUALITY CONTROL

1. **Uses**

   a. Statistical quality control determines whether a shipment or production run of units lies within acceptable limits. Items are either good or bad, i.e., inside or outside of control limits. It is also used to determine whether production processes are out of control.

2. **Acceptance Sampling**

   a. This method determines the probability that the rate of defective items in a batch is less than a specified level.

EXAMPLE

Assume a sample is taken from a population of 500. According to standard acceptance sampling tables, if the sample consists of 25 items and not one is defective, the probability is 93% that the population deviation rate is less than 10%. If 60 items are examined and no defects are found, the probability is 99% that the deviation rate is less than 10%. If two defects in 60 units are observed, the probability is 96% that the deviation rate is less than 10%.

---

3. **Statistical Control Charts**

   a. Statistical control charts are graphic aids for monitoring the status of any process subject to acceptable or unacceptable variations during repeated operations.

      1) They also have applications of direct interest to auditors and accountants, for example, (a) unit cost of production, (b) direct labor hours used, (c) ratio of actual expenses to budgeted expenses, (d) number of calls by sales personnel, or (e) total accounts receivable.

   b. A control chart consists of three lines plotted on a horizontal time scale.

      1) The center line represents the overall mean or average range for the process being controlled. The other two lines are the upper control limit (UCL) and the lower control limit (LCL).

      2) The processes are measured periodically, and the values (X) are plotted on the chart.

         a) If the value falls within the control limits, no action is taken.

         b) If the value falls outside the limits, the result is abnormal, the process is considered out of control, and an investigation is made for possible corrective action.

   c.   Another advantage of the chart is that it makes trends and cycles visible.

      1)   A disadvantage of the chart is that it does not indicate the cause of the variation.

EXAMPLE

The chart below depicts 2 weeks of production by a manufacturer who produces a single precision part each day. To be salable, the part can vary from the standard by no more than ± 0.1 millimeter.

Statistical Control Chart

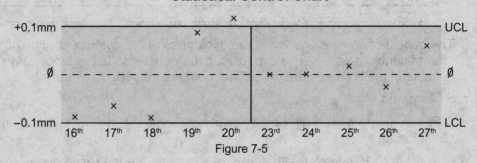

Figure 7-5

The part produced on the 20th had to be scrapped, and changes were made to the equipment to return the process to the controlled state for the following week's production.

---

   d.   Other chart types

      1)   P charts show the percentage of defects in a sample. They are based on an attribute (acceptable/not acceptable) rather than a measure of a variable.

      2)   C charts also are attribute control charts. They show defects per item.

      3)   An R chart shows the range of dispersion of a variable, such as size or weight. The center line is the overall mean.

      4)   An X-bar chart shows the sample mean for a variable. The center line is the average range.

4.   **Variations**

   a.   Variations in a process parameter may have several causes.

      1)   Random variations occur by chance. Present in virtually all processes, they are not correctable because they will not repeat themselves in the same manner. Excessively narrow control limits will result in many investigations of what are simply random fluctuations.

      2)   Implementation deviations occur because of human or mechanical failure to achieve target results.

      3)   Measurement variations result from errors in the measurements of actual results.

      4)   Model fluctuations can be caused by errors in the formulation of a decision model.

      5)   Prediction variances result from errors in forecasting data used in a decision model.

5.   **Benchmarks**

   a.   Establishing control limits based on benchmarks is a common method. A more objective method is to use the concept of expected value. The limits are important because they are the decision criteria for determining whether a deviation will be investigated.

6.   **Cost-Benefit Analysis**

   a.   An analysis using expected value provides a more objective basis for setting control limits. The limits of controls should be set so that the cost of an investigation is less than or equal to the benefits derived.

      1)   The expected costs include investigation cost and the cost of corrective action.

      (Probability of being out of control × Cost of corrective action)
   +   *(Probability of being in control × Investigation cost)*
   _____
      Total expected cost

   b.   The benefit of an investigation is the avoidance of the costs of continuing to operate an out-of-control process. The expected value of benefits is the probability of being out of control multiplied by the cost of not being corrected.

7.   **Pareto Diagrams**

   a.   A Pareto diagram is a bar chart that assists managers in what is commonly called 80:20 analysis.

      1)   The 80:20 rule states that 80% of all effects are the result of only 20% of all causes. In the context of quality control, managers optimize their time by focusing their effort on the sources of most problems.

   b.   The independent variable, plotted on the x axis, is the factor selected by the manager as the area of interest: department, time period, geographical location, etc. The frequency of occurrence of the defect (dependent variable) is plotted on the y axis.

      1)   The occurrences of the independent variable are ranked from highest to lowest, allowing the manager to see at a glance which areas are of most concern.

EXAMPLE

A chief administrative officer uses a Pareto diagram to view which departments are generating the most travel vouchers that have been rejected because of incomplete documentation.

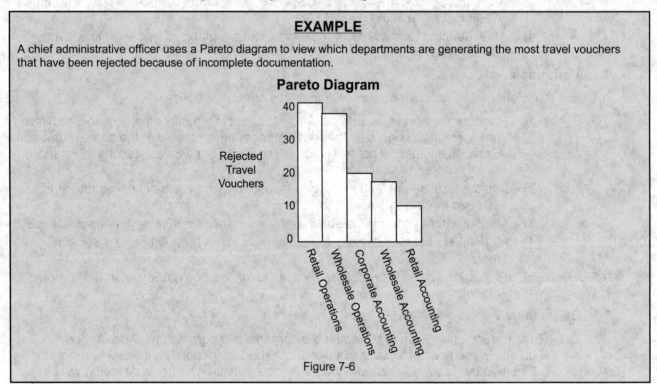

Figure 7-6

8.   **Histograms**

a.   A histogram displays a continuous frequency distribution of the independent variable.

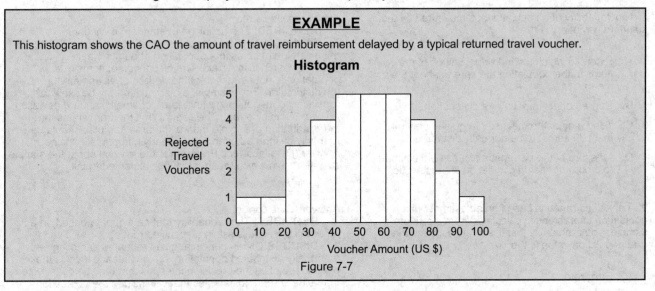

EXAMPLE

This histogram shows the CAO the amount of travel reimbursement delayed by a typical returned travel voucher.

Histogram

Figure 7-7

9.   **Fishbone Diagrams**

a.   A fishbone (Ishikawa) diagram (also called a cause-and-effect diagram) is a total quality management process improvement technique.

1)   Fishbone diagrams are useful in studying causation (why the actual and desired situations differ).

b.   This format organizes the analysis of causation and helps to identify possible interactions among causes.

1)   The head of the skeleton contains the statement of the problem.

2)   The principal classifications of causes are represented by lines (bones) drawn diagonally from the heavy horizontal line (the spine).

3)   Smaller horizontal lines are added in their order of probability in each classification.

c.   Below is a generic fishbone diagram.

Fishbone Diagram

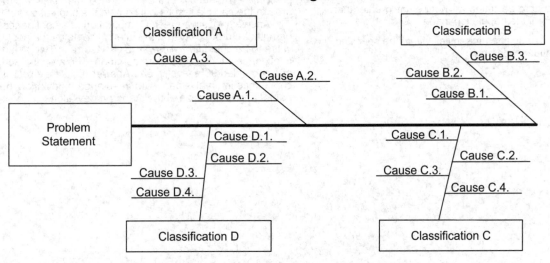

Figure 7-8

Stop and review! You have completed the outline for this subunit. Study multiple-choice questions 19 and 20 on page 165.

QUESTIONS

7.1 Statistical Concepts

1. The variability of a population, as measured by the standard deviation, is the

A. Extent to which the individual values of the items in the population are spread about the mean.

B. Degree of asymmetry of a distribution.

C. Tendency of the means of large samples (at least 30 items) to be normally distributed.

D. Measure of the closeness of a sample estimate to a corresponding population characteristic.

Answer (A) is correct.
   REQUIRED: The definition of standard deviation.
   DISCUSSION: The standard deviation measures the degree of dispersion of items in a population about its mean.
   Answer (B) is incorrect. The dispersion of items in a population is not a function of the degree of asymmetry of the distribution. For example, a distribution may be skewed (positively or negatively) with a large or small standard deviation. Answer (C) is incorrect. The central limit theorem states that the distribution of sample means for large samples should be normally distributed even if the underlying population is not. Answer (D) is incorrect. Precision is the interval about the sample statistic within which the true value is expected to fall.

2. A specified range is based on an estimate of a population characteristic calculated from a random sample. The probability that the range contains the true population value is the

A. Error rate.

B. Lower precision limit.

C. Confidence level.

D. Standard error of the mean.

Answer (C) is correct.
   REQUIRED: The probability that an estimate based on a random sample falls within a specified range.
   DISCUSSION: In principle, given repeated sampling and a normally distributed population, the confidence level is the percentage of all the precision intervals that may be constructed from simple random samples that will include the population value. In practice, the confidence level is regarded as the probability that a precision interval calculated from a simple random sample drawn from a normally distributed population will contain the population value.
   Answer (A) is incorrect. The error rate in an attribute sampling application is the proportion of incorrect items in a population. Answer (B) is incorrect. The lower precision limit is the lower bound of the interval constructed from the sample result at a specified confidence level. Answer (D) is incorrect. The standard error of the mean is the standard deviation of the distribution of sample means.

3. A 90% confidence interval for the mean of a population based on the information in a sample always implies that there is a 90% chance that the

A. Estimate is equal to the true population mean.

B. True population mean is no larger than the largest endpoint of the interval.

C. Standard deviation will not be any greater than 10% of the population mean.

D. True population mean lies within the specified confidence interval.

Answer (D) is correct.
   REQUIRED: The meaning of a confidence interval.
   DISCUSSION: The confidence interval, e.g., 90%, is specified by the auditor. A confidence interval based on the specified confidence level, also called precision, is the range around a sample value that is expected to contain the true population value. In this situation, if the population is normally distributed and repeated simple random samples are taken, the probability is that 90% of the confidence intervals constructed around the sample results will contain the population value.
   Answer (A) is incorrect. Computation of a confidence interval permits the probability that the interval contains the population value to be quantified. Answer (B) is incorrect. Two-sided confidence intervals are more common. The area in each tail of a two-sided 90% level is 5%. Answer (C) is incorrect. The confidence interval is based on the standard deviation, but it has no bearing on the size of the standard deviation.

7.2 Sampling Concepts

4. In preparing a sampling plan for an inventory pricing test, which of the following describes an advantage of statistical sampling over nonstatistical sampling?

    A. Requires nonquantitative expression of sample results.

    B. Provides a quantitative measure of sampling risk.

    C. Minimizes nonsampling risk.

    D. Reduces the level of tolerable error.

Answer (B) is correct.
    REQUIRED: The statement describing an advantage of statistical sampling over nonstatistical sampling.
    DISCUSSION: Statistical and nonstatistical sampling are both used to project the characteristics of a population. However, statistical sampling permits the internal auditor to make a quantitative assessment of how closely the sample represents the population for a given level of reliability.
    Answer (A) is incorrect. Statistical sampling provides quantified results. Answer (C) is incorrect. Nonsampling risk exists in both statistical and nonstatistical sampling. Answer (D) is incorrect. Tolerable error is related to materiality and auditor judgment.

5. To project the frequency of shipments to wrong addresses, an internal auditor chose a random sample from the busiest month of each of the four quarters of the most recent year. What underlying concept of statistical sampling did the auditor violate?

    A. Attempting to project a rate of occurrence rather than an error rate.

    B. Failing to give each item in the population an equal chance of selection.

    C. Failing to adequately describe the population.

    D. Using multistage sampling in conjunction with attributes.

Answer (B) is correct.
    REQUIRED: The concept of statistical sampling violated by sampling from the busiest month.
    DISCUSSION: A random sample is one in which every item in the population has an equal and nonzero chance of being selected for the sample. Here, the auditor deliberately excluded shipments from the slower months.
    Answer (A) is incorrect. Randomness is not associated with a rate of occurrence (often referred to as an error rate). Answer (C) is incorrect. The population is adequately described as the four quarters of the most recent year. Answer (D) is incorrect. Multistage sampling is appropriate when homogeneous subpopulations can be identified and sampled from; sample items are then selected from the randomly selected subpopulations.

6. Which one of the following statements about sampling is true?

    A. A larger sample is always more representative of the underlying population than a smaller sample.

    B. For very large populations, the absolute size of the sample has more impact on the precision of its results than does its size relative to its population.

    C. For a given sample size, a simple random sample always produces the most representative sample.

    D. The limitations of an incomplete sample frame can almost always be overcome by careful sampling techniques.

Answer (B) is correct.
    REQUIRED: The true statement about sampling.
    DISCUSSION: When the size of the population is very large, the absolute size of the sample may vary considerably even though its size relative to the population does not.
    Answer (A) is incorrect. A large sample selected in a biased way is often less representative than a smaller but more carefully selected sample. Answer (C) is incorrect. Simple random sampling does not eliminate sampling risk. Proper execution of a simple random sample increases the probability of drawing a representative sample. Answer (D) is incorrect. Items excluded from the sampling frame cannot be included by an appropriate sampling technique.

7. Random numbers can be used to select a sample only when each item in the population

    A. Can be assigned to a specific stratum.

    B. Is independent of outside influence.

    C. Can be identified with a unique number.

    D. Is expected to be within plus or minus three standard deviations of the population mean.

Answer (C) is correct.
    REQUIRED: The requirement for use of random numbers in sample selection.
    DISCUSSION: A random sample is one in which every item in the population has an equal and nonzero chance of being selected and that selection is not influenced by whether any other item is selected.
    Answer (A) is incorrect. Random-number sampling applies to both simple and stratified sampling. Answer (B) is incorrect. No such requirement exists. Answer (D) is incorrect. By definition, there are a few population items outside plus or minus three standard deviations from the population mean.

8. Systematic selection can be expected to produce a representative sample when

    A. Random number tables are used to determine the items included in the sample.

    B. The population is arranged randomly with respect to the audit objective.

    C. The sample is determined using multiple random starts and includes more items than required.

    D. Judgmental sampling is used by the auditor to offset any sampling bias.

Answer (B) is correct.
    REQUIRED: The condition under which systematic selection produces a representative sample.
    DISCUSSION: A sample selected using a systematic sampling procedure and a random start will behave as if it were a random sample when the population is randomly ordered with respect to the audit objective. Sampling bias due to systematic selection will be small when the population items are not arranged in a pattern.
    Answer (A) is incorrect. Systematic selection is random only with respect to the start. Answer (C) is incorrect. The number of items in a sample is not relevant to the procedures used to select the specific items in the sample. The use of multiple random starts might increase the chance that a sample will behave randomly, but only if the population is arranged randomly. Answer (D) is incorrect. Judgmental sampling will not increase the randomness of a sample but will introduce sampling bias into the sample.

7.3 Attribute Sampling

9. If all other sample size planning factors were exactly the same in attribute sampling, changing the confidence level from 95% to 90% and changing the desired precision from 2% to 5% would result in a revised sample size that would be

    A. Larger.

    B. Smaller.

    C. Unchanged.

    D. Indeterminate.

Answer (B) is correct.
    REQUIRED: The sample size effect of decreasing the confidence level and widening the desired precision interval.
    DISCUSSION: In an attribute test, the confidence level is directly related, and the precision is inversely related, to sample size. Thus, if the confidence level is reduced and precision is widened, sample size will be smaller.
    Answer (A) is incorrect. Increasing the confidence level while narrowing the precision interval would result in a larger sample size. Answer (C) is incorrect. Decreasing the confidence level while widening the precision interval would allow the sample size to be decreased. Answer (D) is incorrect. The revised sample size is determinable.

10. When planning an attribute sampling application, the difference between the expected error rate and the maximum tolerable error rate is the planned

    A. Precision.

    B. Reliability.

    C. Dispersion.

    D. Skewness.

Answer (A) is correct.
    REQUIRED: The difference between the expected error rate and the maximum tolerable error rate.
    DISCUSSION: The precision of an attribute sample (also called the confidence interval or allowance for sampling risk) is an interval around the sample statistic that the auditor expects to contain the true value of the population. In attribute sampling (used for tests of controls), the achieved precision is the difference between the sample deviation rate and the achieved upper deviation limit (customarily determined from a standard table given the sample deviation rate and the sample size).
    Answer (B) is incorrect. Reliability is the confidence level. It is the percentage of times that repeated samples will be representative of the population from which they are taken. Answer (C) is incorrect. Dispersion is the degree of variation in a set of values. Answer (D) is incorrect. Skewness is the lack of symmetry in a frequency distribution.

11. An internal auditor is planning to use attribute sampling to test the effectiveness of a specific internal control related to approvals for cash disbursements. In attribute sampling, decreasing the estimated occurrence rate from 5% to 4% while keeping all other sample size planning factors exactly the same would result in a revised sample size that would be

    A. Larger.

    B. Smaller.

    C. Unchanged.

    D. Indeterminate.

Answer (B) is correct.
    REQUIRED: The sample size effect of decreasing the estimated occurrence rate.
    DISCUSSION: In an attribute test, the expected deviation rate is directly related to sample size. If it is decreased, sample size will decrease.
    Answer (A) is incorrect. Increasing the expected error rate increases the sample size. Answer (C) is incorrect. Changing one variable while holding all other factors constant changes the sample size. Answer (D) is incorrect. Decreasing the expected error rate while holding all other factors constant decreases the sample size.

12. The size of a given sample is jointly a result of characteristics of the population of interest and decisions made by the internal auditor. Everything else being equal, sample size will

    A. Increase if the internal auditor decides to accept more risk of incorrectly concluding that controls are effective when they are in fact ineffective.

    B. Double if the internal auditor finds that the variance of the population is twice as large as was indicated in the pilot sample.

    C. Decrease if the internal auditor increases the tolerable rate of deviation.

    D. Increase as sampling risk increases.

Answer (C) is correct.
    REQUIRED: The true statement about the effect on the sample size resulting from a change in a relevant variable.
    DISCUSSION: In an attribute test, the tolerable deviation rate is inversely related to sample size. If it is increased, sample size will decrease.
    Answer (A) is incorrect. An increase in allowable risk decreases sample size. Answer (B) is incorrect. Doubling the variability of the population will cause the sample size to more than double. Answer (D) is incorrect. Sampling risk increases as the sample size decreases.

7.4 Variables Sampling

13. In a variables sampling application, which of the following will result when confidence level is changed from 90% to 95%?

    A. Standard error of the mean will not be affected.

    B. Nonsampling error will decrease.

    C. Sample size will increase.

    D. Point estimate of the arithmetic mean will increase.

Answer (C) is correct.
    REQUIRED: The effect of raising the confidence level.
    DISCUSSION: In any sampling application (attribute or variables), an increase in the confidence level requires a larger sample.
    Answer (A) is incorrect. The standard error of the mean is the standard deviation of the distribution of sample means. The larger the sample, the lower the degree of variability in the sample. An increase in confidence level from 90% to 95% requires a larger sample. Thus, the standard error of the mean will be affected. Answer (B) is incorrect. By definition, nonsampling error is unaffected by changes in sampling criteria. Answer (D) is incorrect. The estimate of the mean may increase or decrease if sample size changes.

14. An auditor is using the mean-per-unit method of variables sampling to estimate the correct total value of a group of inventory items. Based on the sample, the auditor estimates, with precision of ±4% and confidence of 90%, that the correct total is US $800,000. Accordingly,

    A. There is a 4% chance that the actual correct total is less than US $720,000 or more than US $880,000.

    B. The chance that the actual correct total is less than US $768,000 or more than US $832,000 is 10%.

    C. The probability that the inventory is not significantly overstated is between 6% and 14%.

    D. The inventory is not likely to be overstated by more than 4.4% (US $35,200) or understated by more than 3.6% (US $28,800).

Answer (B) is correct.
    REQUIRED: The proper interpretation of the sample results.
    DISCUSSION: A 90% confidence level implies that 10% of the time the true population total will be outside the computed range. Precision of ±4% gives the boundaries of the computed range: US $800,000 × 4% = US $32,000. Hence, the range is US $768,000 to US $832,000.
    Answer (A) is incorrect. The precision, not the confidence level, is ±4%. Answer (C) is incorrect. Precision is a range of values, not the probability (confidence level) that the true value will be included within that range. Answer (D) is incorrect. The precision percentage is not multiplied by the confidence percentage.

15. An auditor for the state highway and safety department needs to estimate the average highway weight of tractor-trailer trucks using the state's highway system. Which estimation method must be used?

    A. Mean-per-unit.

    B. Difference.

    C. Ratio.

    D. Probability-proportional-to-size.

Answer (A) is correct.
    REQUIRED: The best sampling estimation method to estimate an average weight.
    DISCUSSION: Mean-per-unit sampling estimates the average value of population items, in this case, truck weight.
    Answer (B) is incorrect. Difference estimation compares recorded and audit amounts. Recorded amounts are not relevant to the current procedure. Answer (C) is incorrect. Ratio estimation compares recorded and audit amounts. Recorded amounts are not relevant to the current procedure. Answer (D) is incorrect. Probability-proportional-to-size estimation compares recorded and audit amounts. Recorded amounts are not relevant to the current procedure.

16. When relatively few items of high monetary value constitute a large proportion of an account balance, stratified sampling techniques and complete testing of the high monetary-value items will generally result in a

    A. Simplified evaluation of sample results.

    B. Smaller nonsampling error.

    C. Larger estimate of population variability.

    D. Reduction in sample size.

Answer (D) is correct.
    REQUIRED: The effect of using stratified selection in statistical sampling.
    DISCUSSION: Stratifying a population means dividing it into subpopulations, thereby reducing sample size. Stratifying allows for greater emphasis on larger or more important items.
    Answer (A) is incorrect. While stratifying reduces sample size, stratification requires a combination of sample results from more than one sample, in contrast to simple random sampling. Answer (B) is incorrect. A nonsampling error is an error in "performing" audit procedures, which is independent of sample selection. Answer (C) is incorrect. Stratified sampling, when properly used, will result in a smaller estimate of population variability.

17. The auditor wishes to sample the perpetual inventory records to develop an estimate of the monetary amount of misstatement, if any, in the account balance. The account balance is made up of a large number of small-value items and a small number of large-value items. The auditor has decided to audit all items over US $50,000 plus a random selection of others. This audit decision is made because the auditor expects to find a large amount of errors in the perpetual inventory records but is not sure that it will be enough to justify taking a complete physical inventory. The auditor expects the errors to vary directly with the value recorded in the perpetual records. The most efficient sampling procedure to accomplish the auditor's objectives is

    A. Monetary-unit sampling.

    B. Ratio estimation.

    C. Attribute sampling.

    D. Stratified mean-per-unit sampling.

Answer (B) is correct.
    REQUIRED: The most efficient sampling procedure.
    DISCUSSION: Ratio estimation estimates the population misstatement by multiplying the recorded amount of the population by the ratio of the total audit amount of the sample to its total recorded amount. It is reliable and efficient when small errors predominate and are not skewed. Thus, ratio estimation should be used in this situation because the auditor is not sampling the very large items and the errors are not skewed (they vary directly with the size of the recorded values).
    Answer (A) is incorrect. Monetary-unit (probability-proportional-to-size) sampling becomes less accurate when many errors are expected. Answer (C) is incorrect. Attribute sampling is not used to estimate a monetary amount. Answer (D) is incorrect. Mean-per-unit (MPU) variables sampling averages audit values in the sample and multiplies by the number of items in the population to estimate the population value. When many errors are expected, MPU and stratified MPU are not as efficient as ratio estimation.

18. When an internal auditor uses monetary-unit statistical sampling to examine the total value of invoices, each invoice

    A. Has an equal probability of being selected.

    B. Can be represented by no more than one monetary unit.

    C. Has an unknown probability of being selected.

    D. Has a probability proportional to its monetary value of being selected.

Answer (D) is correct.
    REQUIRED: The effect of using monetary-unit sampling to examine invoices.
    DISCUSSION: Monetary-unit sampling, also called probability-proportional-to-size sampling, results in the selection of every nth monetary unit. Thus, a US $1,000 item is 1,000 times more likely to be selected than a US $1 monetary unit item. The probability of selection of a sampled item is directly proportional to the size of the item.
    Answer (A) is incorrect. Each monetary unit, not each invoice, has an equal probability of being selected (unless all invoices are for the same amount). Answer (B) is incorrect. It is possible for two or more monetary units to be selected from the same item; e.g., a US $4,500 item will be represented by four monetary units if every 1,000th dollar is selected. Answer (C) is incorrect. The probability of selection can be calculated using the monetary value of the item and the monetary value of the population.

7.5 Statistical Quality Control

19. A manufacturer mass produces nuts and bolts on its assembly line. The line supervisors sample every *n*th unit for conformance with specifications. Once a nonconforming part is detected, the machinery is shut down and adjusted. The most appropriate tool for this process is a

    A. Fishbone (Ishikawa) diagram.

    B. Cost of quality report.

    C. ISO 9000 audit.

    D. Statistical quality control chart.

Answer (D) is correct.
    REQUIRED: The most appropriate tool used to verify that runs of units are within acceptable limits.
    DISCUSSION: Statistical quality control is a method of determining whether the shipment or production run of units lies within acceptable limits. It is also used to determine whether production processes are out of control. Statistical control charts are graphic aids for monitoring the status of any process subject to random variations.
    Answer (A) is incorrect. A fishbone diagram is useful for determining the unknown causes of problems, not routine mechanical adjustments. Answer (B) is incorrect. The contents of a cost of quality report are stated in monetary terms. This tool is not helpful for determining when to adjust machinery. Answer (C) is incorrect. An ISO 9000 audit focuses on the quality of the organization's total process, not the routine adjustment of machinery.

20. The director of sales asks for a count of customers grouped in descending numerical rank by (1) the number of orders they place during a single year and (2) the dollar amounts of the average order. The visual format of these two pieces of information is most likely to be a

    A. Fishbone (Ishikawa) diagram.

    B. Cost of quality report.

    C. Kaizen diagram.

    D. Pareto diagram.

Answer (D) is correct.
    REQUIRED: The best visual format used to display the values of two independent variables.
    DISCUSSION: A Pareto diagram (also known as 80:20 analysis) displays the values of an independent variable such that managers can quickly identify the areas most in need of attention.
    Answer (A) is incorrect. A fishbone diagram is useful for determining the unknown causes of problems, not for stratifying quantifiable variables. Answer (B) is incorrect. The contents of a cost of quality report are stated in monetary terms. This report is not helpful for stratifying quantifiable variables. Answer (C) is incorrect. Kaizen diagram is not a meaningful term in this context.

Access the **Gleim CIA Premium Review System** featuring our SmartAdapt technology from your Gleim Personal Classroom to continue your studies. You will experience a personalized study environment with exam-emulating multiple-choice questions.

STUDY UNIT EIGHT
ANALYSIS, EVALUATION, DOCUMENTATION, AND SUPERVISION

(19 pages of outline)

This study unit is the fourth of four covering **Domain III: Performing the Engagement** from The IIA's CIA Exam Syllabus. This domain makes up 40% of Part 2 of the CIA exam and is tested at the **basic** and **proficient** cognitive levels. The relevant portion of the syllabus is highlighted below. (The complete syllabus is in Appendix B.)

		Performing the Engagement (40%)	
		1. Information Gathering	
	A	**Gather and examine relevant information (review previous audit reports and data, conduct walk-throughs and interviews, perform observations, etc.) as part of a preliminary survey of the engagement area**	**Proficient**
	B	Develop checklists and risk-and-control questionnaires as part of a preliminary survey of the engagement area	Proficient
	C	Apply appropriate sampling (nonstatistical, judgmental, discovery, etc.) and statistical analysis techniques	Proficient
		2. Analysis and Evaluation	
	A	**Use computerized audit tools and techniques (data mining and extraction, continuous monitoring, automated workpapers, embedded audit modules, etc.)**	**Proficient**
III	B	Evaluate the relevance, sufficiency, and reliability of potential sources of evidence	Proficient
	C	**Apply appropriate analytical approaches and process mapping techniques (process identification, workflow analysis, process map generation and analysis, spaghetti maps, RACI diagrams, etc.)**	**Proficient**
	D	**Determine and apply analytical review techniques (ratio estimation, variance analysis, budget vs. actual, trend analysis, other reasonableness tests, benchmarking, etc.)**	**Basic**
	E	**Prepare workpapers and documentation of relevant information to support conclusions and engagement results**	**Proficient**
	F	**Summarize and develop engagement conclusions, including assessment of risks and controls**	**Proficient**
		3. Engagement Supervision	
	A	**Identify key activities in supervising engagements (coordinate work assignments, review workpapers, evaluate auditors' performance, etc.)**	**Basic**

8.1 COMPUTERIZED AUDIT TOOLS

1. **Overview**

    a. Internal auditors should use available information technology (IT) to assist in performing audit work. The benefits of using IT include

        1) Reduced audit risk
        2) Increased productivity, resulting in more timely audit engagements
        3) Increased audit opportunities

2. Computer-assisted audit techniques (CAATs) may be systems- or transaction-based or may provide automated methods for extracting and analyzing large amounts of data.

3. **Generalized Audit Software (GAS)**

    a. Using GAS, the auditor loads a copy of the client's production data onto the auditor's own computer to perform various analytical procedures.

        1) For example, the auditor can search for duplicate records, gaps in numerically sequenced records, high-monetary-amount transactions, and suspect vendor numbers. Also, control totals can be calculated, and balances can be stratified for receivables testing.

        2) A limitation of GAS is that it can only be used on hardware with compatible operating systems. An advantage of using GAS is that a complete understanding of the client's hardware and software features or programming language is not required.

        3) Two GAS packages are ACL (Audit Command Language) and IDEA (Interactive Data Extraction and Analysis).

4. **Test Data**

    a. Test data allow the auditor to assess the controls embedded in an application by observing (1) whether the good data are correctly processed and (2) how well the system handles bad data.

        1) Test data, sometimes called a test deck, consist of a set of dummy inputs containing both good and bad data elements. This approach subjects auditor-created data to the client's programs.

        2) Test data must never be mingled with real data, and test data must not be allowed to interfere with production processing. Monitoring by IT personnel is crucial when the auditor uses test data.

5. **Parallel Simulation**

    a. Parallel simulation allows an auditor to determine whether the data are subjected to the processes that the client claims the application performs.

        1) Parallel simulation subjects client data to auditor-created programs.

        2) Parallel simulation requires the auditor to have considerable technical knowledge. The auditor also must have extensive communications with client personnel to learn the designed functions of the application being imitated.

6. **Data Mining and Extraction**

    a. The oldest form of data extraction is the manual copying of client records. Until the widespread use of photocopy machines, it was the only method.

        1) With the easy availability of computing, especially networking technology, data extraction can be performed quickly in very large volumes.

        2) The problem is ensuring that the data extracted are those required for the audit procedure being performed. Control totals and other methods are used for this purpose.

7. **Integrated Test Facility (ITF)**

   a. In this approach, the auditor creates a fictitious entity (a department, vendor, employee, or product) on the client's live production system.

      1) All transactions associated with the dummy entity are processed by the live system, and the auditor can observe the results.

   b. Use of an ITF requires great care to ensure that no transactions associated with the dummy entity are included in production reports and output files.

8. **Embedded Audit Module**

   a. An embedded audit module is an integral part of an application system. It is designed to identify and report actual transactions and other information that meet criteria having audit significance.

      1) An advantage is that it permits **continuous monitoring** of online, real-time systems.

      2) A disadvantage is that audit hooks must be programmed into the operating system and application programs to permit insertion of audit modules.

   b. Continuous monitoring is a management process that monitors whether internal controls are operating effectively on an ongoing basis.

9. **Application Tracing and System Mapping**

   a. Application tracing uses a feature of the programming language in which the application was written.

      1) Tracing aids computer programmers in following the step-by-step operation of a computer program's source code. It can be used by auditors for the same purpose.

   b. System mapping is similar to application tracing. But mapping is performed by another computer program instead of by the auditor.

10. **Spreadsheet Analysis**

    a. Electronic spreadsheets, such as Microsoft Excel, organize information into intersecting rows and columns. This organization permits easy analysis of large amounts of client data.

    b. Internal auditors can use spreadsheets to (1) evaluate "what if" scenarios, (2) create graphs, (3) analyze variances between actual and budgeted amounts, and (4) perform other analytical procedures.

11. **Internet**

    a. The Internet is a useful audit tool for gathering and disseminating audit-related information.

    b. The major use of the Internet by internal auditors is electronic communication.

    c. Users transmitting sensitive information across the Internet must understand the threats that arise that could compromise the confidentiality of the data.

       1) Security measures, such as encryption technology, need to be taken to ensure that the information is viewed only by those authorized to view it.

Stop and review! You have completed the outline for this subunit. Study multiple-choice questions 1 through 3 on page 186.

8.2 ANALYTICAL APPROACHES AND PROCESS MAPPING

1.   **Uses of Flowcharts**

   a.   Flowcharts are graphical representations of the step-by-step progression of information through preparation, authorization, flow, storage, etc. The system depicted may be manual, computerized, or a combination of the two.

   1)   Flowcharting allows the internal auditor to analyze a system and to identify the strengths and weaknesses of internal controls and the appropriate areas of audit emphasis.

   b.   Flowcharting is typically used during the **preliminary survey** to gain an understanding of the client's processes and controls.

2.   **Flowchart Symbols**

   a.   Commonly used document flowchart symbols include the following:

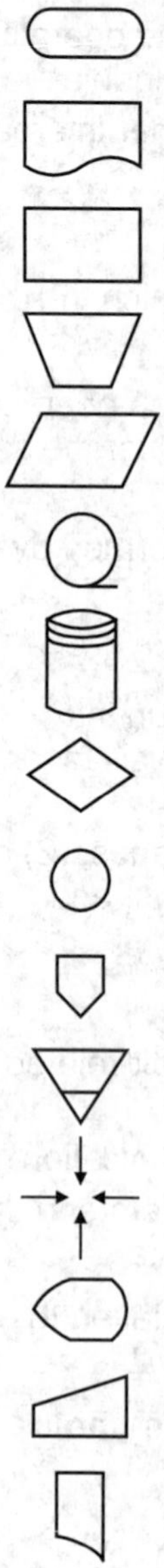

   Starting or ending point or point of interruption

   Input or output of a document or report

   Computer operation or group of operations

   Manual processing operation, e.g., prepare document

   Generalized symbol for input or output used when the medium is not specified

   Hard drive used for input or output

   Hard drive or other digital media used for storage

   Decision symbol indicating a branch in the flow, decision point, or conditional testing

   Connection between points on the same page

   Connection between two pages of the flowchart

   Storage (file) that is not immediately accessible by computer

   Flow direction of data or processing

   Display on a video terminal

   Manual input into a terminal or other online device

   Adding machine tape (batch control)

Figure 8-1

3. **Horizontal Flowcharts**

   a. Horizontal flowcharts (sometimes called **system flowcharts**) depict areas of responsibility (departments or functions) arranged horizontally across the page in vertical columns. Accordingly, activities, controls, and document flows that are the responsibility of a given department or function are shown in the same column. **PO** is a purchase order and **AP** is accounts payable. The following is an example:

Horizontal (System) Flowchart

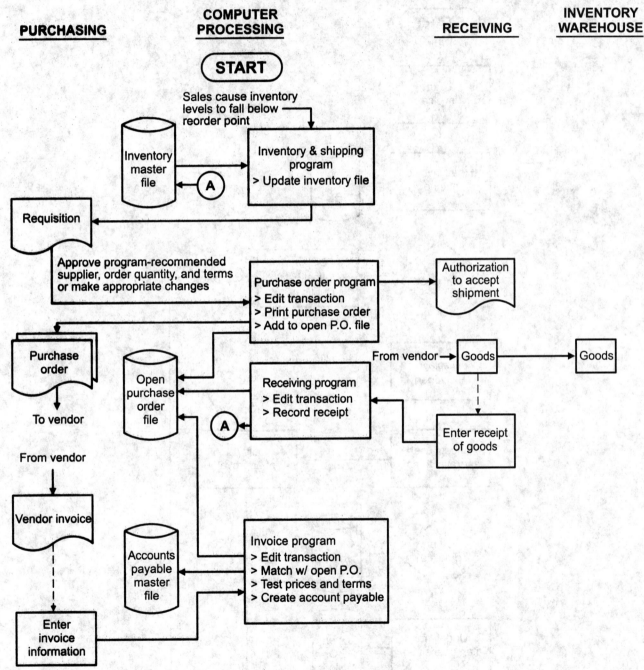

Figure 8-2

4. **Vertical Flowcharts**

    a. Vertical flowcharts, sometimes called **program flowcharts**, present successive steps in a top-to-bottom format.

        1) Their principal use is in the depiction of the specific actions carried out by a computer program.

Vertical (Program) Flowchart

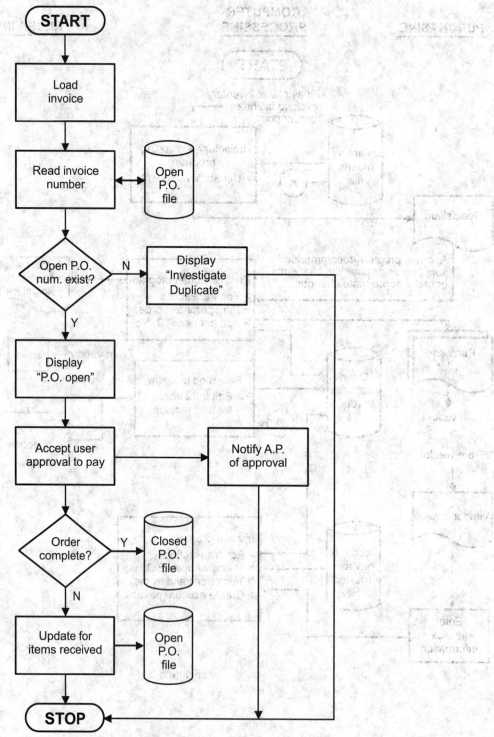

Figure 8-3

5. **Data Flow Diagrams**

   a. Data flow diagrams show how data flow to, from, and within an information system and the processes that manipulate the data. A data flow diagram can be used to depict lower-level details as well as higher-level processes.

      1) A system can be divided into subsystems, and each subsystem can be further subdivided at levels of increasing detail. Thus, any process can be expanded as many times as necessary to show the required level of detail.

      2) The symbols used in data flow diagrams are presented below:

Data Flow Diagram Symbols

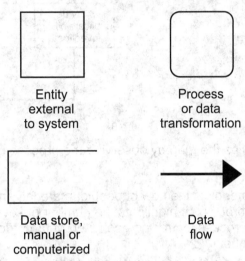

Figure 8-4

      a) No symbol is needed for documents or other output because data flow diagrams depict only the flow of data. For the same reason, no distinction is made between manual and online storage.

6. **Process Mapping**

   a. A process map is the pictorial representation or narrative description of a client process. During the **preliminary survey**, reviewing the process map aids the internal auditor in assessing the efficiency of processes and controls.

      1) Narratives should be used only for simple processes.

   b. Pictorial process mapping uses the three most common flowcharting symbols:

Process Mapping Symbols

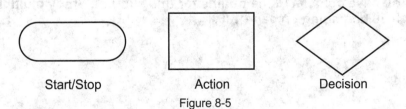

Start/Stop   Action   Decision

Figure 8-5

c. Below is an example of a process map prepared by the client or auditor for processing an invoice against a purchase order (PO). Approved invoices ultimately are forwarded to accounts payable (AP).

Process Map for Invoice Processing in Purchasing Department

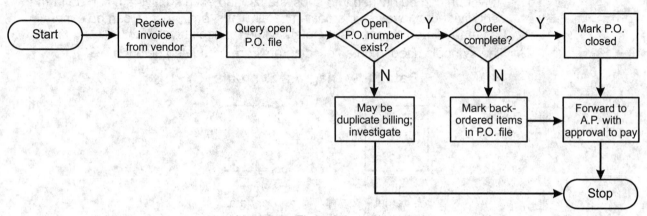

Figure 8-6

d. The auditor verifies the map by observing the process (a functional **walk-through**).

7. **Spaghetti Map**

a. A spaghetti map depicts the flow of people, material, and information from the first to last steps of a process. It highlights the number of key steps and spatial relationships of a particular process by tracing each step of the process. The resulting traces resemble "spaghetti."

b. The goal is to identify the inefficiencies in a process, eliminate the superfluous steps, and create more streamlined process paths.

8. **RACI Diagram**

a. A RACI diagram is used to clarify decision-making assignments in cross-functional or departmental projects and processes.

1) **R – Responsible.** A person who is responsible for performing the particular task.

2) **A – Accountable.** A person who is the final decision maker and is ultimately accountable for the task.

3) **C – Consulted.** A person who must be consulted before completing the task or making a decision.

4) **I – Informed.** A person who is informed after a decision is made or when the task is completed.

Stop and review! You have completed the outline for this subunit. Study multiple-choice questions 4 through 10 beginning on page 186.

8.3 ANALYTICAL REVIEW TECHNIQUES

Performance Standard 2320
Analysis and Evaluation

Internal auditors must base conclusions and engagement results on appropriate analyses and evaluations.

---

1. Analysis and evaluation are required to some extent in (a) planning the engagement and developing the work program and (b) performing procedures. Planning may involve obtaining information by performing procedures, e.g., a risk-and-control matrix and evaluation of control design.

    a. The work program and workpapers are linked. Examples of workpapers are

        1) A planning memo
        2) Flowcharts or narratives
        3) A process-risk map
        4) A risk-and-control matrix connecting risks, controls, evidence, and conclusions

2. **Analytical Procedures**

    a. Specific guidance is in Implementation Guide 2320, *Analysis and Evaluation*.

        1) Use of analytical procedures as a planning tool or to perform the engagement requires developing expectations against which specified information can be compared. The information used to form an expectation should be reliable (e.g., independent of the source of the information tested).

            a) The premise of analytical procedures is that certain relationships between different kinds of information are reasonably expected to continue unless invalidated by known conditions.

        2) "Examples of analytical procedures include:

            a) Ratio, trend, and regression analysis.
            b) Reasonableness tests.
            c) Period-to-period comparisons.
            d) Forecasts.
            e) Benchmarking information against similar industries or organizational units."

        3) Any significant variances from auditor-developed expectations should be investigated.

            a) Matters that cannot be explained may require follow-up and possible communication to senior management and the board.

    b. When determining the extent to which analytical procedures should be used, internal auditors consider the

        1) Significance of the area being examined,
        2) Assessment of risk management in the audited area,
        3) Adequacy of the internal control system,
        4) Availability and reliability of financial and nonfinancial information,
        5) Precision with which the results of analytical audit procedures can be predicted,
        6) Availability and comparability of information regarding the industry in which the organization operates, and
        7) Extent to which other procedures provide evidence.

3. **Ratio Analysis**

    a. One of the most common analytical procedures is ratio analysis, the comparison of one financial statement element with another. Ratios are used frequently to assess an organization's liquidity and profitability.

    b. **Liquidity** is the ability to meet current obligations as they come due and continue operating in the short run. The following ratios are measures of an organization's relative liquidity (the higher the ratio, the higher the liquidity) based on balance sheet amounts:

        1) The **current ratio** equals the balance of current assets divided by the balance of current liabilities.

        $$\frac{Current\ assets}{Current\ liabilities}$$

        2) The **accounts receivable turnover ratio** measures the number of times the organization's average balance in receivables is converted to cash during a fiscal year (or financial statement cycle).

        $$\frac{Net\ credit\ sales}{Average\ accounts\ receivable}$$

            a) Average accounts receivable equals beginning accounts receivable plus ending accounts receivable, divided by 2.

        3) The **inventory turnover ratio** measures the number of times the organization's average balance in inventory is converted to cash in the space of a year (or financial statement cycle).

        $$\frac{Cost\ of\ goods\ sold}{Average\ inventory}$$

            a) Average inventory equals beginning inventory plus ending inventory, divided by 2.

    c. **Total asset turnover** measures net sales generated relative to total assets.

        $$\frac{Net\ sales}{Average\ total\ assets}$$

        1) If net sales increase and all other factors remain the same, the asset turnover ratio improves because more sales are being generated by the same amount of assets.

    d. **Profitability** is measured by three common percentages based on income statement amounts:

        1) **Gross profit margin** is the ratio of gross margin to sales. The key issue is the relationship of gross profit to the increase or decrease in sales. For example, a 10% increase in sales should be accompanied by at least a 10% increase in the gross profit.

        $$\frac{Gross\ profit}{Sales}$$

        2) **Operating profit margin** is the ratio of operating profit to sales.

        $$\frac{Operating\ profit}{Sales}$$

        3) **Net profit margin** is the ratio of net profit to sales. This percentage is particularly important because it measures the proportion of the organization's revenues that it can pass on to its owners.

        $$\frac{Net\ profit}{Sales}$$

    e. Sometimes ratio analysis is used to relate a financial statement item to nonfinancial data. An example is average sales per retail location.

4.   **Ratio Comparisons**

a.   Ratios by themselves reveal little about the organization.

1)   **Trend** analysis tracks the changes in a ratio over time, e.g., the last 3 fiscal years. It helps assess the effects of changes in the overall economy or the relative success of a marketing campaign.

2)   **Period-to-period** analysis compares performance for similar time periods, e.g., the third quarter of the current year and the third quarter of the prior year. This approach is especially informative in seasonal industries, such as retailing and agriculture.

3)   **Industry** analysis compares the organization's ratios with those of competitors or with the published averages for the entire industry. These must be used with caution because different organizations in the same industry may have different cost structures.

5.   **Other Analytical Procedures**

a.   **Regression analysis** determines the degree of relationship, if any, between two variables, such as that between sales and cost of goods sold. The degree of relationship can be used as a benchmark to test for reasonableness.

b.   **Variance analysis** studies the difference (favorable or unfavorable) between an amount based on an actual result and the corresponding budgeted amount. It is a method of planning and control that focuses attention on the causes of significant deviations from expectations.

1)   Variance analysis is a form of **reasonableness test** used in accounting applications.

c.   **Benchmarking** compares some aspect of an organization's performance with best-in-class performance. (Benchmarking is covered in detail in Study Unit 3, Subunit 5.)

d.   **Benford's law** (or First-Digit Law) states that leading digits in a data set are disproportionately more likely to be lower numbers (e.g., 1, 2, or 3). Consequently, internal auditor analyses that reveal a contrary state could be indicative of fraud and may result in expanded procedures.

EXAMPLE

An internal auditor reviews the accounts receivables system and determines that credit requirements for new customers have been loosened. The result is an increase in sales and accounts receivable. To determine (1) whether further investigation is justified and (2) what should be investigated, the auditor should review the reasonableness of the accounts receivables balance and the effects of the new credit requirements on the accounts receivable turnover ratio. Amounts can be compared with those for prior periods and for similar organizations in the same industry.

Internal auditors have many resources for analyzing and interpreting data. Analytical procedures often provide the internal auditor with an efficient and effective means of obtaining evidence. The assessment results from comparing information with expectations identified or developed by the internal auditor.

Stop and review! You have completed the outline for this subunit. Study multiple-choice questions 11 through 13 on page 189.

8.4 WORKPAPERS -- PURPOSE AND CHARACTERISTICS

> **Performance Standard 2330**
> **Documenting Information**
>
> Internal auditors must document sufficient, reliable, relevant, and useful information to support the engagement results and conclusions.

1. **General Guidelines**

   a. Engagement workpapers

      1) Aid in the planning, performance, and review of engagements
      2) Provide the principal support for engagement results
      3) Document whether engagement objectives were achieved
      4) Support the accuracy and completeness of the work performed
      5) Provide a basis for the internal audit activity's quality assurance and improvement program
      6) Facilitate third-party review

2. **Workpapers**

   a. The content of workpapers is prescribed in IG 2330, *Documenting Information*.

      1) **Purpose.** Workpapers document the engagement process from planning to drawing conclusions.
      2) **Uniformity.** The content, organization, and format of workpapers depend on the organization and the engagement. But consistency should be maintained within the internal audit activity to permit sharing of information and coordination of activities.
      3) **Responsibility.** In accordance with Standard 2040 and Standard 2050, the CAE should establish policies and procedures for workpapers for different engagements.

         a) Standard formats with any needed flexibility improve efficiency and consistency.

      4) **Characteristics.** Standard 2310 requires internal auditors to identify sufficient, reliable, relevant, and useful information. This requirement also applies to information in workpapers that relates to objectives, observations, conclusions, and recommendations.

         a) The sufficiency and relevance characteristics "enable a prudent, informed person, such as another internal auditor or an external auditor, to reach the same conclusions."
         b) Well-organized workpapers allow reperformance of the work and support conclusions and results.

      5) **Content.** Workpapers may include the following:

         a) Indexing
         b) Titles indicating the subject matter of the engagement
         c) Time of the engagement
         d) Scope of work
         e) Purpose
         f) Sources of information
         g) The population, sample size, and means of selection
         h) Analytical methods

        i)   Results of tests and analyses

        j)   Conclusions cross-referenced to observations

        k)   Recommended follow-up

        l)   Names of the internal auditor(s)

        m)   Review notation and name of the reviewer(s)

6) **Review.** Review of workpapers is a means of staff development.

    a)   The review may determine compliance with the *Standards* and quality control guidelines.

3. **Best Practices**

    a.   Each workpaper must, at a minimum, identify the engagement and describe the contents or purpose of the workpaper, for example, in the heading.

        1)   Also, each workpaper should be signed (initialed) and dated by the internal auditor and contain an index or reference number.

    b.   Workpapers should be consistently and efficiently prepared to facilitate review. They should be

        1)   Neat, not crowded, and written on only one side (if written at all).

        2)   Uniform in size and appearance.

        3)   Economical, avoiding unnecessary copying, listing, or scheduling.

            a)   They should use copies of engagement clients' records if applicable.

        4)   Arranged in a logical and uniform style.

            a)   The best organization is that of the work program. Each section should have statements of purpose and scope followed by observations, conclusions, recommendations, and corrective action.

        5)   Clear, concise, and complete.

        6)   Restricted to matters that are relevant and significant.

        7)   Written in a simple style.

    c.   While clarity, concision, and accuracy are desirable qualities of workpapers, completeness and support for conclusions are the most important considerations.

4. **Other Content**

    a.   Workpapers should document such matters as how sampling populations were defined and how statistical samples were selected.

    b.   Furthermore, verification symbols (tick marks) are likely to appear on most workpapers and should be explained.

5. **Indexing**

    a.   Indexing permits cross-referencing. It is important because it simplifies supervisory review either during the engagement or subsequently by creating a trail of related items through the workpapers.

        1)   Indexing facilitates preparation of final engagement communications, later engagements for the same client, and internal and external assessments of the internal audit activity.

6. **Summaries**

    a.   Internal auditors summarize information in workpapers. Summaries help to coordinate workpapers related to a subject by providing concise statements of the most important information. Thus, they provide for an orderly and logical flow of information and facilitate efficient supervisory review.

7. **Permanent Files**

    a. The following are typical items contained in the permanent or carry-forward files:

        1) Previous engagement communications, responses, and results of follow-up
        2) Engagement communications provided by other organizational subunits
        3) Reviews of the long-term engagement work schedule by senior management
        4) Results of post-engagement reviews
        5) Auditor observations during past engagements that may have future relevance
        6) The chart of accounts with items referenced to engagement projects
        7) Management's operating reports
        8) Applicable engagement work programs and questionnaires
        9) Long-term contracts
        10) Flowcharts of operations
        11) Historical financial information
        12) Project control information
        13) Correspondence about the engagement project
        14) Updated organizational charter, bylaws, minutes, etc.

8. **Computerized Workpapers**

    a. Electronic workpapers have the following advantages:

        1) Uniformity of format
        2) Ease of storage
        3) Searchability and automated cross-indexing
        4) Backup and recovery functions
        5) Built-in audit methodologies, such as sampling routines

    b. However, the use of electronic media involves security issues that do not arise when workpapers exist only on paper.

        1) Electronic workpapers and reviewer comments should be protected from unauthorized access and change.

        2) Information recorded by scanning workpapers should be adequately controlled to ensure its continued integrity.

        3) Workpaper retention policies should consider changes made in the original operating system, other software, and hardware to ensure the continued retrievability of electronic workpapers throughout the retention cycle.

    c. Software packages have moved beyond the simple storage and retrieval of workpapers.

Stop and review! You have completed the outline for this subunit. Study multiple-choice questions 14 through 17 on page 190.

8.5 WORKPAPERS -- REVIEW, CONTROL, AND RETENTION

> ### Implementation Standard 2330.A1
> The chief audit executive must control access to engagement records. The chief audit executive must obtain the approval of senior management and/or legal counsel prior to releasing such records to external parties, as appropriate.

1. **Review of Workpapers**

    a. Workpapers facilitate supervision of the engagement. They are a means of communication between internal auditors and the auditor in charge.

      b.   All workpapers are reviewed to ensure that (1) they support engagement communications and (2) all necessary procedures are performed.

          1)   The reviewer initials and dates each workpaper to provide evidence of review. Other methods include

              a)   Completing a review checklist,
              b)   Preparing a memorandum on the review, or
              c)   Evaluating and accepting reviews within the workpaper software.

      c.   Written review notes record questions arising from the review. When clearing review notes, the auditor ensures that the workpapers provide adequate evidence that questions raised have been resolved. The reviewer may

          1)   Retain the notes as a record of questions raised, steps taken, and results.
          2)   Discard the notes after questions are resolved and workpapers are amended to provide requested information.

2. Control of Workpapers

      a.   The primary objective of maintaining security over workpapers is to prevent unauthorized changes or removal of information.

          1)   The workpapers are essential to the proper functioning of the internal audit activity. Among many other purposes, they document the information obtained, the analyses made, and the support for the conclusions and engagement results.

          2)   Unauthorized changes or removal of information would seriously compromise the integrity of the internal audit activity's work. For this reason, the chief audit executive must ensure that workpapers are kept secure.

      b.   Workpapers contain sensitive information, but they generally are not protected from disclosure in civil and criminal legal matters. Thus, auditors do not have the equivalent of the attorney-client privilege.

      c.   Engagement records include reports, supporting documents, review notes, and correspondence, regardless of storage media. These records or workpapers are the property of the organization. The internal audit activity controls workpapers and provides access to authorized personnel only.

3. Access

      a.   When engagement objectives will not be compromised, the internal auditor may show all or part of the workpapers to the client.

          1)   For instance, the results of certain engagement procedures may be shared with the client to encourage corrective action.

      b.   One potential use of engagement workpapers is to provide support in the organization's pursuit of insurance claims, fraud cases, or lawsuits.

          1)   In such cases, management and other members of the organization may request access to engagement workpapers. This access may be necessary to substantiate or explain engagement observations and recommendations or to use engagement documentation for other business purposes.

      c.   Internal auditors are encouraged to consult legal counsel in matters involving legal issues. Requirements may vary significantly in different jurisdictions.

4.   **Retention of Workpapers**

> **Implementation Standard 2330.A2**
>
> The chief audit executive must develop retention requirements for engagement records, regardless of the medium in which each record is stored. These retention requirements must be consistent with the organization's guidelines and any pertinent regulatory or other requirements.

    a.   Record retention requirements vary among jurisdictions and legal environments.

    b.   The CAE should develop a written retention policy that meets organizational needs and legal requirements of the jurisdictions where the organization operates.

    c.   The record retention policy should include appropriate arrangements for the retention of records related to engagements performed by external service providers.

    d.   Workpapers should be destroyed after they have served their purpose. Any parts having continuing value should be brought forward to current workpapers or to the permanent file.

Stop and review! You have completed the outline for this subunit. Study multiple-choice questions 18 and 19 on page 191.

8.6 DRAWING CONCLUSIONS

1.   After performing procedures, the internal auditor applies experience, logic, and professional skepticism to analyzing and evaluating the evidence obtained (findings). The internal auditor then draws conclusions.

    a.   Conclusions and opinions are evaluations of the effects of the observations and recommendations regarding the activities reviewed. Conclusions and opinions put the observations and recommendations in perspective based upon their overall implications and are clearly identified in the report.

        1)   The terms "conclusion" and "opinion" are interchangeable.

    b.   Conclusions may address the entire scope of an engagement or its specific elements. Thus, the internal auditor may draw conclusions based on the results of a procedure, a group of procedures, or the whole engagement.

2.   **Root Cause Analysis**

    a.   When audit procedures detect an unfavorable condition (noncompliance, fraud, opportunity loss, misstatement, etc.), internal auditors are encouraged to identify the root cause. IG 2320, *Analysis and Evaluation*, provides the following guidance on root cause analysis:

        1)   **Purpose.** A root cause analysis identifies the underlying reason for the unfavorable condition.

            a)   The analysis improves the effectiveness and efficiency of governance, risk management, and controls.

        2)   **Cost-benefit.** Due professional care should be exercised by weighing effort (e.g., time, cost, and expertise) against possible benefits. Root cause analysis is subject to a cost (effort) – benefit constraint.

        3)   **Application.** A root cause analysis may be difficult and subjective or as simple as asking one or more "why" questions to identify variance.

        4)   **Professional judgment.** Root causes generally result from decisions, acts, or failures to act by a person or group. But a root cause may be elusive even after extensive analysis of quantitative or qualitative information. Furthermore, two or more mistakes of varying significance may collectively be the root cause. In other cases, the search for the root cause may involve a broader problem, e.g., organizational culture. Accordingly, input may be sought from internal and external stakeholders.

        5)   **Multiple root causes.** In some circumstances, the internal auditors' objective and independent analysis may identify multiple root causes for management's consideration.

        6)   **Management assistance.** The resources (e.g., time and expertise) of the internal audit activity may be inadequate to complete a root cause analysis. In these cases, the CAE may recommend that management determine the root cause.

3.   **Examples**

    a.   Below is an example of the process of moving from a finding to a conclusion for a specific engagement objective:

        1)   The engagement work program called for the auditor to examine all purchase orders exceeding US $100,000 to determine whether they were approved by the appropriate division vice president. The results of the procedure are stated as a finding:

            Of 38 purchase orders over US $100,000 examined, 3 lacked required vice presidential approval, an exception rate of 7.9%.

           a)   The finding (observation) is a relevant statement of fact about the results of audit work without interpretation or commentary.

        2)   From the finding, the internal auditor can draw a conclusion that informs the reader of the implications of the finding for one or more engagement objectives:

            The system of internal controls over purchases of material dollar amounts in the Eastern Division is not functioning as designed.

        3)   The relationship of a finding and a conclusion need not be one-to-one. If the auditor finds it useful, multiple findings can be used to support a single conclusion:

            Of 38 purchase orders over US $100,000 examined, 3 lacked required vice presidential approval, an exception rate of 7.9%. Of 115 purchase orders less than US $100,000 randomly selected and examined, 12 lacked required approvals, an exception rate of 10.4%. Given these findings, the system of internal controls over all purchases in the Eastern Division is not functioning as designed.

    b.   Auditor judgment is the essential element in moving from a finding to a conclusion. No formula can tell an auditor whether a certain exception rate is indicative of a working or failing control.

        1)   Depending on context, decisions about materiality, and knowledge of the auditee, the findings in the example above could have resulted in positive, not negative, conclusions.

4.   **Report Test Results to Auditor in Charge**

    a.   The auditor in charge of the engagement is responsible for coordinating the results of audit work and ensuring that work performed supports conclusions and opinions.

        1)   For this reason, internal audit staff must report the results of audit work to the auditor in charge.

Stop and review! You have completed the outline for this subunit. Study multiple-choice questions 20 and 21 on page 191.

8.7 SUPERVISION

1.   **Supervision at the Engagement Level**

> ### Performance Standard 2340
> ### <u>Engagement Supervision</u>
>
> Engagements must be properly supervised to ensure objectives are achieved, quality is assured, and staff is developed.

a.   Supervision is needed at all levels of the internal audit activity from planning to performance to reporting results. The CAE may delegate the task of supervision on individual engagements.

> ### Interpretation of Standard 2340
>
> The extent of supervision required will depend on the proficiency and experience of internal auditors and the complexity of the engagement. The chief audit executive has overall responsibility for supervising the engagement, whether performed by or for the internal audit activity, but may designate appropriately experienced members of the internal audit activity to perform the review. Appropriate evidence of supervision is documented and retained.

b.   Further guidance is provided in IG 2340, *Engagement Supervision*.

1)   Supervision by the CAE is relevant to all phases of the engagement. The process includes

a)   Ensuring auditors collectively possess the required knowledge, skills, and other competencies.

b)   Providing instructions during planning and approving the engagement program.

c)   Ensuring the work program is completed (unless changes are justified and authorized) and objectives are met.

d)   Determining workpapers support observations, conclusions, and recommendations.

e)   Ensuring communications are accurate, objective, clear, concise, constructive, and timely.

f)   Developing internal auditors' proficiency.

2)   The CAE is responsible for all internal audit engagements and significant professional judgments. The CAE adopts suitable means to

a)   Minimize the risk of inconsistent professional judgments or other actions inconsistent with those of the CAE and

b)   Resolve differences in professional judgment between the CAE and staff members.

i)   The means of conflict resolution may include

- Discussion of facts,
- Inquiries or research,
- Workpaper documentation of differences, and,
- For an ethical issue, referral to an individual responsible for such matters.

2.   **Relationships**

a.   To ensure complete cooperation, senior management is responsible for notifying other departments of the existence of the internal audit activity.

1)   Partnering with management at all levels is one of the best ways for internal auditors to obtain information.

2)   Employees are another source of information.

    b.   Internal auditors need effective interpersonal skills to promote the internal audit activity throughout the organization. According to The IIA Competency Framework, internal auditors nurture relationships when they

        1)   Cultivate and maintain extensive informal networks,
        2)   Create opportunities and events to help people build relationships with each other,
        3)   Compliment and affirm others,
        4)   Build relationships by sharing personal experiences and perspectives,
        5)   Keep others in the loop,
        6)   Seek opportunities for contact that build relationships,
        7)   Initiate and participate in conversations that enhance approachability,
        8)   Are recognized as approachable and resourceful individuals, and
        9)   Use diplomacy and tact.

    c.   Internal auditors rely on collaboration and cooperation among departments and other groups to work toward shared goals. During an engagement, internal auditors have a unique opportunity to build credibility and to promote the goals of adding value and improving the organization's operations.

3.   **Coordination during the Engagement**

    a.   The auditor-in-charge should coordinate work assignments among audit team members during the engagement.

    b.   Coordination during the engagement ensures that engagement objectives will be met efficiently and effectively.

4.   **Staff Performance Evaluations**

    a.   The CAE is responsible for ensuring that the internal audit activity has sufficient resources, including employees with the knowledge, skills, and other competencies appropriate for planned activities.

        1)   Thus, as part of the resource management process, a written appraisal of each internal auditor's performance is required at least annually.

        2)   Furthermore, at the conclusion of any major audit engagement, supervisory personnel should complete performance appraisals for all audit staff who worked on the engagement.

            a)   Such appraisals help (1) the CAE to assess future training needs and current staff abilities and (2) staff to identify areas of personal strength and weakness.

    b.   Best practices include the following:

        1)   It is appropriate and advisable to notify internal auditors of an upcoming appraisal.

        2)   Evaluators should use objective language and not use generalizations. Rather, the evaluators should cite specific information and be prepared to support assertions with evidence.

        3)   All appraisals should be documented.

    c.   The halo effect is a generalization from the perception of one trait to others.

        1)   If an employee's performance appraisal of any given subordinate tends to be consistently high, consistently low, or consistently in the middle across the performance dimensions, a halo bias may exist in the way the subordinate is being rated.

            a)   Appraisal ratings are not likely to remain consistent if the forms have too many leading questions.

Stop and review! You have completed the outline for this subunit. Study multiple-choice questions 22 through 24 on page 192.

QUESTIONS

8.1 Computerized Audit Tools

1. An auditor is **least** likely to use computer software to

A. Construct parallel simulations.

B. Access client data files.

C. Prepare spreadsheets.

D. Assess computer control risk.

Answer (D) is correct.
REQUIRED: The task least likely to be done with computer software.
DISCUSSION: The auditor is required to evaluate the adequacy and effectiveness of the system of internal control and to assess risk to plan the audit. This assessment is a matter of professional judgment that cannot be accomplished with a computer alone.
Answer (A) is incorrect. Parallel simulation involves using an auditor's program to reproduce the logic of management's program. Answer (B) is incorrect. Computer software makes accessing company files much faster and easier. Answer (C) is incorrect. Many audit spreadsheet programs are available.

2. Which of the following **cannot** be performed by an auditor using generalized audit software (GAS)?

A. Identifying missing check numbers.

B. Correcting erroneous data elements, making them suitable for audit testwork.

C. Matching identical product information in separate data files.

D. Aging accounts receivable.

Answer (B) is correct.
REQUIRED: The task that generalized audit software cannot perform.
DISCUSSION: GAS can help an auditor identify erroneous data, but correcting them before performing testwork is inappropriate.
Answer (A) is incorrect. Identifying gaps is a function of major GAS packages. Answer (C) is incorrect. Merging files is a function of GAS packages. Answer (D) is incorrect. Aging is a function of GAS packages.

3. Which of the following is the primary reason that many auditors hesitate to use embedded audit modules?

A. Embedded audit modules cannot be protected from computer viruses.

B. Auditors are required to monitor embedded audit modules continuously to obtain valid results.

C. Embedded audit modules can easily be modified through management tampering.

D. Auditors are required to be involved in the system design of the application to be monitored.

Answer (D) is correct.
REQUIRED: The primary reason many auditors hesitate to use embedded audit modules.
DISCUSSION: Continuous monitoring and analysis of transaction processing can be achieved with an embedded audit module. To be successful, the internal auditor may need to be involved in the design of the application. Designing the system may impair independence unless the client makes all management decisions.
Answer (A) is incorrect. Embedded audit modules are no more vulnerable to computer viruses than any other software. Answer (B) is incorrect. The advantage of embedded audit modules is that auditors are not required to monitor them continuously to obtain valid results. Answer (C) is incorrect. Embedded audit modules cannot be easily modified through management tampering.

8.2 Analytical Approaches and Process Mapping

4. Of the following, which is the most efficient source for an auditor to use to evaluate a company's overall control system?

A. Control flowcharts.

B. Copies of standard operating procedures.

C. A narrative describing departmental history, activities, and forms usage.

D. Copies of industry operating standards.

Answer (A) is correct.
REQUIRED: The most efficient source for an auditor to use to evaluate a company's overall control system.
DISCUSSION: Control flowcharting is a graphical means of representing the sequencing of activities and information flows with related control points. It provides an efficient and comprehensive method of describing relatively complex activities, especially those involving several departments.
Answer (B) is incorrect. Copies of procedures and related forms do not provide an efficient overview of processing activities. Answer (C) is incorrect. A narrative review covering the history and forms usage of the department is not as efficient or comprehensive as flowcharting for the purpose of communicating relevant information about controls. Answer (D) is incorrect. Industry standards do not provide a picture of existing practice for subsequent audit activity.

5. Which of the following tools would best give a graphical representation of a sequence of activities and decisions?

A. Flowchart.

B. Control chart.

C. Histogram.

D. Run chart.

Answer (A) is correct.

REQUIRED: The best tool for a graphical representation of a sequence of activities and decisions.

DISCUSSION: Flowcharting is an essential aid in the program development process that involves a sequence of activities and decisions. A flowchart is a pictorial diagram of the definition, analysis, or solution of a problem in which symbols are used to represent operations, data flow, equipment, etc.

Answer (B) is incorrect. A control chart is used to monitor deviations from desired quality measurements during repetitive operations. Answer (C) is incorrect. A histogram is a bar chart showing conformance to a standard bell curve. Answer (D) is incorrect. A run chart tracks the frequency or amount of a given variable over time.

6. The diamond-shaped symbol is commonly used in flowcharting to show or represent a

A. Process or a single step in a procedure or program.

B. Terminal output display.

C. Decision point, conditional testing, or branching.

D. Predefined process.

Answer (C) is correct.

REQUIRED: The meaning of the diamond-shaped symbol used in flowcharting.

DISCUSSION: Flowcharts illustrate in pictorial fashion the flow of data, documents, and/or operations in a system. Flowcharts may summarize a system or present great detail, e.g., as found in program flowcharts. The diamond-shaped symbol represents a decision point or test of a condition in a program flowchart, that is, the point at which a determination must be made as to which logic path (branch) to follow.

Answer (A) is incorrect. The rectangle is the appropriate symbol for a process or a single step in a procedure or program. Answer (B) is incorrect. A terminal display is signified by a symbol similar to the shape of a cathode ray tube. Answer (D) is incorrect. A predefined processing step is represented by a rectangle with double lines on either side.

7. An auditor's flowchart of a client's accounting system is a diagrammatic representation that depicts the auditor's

A. Assessment of the risks of material misstatement.

B. Identification of weaknesses in the system.

C. Assessment of the control environment's effectiveness.

D. Understanding of the system.

Answer (D) is correct.

REQUIRED: The purpose of an auditor's flowchart.

DISCUSSION: The auditor should document (1) the understanding of the entity and its environment and the components of internal control, (2) the sources of information regarding the understanding, and (3) the risk assessment procedures performed. The form and extent of this documentation are influenced by the nature and complexity of the entity's controls. For example, documentation of the understanding of internal control of a complex information system in which many transactions are electronically initiated, authorized, recorded, processed, or reported may include questionnaires, flowcharts, or decision tables.

Answer (A) is incorrect. The conclusions about the assessments of the RMMs should be documented. These are professional judgments of the auditor documented in the workpapers. Answer (B) is incorrect. The flowchart is a tool to document the auditor's understanding of internal control, but it does not specifically identify weaknesses in the system. Answer (C) is incorrect. The auditor's judgment is the ultimate basis for concluding that controls are effective.

8. When documenting internal control, the independent auditor sometimes uses a systems flowchart, which can best be described as a

A. Pictorial presentation of the flow of instructions in a client's internal computer system.

B. Diagram that clearly indicates an organization's internal reporting structure.

C. Graphic illustration of the flow of operations that is used to replace the auditor's internal control questionnaire.

D. Symbolic representation of a system or series of sequential processes.

Answer (D) is correct.

REQUIRED: The best description of a systems flowchart.

DISCUSSION: A systems flowchart is a symbolic representation of the flow of documents and procedures through a series of steps in the accounting process of the client's organization.

Answer (A) is incorrect. A pictorial presentation of the flow of instructions in a client's internal computer system is a computer program flowchart. Answer (B) is incorrect. The organizational chart depicts the client's internal reporting structure. Answer (C) is incorrect. A flowchart does not necessarily replace the auditor's internal control questionnaire. Controls beyond those depicted on the systems flowchart must also be considered by the auditor, and information obtained from the questionnaire may be used to develop the flowchart.

Questions 9 and 10 are based on the following information.

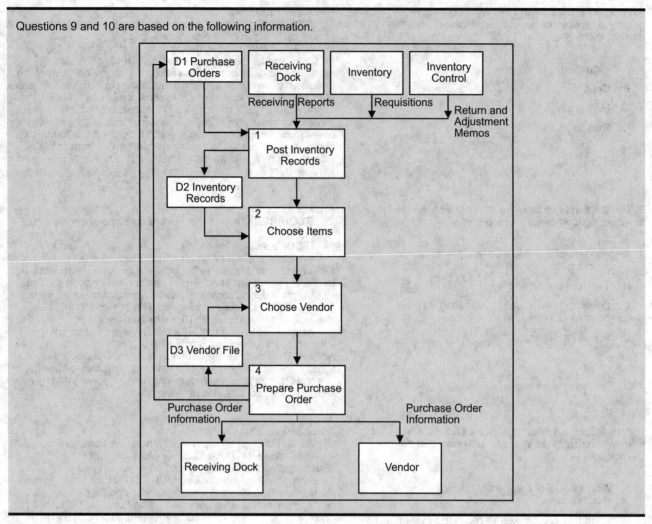

9. This figure shows how

A. Physical media are used in the system.

B. Input/output procedures are conducted.

C. Data flow within and out of the system.

D. Accountability is allocated in the system.

Answer (C) is correct.
REQUIRED: The nature of the figure.
DISCUSSION: A data flow diagram shows how data flow to, from, and within a system and the processes that manipulate the data.
Answer (A) is incorrect. The figure does not show physical media or input/output procedures (manifestations of how the system works rather than what it accomplishes). Flowcharts depict these matters. Answer (B) is incorrect. The figure is a data flow diagram; it depicts the flow of data within and out of the system. Flowcharts show how input/output procedures are conducted. Answer (D) is incorrect. The figure does not show how accountability is allocated in the system. Accountability transfers are usually shown in flowcharts.

10. This data flow diagram could be expanded to show the

A. Edit checks used in preparing purchase orders from stock records.

B. Details of the preparation of purchase orders.

C. Physical media used for stock records, the vendor file, and purchase orders.

D. Workstations required in a distributed system for preparing purchase orders.

Answer (B) is correct.
REQUIRED: The result that can be achieved by expanding the figure.
DISCUSSION: A data flow diagram can be used to depict lower-level details as well as higher-level processes. A system can be divided into subsystems, and each subsystem can be further subdivided at levels of increasing detail. Thus, any process can be expanded as many times as necessary to show the required level of detail.
Answer (A) is incorrect. A data flow diagram does not depict edit checks. Answer (C) is incorrect. Flowcharts, not data flow diagrams, show the physical media on which data such as stock records, the vendor file, and purchase orders are maintained. Answer (D) is incorrect. Flowcharts, not data flow diagrams, show the workstations through which data pass and the sequence of activities.

8.3 Analytical Review Techniques

11. Accounts payable schedule verification may include the use of analytical information. Which of the following is analytical information?

A. Comparing the schedule with the accounts payable ledger or unpaid voucher file.

B. Comparing the balance on the schedule with the balances of prior years.

C. Comparing confirmations received from selected creditors with the accounts payable ledger.

D. Examining vendors' invoices in support of selected items on the schedule.

Answer (B) is correct.
REQUIRED: The analytical information.
DISCUSSION: Analytical procedures are used to compare information with expectations. Such procedures include period-to-period comparisons. Thus, comparing the balance on a schedule with the balances from prior years creates analytical information.
Answer (A) is incorrect. Comparing the schedule with the accounts payable ledger or unpaid voucher file is a test of details. Answer (C) is incorrect. Comparing confirmations received from selected creditors with the accounts payable ledger is a test of details. Answer (D) is incorrect. Examining vendors' invoices in support of selected items on the schedule is a test of details.

12. Analytical procedures enable the internal auditor to predict the balance or quantity of an item. Information to develop this estimate can be obtained by all of the following **except**

A. Tracing transactions through the system to determine whether procedures are being applied as prescribed.

B. Comparing financial data with data for comparable prior periods, anticipated results (e.g., budgets and forecasts), and similar data for the industry in which the entity operates.

C. Studying the relationships of elements of financial data that would be expected to conform to a predictable pattern based upon the entity's experience.

D. Studying the relationships of financial data with relevant nonfinancial data.

Answer (A) is correct.
REQUIRED: The procedure not a source of information for analytical procedures.
DISCUSSION: Tracing transactions through the system is a test of controls directed toward the operating effectiveness of internal control, not an analytical procedure.
Answer (B) is incorrect. The basic premise of analytical procedures is that plausible relationships among data may be reasonably expected to exist and continue in the absence of known conditions to the contrary. Well-drafted budgets and forecasts prepared at the beginning of the year should therefore be compared with actual results, and engagement client information should be compared with data for the industry in which the engagement client operates. Answer (C) is incorrect. The internal auditor should expect financial ratios and relationships to exist and to remain relatively stable in the absence of reasons for variation. Answer (D) is incorrect. Financial information is related to nonfinancial information; e.g., salary expense should be related to the number of hours worked.

13. An internal auditor's preliminary analysis of accounts receivable turnover revealed the following rates:

Year 1	Year 2	Year 3
7.3	6.2	4.3

Which of the following is the most likely cause of the decrease in accounts receivable turnover?

A. Increase in the cash discount offered.

B. Liberalization of credit policy.

C. Shortening of due date terms.

D. Increased cash sales.

Answer (B) is correct.
REQUIRED: The most likely cause of a decrease in accounts receivable turnover.
DISCUSSION: The accounts receivable turnover ratio equals net credit sales divided by average accounts receivable. Accounts receivable turnover will decrease if net credit sales decrease or average accounts receivable increase. Liberalization of credit policy will increase receivables.
Answer (A) is incorrect. An increase in cash sales that reduces credit sales as a result of an increased cash discount has an indeterminate effect on the turnover ratio. Both the numerator and the denominator are decreased but not necessarily by the same amount. An increase in cash sales not affecting credit sales has no effect on the ratio. Answer (C) is incorrect. Shortening due dates decreases the average accounts receivable outstanding and increases the ratio if other factors are held constant. Answer (D) is incorrect. Increased cash sales have an indeterminate effect on the turnover ratio.

8.4 Workpapers -- Purpose and Characteristics

14. An internal auditor's workpapers should support the observations, conclusions, and recommendations to be communicated. One of the purposes of this requirement is to

A. Provide support for the internal audit activity's financial budget.

B. Facilitate quality assurance reviews.

C. Provide control over workpapers.

D. Permit the audit committee to review observations, conclusions, and recommendations.

Answer (B) is correct.
   REQUIRED: The purpose of the requirement that workpapers support the observations, conclusions, and recommendations to be communicated.
   DISCUSSION: As a means of developing internal audit staff, supervisory review of workpapers may be a basis for assessing the internal audit activity's quality assurance and improvement program. Thus, they facilitate quality assurance reviews.
   Answer (A) is incorrect. Financial budgets are based on the planned scope of internal audit work. Answer (C) is incorrect. Control over workpapers is obtained by other means. Answer (D) is incorrect. Audit committees rarely review the full draft of a final engagement communication, much less the supporting workpapers.

15. The internal auditor prepares workpapers primarily for the benefit of

A. The external auditor.

B. The internal audit activity.

C. The engagement client.

D. Senior management.

Answer (B) is correct.
   REQUIRED: The primary beneficiary of the internal auditor's workpapers.
   DISCUSSION: Internal auditors must document sufficient, reliable, relevant, and useful information to support the engagement results and conclusions (Perf. Std. 2330). Thus, internal auditors prepare workpapers primarily for the benefit of the internal audit activity.

16. Engagement workpapers are indexed by means of reference numbers. The primary purpose of indexing is to

A. Permit cross-referencing and simplify supervisory review.

B. Support the final engagement communication.

C. Eliminate the need for follow-up reviews.

D. Determine that workpapers adequately support observations, conclusions, and recommendations.

Answer (A) is correct.
   REQUIRED: The primary purpose of indexing.
   DISCUSSION: Indexing permits cross-referencing. It is important because it simplifies supervisory review either during the engagement or subsequently by creating a trail of related items through the workpapers. It thus facilitates preparation of final engagement communications, later engagements for the same engagement client, and internal and external assessments of the internal audit activity.
   Answer (B) is incorrect. The workpapers as a whole should support the final engagement communication. Answer (C) is incorrect. Follow-up is necessitated by engagement client conditions, not the state of workpapers. Answer (D) is incorrect. The purpose of supervisory review of workpapers is to determine that workpapers adequately support observations, conclusions, and recommendations.

17. Which of the following conditions constitutes inappropriate preparation of workpapers?

A. All forms and directives used by the engagement client are included in the workpapers.

B. Flowcharts are included in the workpapers.

C. Engagement observations are cross-referenced to supporting documentation.

D. Tick marks are explained in notes.

Answer (A) is correct.
   REQUIRED: The wrong method to prepare workpapers.
   DISCUSSION: Performance Standard 2330 states that internal auditors must document sufficient, reliable, relevant, and useful information to support the engagement results and conclusions. Thus, workpapers should be confined to information that is material and relevant to the engagement and the observations, conclusions, and recommendations. Thus, forms and directives used by the engagement client should be included only to the extent they support the observations, conclusions, and recommendations and are consistent with engagement objectives.
   Answer (B) is incorrect. A graphic representation of the engagement client's controls, document flows, and other activities is often vital for understanding operations and is therefore a necessary part of the documentation. Answer (C) is incorrect. Cross-referencing is essential to the orderly arrangement and understanding of workpapers and reduces duplication. Answer (D) is incorrect. Tick marks are verification symbols that should be standard throughout the engagement. They should be described in a note.

8.5 Workpapers -- Review, Control, and Retention

18. Which of the following actions constitutes a violation of the confidentiality concept regarding workpapers? An internal auditor

A. Takes workpapers to his or her hotel room overnight.

B. Shows workpapers on occasion to engagement clients.

C. Allows the external auditor to copy workpapers.

D. Misplaces workpapers occasionally.

Answer (D) is correct.
REQUIRED: The action violating the confidentiality concept regarding workpapers.
DISCUSSION: The internal audit activity controls engagement workpapers and provides access to authorized personnel only. By misplacing workpapers occasionally, the internal auditor is thus violating the confidentiality concept.
Answer (A) is incorrect. Continuous physical control of workpapers during fieldwork may be appropriate. Answer (B) is incorrect. Engagement clients may be shown workpapers with the CAE's approval. Answer (C) is incorrect. Internal and external auditors commonly grant access to each others' work programs and workpapers.

19. Workpapers should be disposed of when they are of no further use. Retention policies must

A. Specify a minimum retention period of 3 years.

B. Be prepared by the audit committee.

C. Be approved by legal counsel.

D. Be approved by the external auditor.

Answer (C) is correct.
REQUIRED: The true statement about retention of workpapers.
DISCUSSION: The chief audit executive must develop retention requirements for engagement records, regardless of the medium in which each record is stored. These retention requirements must be consistent with the organization's guidelines and any pertinent regulatory or other requirements (Impl. Std. 2330.A2). Thus, approval by the organization's legal counsel is appropriate.
Answer (A) is incorrect. Workpapers should not be retained for an arbitrary period. The duration of retention is a function of usefulness, including legal considerations. Answer (B) is incorrect. The CAE must develop retention policies. Answer (D) is incorrect. Retention policies need not be approved by the external auditor.

8.6 Drawing Conclusions

20. "Except for the missing documentation noted above, the system of internal controls over petty cash is functioning as intended." The preceding statement is an example of a(n)

A. Observation.

B. Objective.

C. Conclusion.

D. Finding.

Answer (C) is correct.
REQUIRED: The appropriate description of the statement.
DISCUSSION: A conclusion or opinion is the auditor's interpretation of the results of the engagement. It allows the reader to understand the meaning of what the auditor discovered.
Answer (A) is incorrect. A finding (observation) is a relevant statement of fact about the results of an internal audit without interpretation or commentary. Answer (B) is incorrect. The IIA Glossary defines engagement objectives as broad statements developed by internal auditors that define intended engagement accomplishments. Answer (D) is incorrect. A finding (observation) is an objective statement of fact about the results of an internal audit without interpretation or commentary.

21. The single most important factor in drawing a useful conclusion or stating a useful opinion in an engagement report is

A. Use of statistical sampling techniques.

B. Senior management interest in the engagement outcome.

C. Auditee management assurances.

D. Auditor judgment.

Answer (D) is correct.
REQUIRED: The single most important factor in drawing a useful conclusion or stating a useful opinion in an engagement report.
DISCUSSION: Auditor judgment is the essential element in moving from a finding/observation to a conclusion or opinion. No formula can tell an auditor whether a certain exception rate is indicative of a working or failing control.
Answer (A) is incorrect. Statistical sampling allows the auditor to state the results of the engagement with a certain level of confidence, but it is not a substitute for auditor judgment. Answer (B) is incorrect. The level of interest of senior management in the engagement must not affect the auditor's judgment in drawing conclusions and stating opinions. Answer (C) is incorrect. Assurances provided by auditee management are among many factors used by internal auditors as input into forming findings/observations and the resulting conclusions/opinions.

8.7 Supervision

22. Which of the following activities does **not** constitute engagement supervision?

- A. Preparing a preliminary engagement work program.
- B. Providing appropriate instructions to the internal auditors.
- C. Reviewing engagement workpapers.
- D. Ensuring that engagement communications meet appropriate criteria.

Answer (A) is correct.
    REQUIRED: The activity not constituting supervision.
    DISCUSSION: Preparing a preliminary engagement work program is part of engagement planning, not an aspect of engagement supervision.
    Answer (B) is incorrect. Providing appropriate instructions to the internal auditors is an aspect of engagement supervision. Answer (C) is incorrect. Reviewing engagement workpapers is an aspect of engagement supervision. Answer (D) is incorrect. Ensuring that engagement objectives are achieved is an aspect of engagement supervision.

23. Supervision of an internal audit engagement should include

- A. Determining that engagement workpapers adequately support the engagement observations.
- B. Assigning staff members to the particular engagement.
- C. Determining the scope of the engagement.
- D. Appraising each internal auditor's performance on at least an annual basis.

Answer (A) is correct.
    REQUIRED: The extent of supervision of an engagement.
    DISCUSSION: Among other things, supervision includes ensuring that (1) the approved engagement work program is completed unless changes are justified and authorized, and (2) workpapers adequately support engagement observations, conclusions, and recommendations.
    Answer (B) is incorrect. Engagement resource allocation is a planning function, not a supervisory function. Answer (C) is incorrect. Determining the engagement scope is a planning function, not a supervisory function. Answer (D) is incorrect. Appraising performance on an annual basis is not a supervisory function of a specific engagement but is part of the management of the human resources of the internal audit activity.

24. Which of the following best describes engagement supervision?

- A. The manager of each engagement has the ultimate responsibility for supervision.
- B. Supervision is primarily exercised at the final review stage of an engagement to ensure the accuracy of the engagement communications.
- C. Supervision is most important in the planning phase of the engagement to ensure appropriate coverage.
- D. Supervision is a continuing process beginning with planning and ending with the conclusion of the engagement.

Answer (D) is correct.
    REQUIRED: The best description of engagement supervision.
    DISCUSSION: The CAE (or designee) provides appropriate engagement supervision. Supervision is a process that begins with planning and continues throughout the engagement.
    Answer (A) is incorrect. The CAE has the ultimate responsibility for supervision. Answer (B) is incorrect. Supervision begins with planning and continues throughout the engagement. Answer (C) is incorrect. Supervision is equally important in all phases of the engagement.

 Access the **Gleim CIA Premium Review System** featuring our SmartAdapt technology from your Gleim Personal Classroom to continue your studies. You will experience a personalized study environment with exam-emulating multiple-choice questions.

STUDY UNIT NINE
COMMUNICATING RESULTS
AND MONITORING PROGRESS

(18 pages of outline)

This study unit covers **Domain IV: Communicating Engagement Results and Monitoring Progress** from The IIA's CIA Exam Syllabus. This domain makes up 20% of Part 2 of the CIA exam and is tested at the **basic** and **proficient** cognitive levels. The relevant portion of the syllabus is highlighted below. (The complete syllabus is in Appendix B.)

		Communicating Engagement Results and Monitoring Progress (20%)	
		1. Communicating Engagement Results and the Acceptance of Risk	
IV	A	Arrange preliminary communication with engagement clients	Proficient
	B	Demonstrate communication quality (accurate, objective, clear, concise, constructive, complete, and timely) and elements (objectives, scope, conclusions, recommendations, and action plan)	Proficient
	C	Prepare interim reporting on the engagement progress	Proficient
	D	Formulate recommendations to enhance and protect organizational value	Proficient
	E	Describe the audit engagement communication and reporting process, including holding the exit conference, developing the audit report (draft, review, approve, and distribute), and obtaining management's response	Basic
	F	Describe the chief audit executive's responsibility for assessing residual risk	Basic
	G	Describe the process for communicating risk acceptance (when management has accepted a level of risk that may be unacceptable to the organization)	Basic
		2. Monitoring Progress	
	A	Assess engagement outcomes, including the management action plan	Proficient
	B	Manage monitoring and follow-up of the disposition of audit engagement results communicated to management and the board	Proficient

9.1 COMMUNICATION WITH CLIENTS

1. **Engagement Communications**

   a. The following are purposes of engagement communications:

      1) Inform (tell what was found),

      2) Persuade (convince management of the worth and validity of the audit findings), and

      3) Get results (move management toward change and improvement).

   b. Providing useful and timely information and promoting improvements in operations are goals of internal auditors.

      1) To accomplish these goals, engagement communications should meet the expectations, perceptions, and needs of operating and senior management.

      2) For the benefit of senior management, the communication should provide appropriately generalized information regarding matters of significance to the organization as a whole. For the benefit of operating management, the communication should emphasize details of operations.

   c. Internal auditors should be skilled in oral and written communications to clearly and effectively convey such matters as engagement objectives, evaluations, conclusions, and recommendations.

2. **Preliminary Communication**

   a. The CAE generally notifies client management about the timing of the audit, the reasons for it, the preliminary scope, and the estimated client resources needed.

      1) For an assurance service, the person or group directly involved with the entity, operation, function, system, or other subject matter under review is the process owner.

      2) For a consulting service, the person or group seeking advice is the engagement client (Introduction to the *Standards*).

      3) For the sake of convenience, The IIA and this text use the term **engagement client** for both assurance and consulting services.

   b. Before this communication, the internal audit activity gathers basic information about the client, for example, about its industry, principal personnel, processes, major inputs and outputs, and control environment.

      1) Some information may be acquired by sending a questionnaire to the client early in the audit process. The answers are then discussed at the preliminary meeting.

      2) This preliminary notice is omitted when the engagement involves such activities as a surprise cash count or procedures related to suspected fraud.

   c. If the results of a preliminary survey and limited testing reveal no deficiencies, the internal audit activity should send a memorandum communication to the client summarizing the preliminary survey results and indicating that the engagement has been canceled.

3. **Interim Communication**

   a. Interim (progress) communications provide a prompt means of documenting a situation requiring immediate action.

      1) They are preliminary and should indicate that

         a) Only current information, that is, an incomplete study, is the basis for such communications.

         b) The final engagement communication will follow up on the topics covered.

      2) Progress communications prepared by the internal audit staff should be reviewed by the chief audit executive or other supervisory personnel.

   3) Progress communications about deficiency observations should have the same structure as communications on observations. Deficiencies are described in records of engagement observations and are communicated to management in the form of a single-page executive summary.

   4) Progress communications also may be used to report the status of long, sensitive, or otherwise special engagements to the clients and senior management.

  b. **Interim reports** (oral or written) transmitted formally or informally communicate

   1) Information needing immediate attention,

   2) A change in the scope of the engagement, or

   3) The progress of a long-duration engagement.

  c. The use of interim reports does not reduce or eliminate the need for a final report.

Stop and review! You have completed the outline for this subunit. Study multiple-choice questions 1 and 2 on page 211.

9.2 OBSERVATIONS AND RECOMMENDATIONS

1. After identifying, analyzing, evaluating, and documenting engagement information, the internal auditor makes observations and forms conclusions about the engagement objectives based on the information.

  a. Recommendations are based on observations and conclusions and may be general or specific. They are made to enhance and protect organizational value. Specifically, they call for action to correct existing conditions or improve operations and may suggest approaches to correcting or enhancing performance as a guide for management in achieving desired results.

  NOTE: The word "findings" is often used as a synonym for "observations" on the CIA exam.

2. **Four Attributes of Observations and Recommendations**

  a. Observations and recommendations result from comparing criteria (the correct state) with condition (the current state). When conditions meet the criteria, communication of satisfactory performance may be appropriate. Observations and recommendations are based on the following attributes:

   1) **Criteria** are the standards, measures, or expectations used in making an evaluation or verification (the correct state). Examples of criteria for evaluating operations include

    a) Organizational policies and procedures delegating authority and assigning responsibilities,

    b) Textbook illustrations of generally accepted practices, and

    c) Codification of best practices in similar organizations.

   2) The **condition** is the factual evidence that the internal auditor found in the examination (the current state).

   3) The **cause** is the reason for the difference between expected and actual conditions.

    a) A recommendation in a final engagement communication should address the cause attribute.

   4) The **effect** is the risk or exposure the organization or others encounter because the condition is not consistent with the criteria (the impact of the difference).

    a) In determining the risk or exposure, internal auditors consider the effect their observations and recommendations may have on the organization's operations and financial statements.

  b. Observations and recommendations also may include client accomplishments, related issues, and supportive information.

3. **Favorable observations** should be short and simple. For example, "Production schedules, levels, and quality were at or ahead of budgeted levels in every case."

4. **Unfavorable observations** need further explanation to justify recommended changes. The following are examples:

   a. **Summary**

      1) Because of inaccurate inventory records, the supply department bought unneeded supplies costing US $75,000.

   b. **Criteria**

      1) Established procedures provide that excess materials returned by the production department shall be entered on the records of the supply department to show the levels of inventory currently on hand and available for issuance.

   c. **Condition (facts)**

      1) Our tests disclosed that, for a period of 6 months, supplies returned from production had not been entered on the supply department's records.

   d. **Cause**

      1) We found that the employees responsible for the posting of returned supplies had not been instructed in their duties. In addition, supervisors had not been monitoring the process.

   e. **Effect**

      1) As a result of the inaccurate inventory records, the organization bought unneeded supplies costing about US $75,000.

   f. **Recommendation**

      1) We reviewed the conditions with the manager of the supply department, and he agreed to bring the inventory records up to date, issue job instructions to the workers spelling out the need to record returned supplies, and instruct supervisors to monitor the process in the future and to submit written reports on their periodic reviews.

   g. **Corrective action taken**

      1) Before we concluded our examination, the manager took all three steps. Our subsequent spot checks showed that the action was effective. We therefore consider this observation closed.

Stop and review! You have completed the outline for this subunit. Study multiple-choice questions 3 through 6 beginning on page 211.

9.3 COMMUNICATING ENGAGEMENT RESULTS

1. **Final Engagement Communication**

   a. Internal auditors are expected to make known the results of their work.

> **Performance Standard 2400**
> **Communicating Results**
>
> Internal auditors must communicate the results of engagements.

   b. The CAE, auditor-in-charge of the engagement, or other auditor with sufficient experience communicates results to the engagement client.

   c. The IIA provides specific criteria to be included with the results of engagements.

Performance Standard 2410
Criteria for Communicating

Communications must include the engagement's objectives, scope, and results.

Implementation Standard 2410.A1

Final communication of engagement results must include applicable conclusions, as well as applicable recommendations and/or action plans. Where appropriate, the internal auditors' opinion should be provided. An opinion must take into account the expectations of senior management, the board, and other stakeholders and must be supported by sufficient, reliable, relevant, and useful information.

---

d. According to IG 2410, *Criteria for Communicating*, planning of the final communication includes consideration of all discussions with management of the area audited.

　　1) Thus, the final engagement communication should consider client responses to audit observations that are received before the final communication has been issued.

e. Specific guidance on the elements of final communications is provided below.

　　1) A final communication may vary by organization or type of engagement. However, it contains at least the purpose, scope, and results of the engagement.

　　2) A final communication may include background information, such as activities reviewed and the status of observations, conclusions, recommendations from prior reports, and summaries of the communication's content.

　　3) **Purpose** statements describe the objectives and may explain why the engagement was conducted and what it was expected to achieve.

　　4) **Scope** statements identify the audited activities and may include the time period reviewed and related activities not reviewed to define the engagement. They also may describe the nature and extent of engagement work.

　　5) **Results** include observations, conclusions, opinions, recommendations, and action plans.

　　6) **Observations** (findings) are relevant statements of fact. A final communication contains those observations necessary for understanding the conclusions and recommendations. Less significant matters may be communicated informally.

　　7) **Conclusions and opinions** are evaluations of the effects of the observations and recommendations. They are clearly identified. Conclusions may address the entire engagement scope or specific aspects. They may cover (but are not limited to) whether

　　　　a) Operating or program objectives conform with the organization's,

　　　　b) Those objectives are being met, and

　　　　c) The activity under review is functioning as intended.

　　8) An overall opinion on the engagement is **not mandatory**. An opinion should only be included when it is appropriate, for example, when it improves communication with the users of the reports.

　　　　a) An opinion may include an overall assessment of controls or be limited to specific controls or aspects of the engagement.

　　9) The internal auditor reaches agreement with the client about results and any necessary plan of corrective action. Disagreements are fully disclosed, including both positions and the reasons.

　　　　a) The client's comments about results may be presented in the report.

10) A signed report is issued at the end of the engagement.

    a) Summary reports, which provide highlights of the engagement results, are appropriate for levels above the client. They may be issued separately from, or with, the final communication.

    b) The auditor authorized to sign is designated by the CAE.

    c) If reports are distributed electronically, the internal audit activity keeps a signed report on file.

        i) The term "signed" means a manual or electronic signature in the report or on a cover letter.

Implementation Standard 2410.A2

Internal auditors are encouraged to acknowledge satisfactory performance in engagement communications.

---

f. Internal auditors should provide positive feedback to engagement clients when appropriate. This practice helps to develop good relations with clients and may improve their receptiveness to the audit findings.

g. Additionally, client accomplishments included in the final communication may be necessary to present fairly the existing conditions and provide perspective and balance.

Stop and review! You have completed the outline for this subunit. Study multiple-choice questions 7 through 9 beginning on page 213.

9.4 COMMUNICATION QUALITIES AND OVERALL OPINIONS

1. **Definitions of the Qualities of Communications**

Performance Standard 2420
Quality of Communications

Communications must be accurate, objective, clear, concise, constructive, complete, and timely.

---

a. The IIA issued an Interpretation of the Performance Standard above to define each quality.

Interpretation of Standard 2420

- Accurate communications are free from errors and distortions and are faithful to the underlying facts.
- Objective communications are fair, impartial, and unbiased and are the result of a fair-minded and balanced assessment of all relevant facts and circumstances.
- Clear communications are easily understood and logical, avoiding unnecessary technical language and providing all significant and relevant information.
- Concise communications are to the point and avoid unnecessary elaboration, superfluous detail, redundancy, and wordiness.
- Constructive communications are helpful to the engagement client and the organization and lead to improvements where needed.
- Complete communications lack nothing that is essential to the target audience and include all significant and relevant information and observations to support recommendations and conclusions.
- Timely communications are opportune and expedient, depending on the significance of the issue, allowing management to take appropriate corrective action.

---

    b.   Consistent with the *Standards* and IG 2420, *Quality of Communications*, the following are characteristics of high-quality communications:

        1)   Data and evidence are processed with care and precision.

        2)   Observations, conclusions, and recommendations are unbiased.

        3)   Unnecessary technical language is avoided, and context for all significant and relevant information is provided.

        4)   Communications are meaningful but concise.

        5)   The content and tone are useful and positive, and objectives are focused.

        6)   Communications are consistent with the entity's style and culture.

        7)   Results are not unduly delayed.

2.   **Other Characteristics of Effective Communications**

    a.   The presentation should be **coherent**, that is, logically ordered and integrated.

    b.   Sentences should be short and use simple but appropriate vocabulary.

    c.   Good writing is **consistent**. Inconsistent style, sentence structure, format, and vocabulary are confusing.

    d.   Active-voice verbs are generally (not always) preferable to passive-voice verbs. The active voice is more concise, vivid, and interesting.

    e.   The Seven Seas (7 Cs) is a useful memory aid. Good writing is

        1)   Clear.

        2)   Correct (accurate and objective).

        3)   Concise.

        4)   Consistent.

        5)   Constructive.

        6)   Coherent.

        7)   Complete and timely.

    f.   Emphasis

        1)   Successful communication between the internal auditor and the engagement client partially depends on achieving appropriate emphasis. Both parties should be aware of the most important points in their discussion.

        2)   Graphic illustrations (e.g., pictures, charts, or graphs), oral and written repetition (e.g., summaries) and itemized lists (bulleted or numbered) are good ways of emphasizing information.

        3)   Using audiovisual aids to support a discussion of major points results in the most retention of information. One study concluded that 85% of the information presented in this way will be remembered after 3 hours, and 65% after 3 days.

    g.   Word selection (diction) can affect the recipient of an engagement communication in either written or oral form.

        1)   In general, language should be fact-based and neutral. But if the internal auditor's objective is to persuade an individual to accept recommendations, words with strong or emotional connotations should be used.

            a)   However, words that are connotation-rich have strong but unpredictable effects. A common example is using the word "fraud" rather than the more neutral "irregularity."

        2)   Using too strong a word or a word inappropriate for the particular recipient may induce an unwanted response. Thus, high-connotation language should be chosen carefully to appeal to the specific recipient.

3.   **Errors and Omissions**

Performance Standard 2421
Errors and Omissions

If a final communication contains a significant error or omission, the chief audit executive must communicate corrected information to all parties who received the original communication.

---

    a.   The correction of an error or omission in an internal audit communication need not be in written form.

4.   **The Conformance Phrase**

Performance Standard 2430
Use of "Conducted in Conformance with the *International Standards for the Professional Practice of Internal Auditing*"

Indicating that engagements are "conducted in conformance with the *International Standards for the Professional Practice of Internal Auditing*" is appropriate only if supported by the results of the quality assurance and improvement program.

---

5.   **Nonconformance**

Performance Standard 2431
Engagement Disclosure of Nonconformance

When nonconformance with the Code of Ethics or the *Standards* impacts a specific engagement, communication of the results must disclose the:

● Principle(s) or rule(s) of conduct of the Code of Ethics or Standard(s) with which full conformance was not achieved.

● Reason(s) for nonconformance.

● Impact of nonconformance on the engagement and the communicated engagement results.

---

6.   **Overall Opinions**

    a.   In contrast to an engagement opinion, an overall opinion considers multiple engagements. The IIA Glossary defines an overall opinion as follows:

The rating, conclusion, and/or other description of results provided by the chief audit executive addressing, at a broad level, governance, risk management, and/or control processes of the organization. An overall opinion is the professional judgment of the chief audit executive based on the results of a number of individual engagements and other activities for a specific time interval.

Performance Standard 2450
Overall Opinions

When an overall opinion is issued, it must take into account the strategies, objectives, and risks of the organization; and the expectations of senior management, the board, and other stakeholders. The overall opinion must be supported by sufficient, reliable, relevant, and useful information.

> ### Interpretation of Standard 2450
>
> The communication will include:
>
> - The scope, including the time period to which the opinion pertains.
> - Scope limitations.
> - Consideration of all related projects, including the reliance on other assurance providers.
> - A summary of the information that supports the opinion.
> - The risk or control framework or other criteria used as a basis for the overall opinion.
> - The overall opinion, judgment, or conclusion reached.
>
> The reasons for an unfavorable overall opinion must be stated.

    b.   The outline in this section is based on Practice Guide, *Formulating and Expressing Internal Audit Opinions.*

    c.   Internal auditors may be asked by stakeholders to express macro opinions or micro opinions, depending on the scope of the engagement.

        1)   The assurance for the organization as a whole is a **macro opinion**. It is usually based on multiple audit projects. For example, a macro opinion may be expressed on

            a)   The overall system of internal control over financial reporting

            b)   Controls over compliance with laws and regulations, such as health and safety, when they are performed in multiple countries or subsidiaries

            c)   Controls, such as budgeting and performance management, when they are performed in multiple subsidiaries and coverage extends to the majority of assets, revenues, etc.

        2)   The assurance for a component of operations is a **micro opinion**. It is usually based on one or a few audit projects. For example, a micro opinion may be expressed on

            a)   An individual business process or activity in one organization, department, or location.

            b)   Internal control at a reporting unit when all work is performed in one audit.

            c)   Compliance with policies, laws, and regulations regarding data privacy when the work is performed in one or a few business units.

        3)   The need for audit opinions and the ability to express them depends on, among other things,

            a)   The needs of stakeholders;

            b)   The scope, nature, timing, and extent of audit work;

            c)   The sufficiency of resources to complete the work; and

            d)   Assessing the results.

    d.   **Stakeholder requirements** for opinions should be clarified by the CAE with senior management and the board. Thus, the nature of the service to be performed should be determined prior to the engagement.

        1)   Discussions with stakeholders about an opinion may include

            a)   Why it is being requested.

            b)   The timing for issuance and type of opinion.

            c)   The form of opinion (e.g., written or verbal).

            d)   The level of assurance.

            e)   The period covered.

            f)   The scope (e.g., whether it is limited to operational controls).

                i)   The scope definition commonly extends to (a) the parts of the entity covered, (b) controls addressed, and (c) the time period or moment in time for which the opinion is expressed.

g) Suitable criteria to be used, i.e., a framework of factors relevant to the auditee against which outcomes may be measured.

   i) The internal audit activity determines whether the entity has identified appropriate governance, risk management, and control practices. Thus, the auditee should provide a statement of risk tolerance or risk appetite and materiality thresholds. Without these principles, an opinion should not be expressed.

h) Potential users.

e. The following are factors that affect the expression of an opinion.

   1) The characteristics of macro and micro opinions.
   2) Whether positive or negative assurance will be expressed.
   3) The purpose and use of any special requests.
   4) The audit evidence to support the opinion and the time required for the work.
   5) Agreement with stakeholders on the criteria used.
   6) The need to develop an approach to provide sufficient, relevant evidence. This approach may combine the results of previous audits or identify areas of significance and risk.

      a) If multiple projects are required, they should be identified.

   7) The consideration of related projects (including reliance on the work of others or self-assessments) and allowing time for the final assessment.
   8) Whether resources and skills are adequate. If not, the auditor may (a) decline to express the opinion or (b) qualify the opinion (by excluding certain areas or risks from the scope).

      a) Discussions with management and communication of the plan, including its timing and scope and the criteria to be used.

f. **Evaluating results** of audit work completed may involve rating individual audit findings and their significance relative to a project, risk category, or the organization as a whole.

   1) The auditor considers the magnitude or significance (materiality) of a key business objective that is fundamental to the opinion, including the residual risk that it will not be achieved.
   2) The implications of audit issues or findings (impact) are considered and understood in the context of the opinion to be given (micro or macro).
   3) Another factor to be considered in a macro opinion is rating the risks that the controls in place will not permit management's objectives to be achieved.

g. The **use of grades** in expressing an opinion requires careful wording, particularly terms such as "adequate" or "inadequate" and "satisfactory" or "unsatisfactory." Wording should be clear and well defined.

   1) General terms may not sufficiently define the meaning. For example, the term "effective" usually refers to effectiveness in design and operation. The opinion needs to indicate whether both meanings are included.
   2) Clarity is improved if the organization has adopted a broadly understood definition of internal controls, such as the COSO model.
   3) Use of a grading scale generally requires a well-defined evaluation structure. For example, an opinion may state how much better or worse controls are than a defined benchmark.
   4) Increased precision in the information provided in an opinion normally increases the amount of evidence needed to support the opinion.

    h.   Macro opinions are generally in writing and in the form of **positive assurance**.

        1)   The CAE provides macro opinions because (s)he has an overview of micro audit results.

        2)   Positive assurance (reasonable assurance) is the highest level and requires the highest level of evidence.

            a)   The assertion may be binary, for example, that controls are (are not) effective, or risks are (are not) effectively managed.

        3)   Variations in positive assurance may include the use of commonly understood grades of the effectiveness of control or risk management.

            a)   Examples include color coding (red-yellow-green) or a grading scale (1 to 4).

        4)   A **qualified opinion** indicates an exception to the general opinion, for example, that controls were satisfactory with the exception of accounts payable controls.

    i.   **Negative assurance**, sometimes referred to as limited assurance, is a statement that nothing came to the auditor's attention about an objective, such as the effectiveness of internal control or adequacy of a risk management process.

        1)   The internal auditor takes no responsibility for the sufficiency of the audit scope and procedures.

        2)   Occasionally, internal auditing may be asked for an informal opinion (oral opinion) on the adequacy of governance, risk management, or control policies and processes, either at the macro or micro level.

            a)   If possible, the expression of such an opinion should be based on objective evidence.

            b)   The same factors are considered as in expressing a written opinion.

            c)   In some instances, internal auditing should decline to issue an oral opinion, especially given a lack of sufficient evidence or work to support the opinion.

    j.   If the CAE intends to rely on the **work of others**, appropriate steps should be taken, including assessing the competency, independence, and objectivity of the other assurance providers.

        1)   Such reliance should be included in discussions with key stakeholders and, if significant, the board.

    k.   The use of opinions has **legal** significance because of the increased reliance on internal audit reports. However, reliance might result in legal liability if a control failure is discussed after issuance of the report. Moreover, the CAE's certification credentials may have legal implications if noncompliance issues arise.

        1)   Thus, the CAE should use appropriate language in the report and provide a disclaimer that notifies the reader of any limitations on the assurance given.

            a)   The CAE should state that it is not possible to provide absolute assurance and should encourage readers to consider all legal implications.

Stop and review! You have completed the outline for this subunit. Study multiple-choice questions 10 and 11 on page 214.

9.5 EXIT CONFERENCE AND MANAGEMENT'S RESPONSE

1. **Exit Conferences**

   a. Internal auditors discuss observations, conclusions, and recommendations with engagement clients and appropriate levels of management before the CAE issues the final communication. The discussion usually occurs during the engagement or at post-engagement (exit) conferences.

      1) Internal auditors are in charge of the exit conference and therefore should lead the discussions.

      2) The conference participants should include representatives from management who have detailed knowledge about the process or area under review and who can authorize implementation of corrective action.

   b. The primary purpose of an exit conference is to present audit findings (i.e., observations, conclusions, and recommendations). Secondary purposes are, among others, to

      1) Improve relations with the engagement client(s).

      2) Review and verify the appropriateness of the engagement communication based upon client input, which ensures the accuracy of the information used by internal auditors.

      3) Resolve conflicts.

      4) Identify management's actions and responses or generate commitment for appropriate managerial action.

      5) Enhance the effectiveness of internal auditing engagements.

   c. The internal auditor should document the exit conference because the information may be needed if a dispute later arises.

2. **Management's Review and Response**

   a. Reviews of drafts of communications with engagement clients (management or others) are a courtesy to them and a form of insurance for the engagement.

   b. Clients may have discussed all such matters during the engagement. They should be given the opportunity to read what will be sent to their superiors. Moreover, seeing the draft report may cause clients to view the results differently.

   c. Reviewing results in draft form with the client may detect omissions or inaccuracies before the final communication is issued.

      1) Documenting these discussions and reviews can be valuable in preventing or resolving disputes.

   d. The auditor carefully considers the following before the review:

      1) The person(s) with whom the draft should be reviewed.

      2) The feasibility of performing some reviews on a group basis.

      3) The timing and order of the reviews.

      4) Sending the draft to the client before the meeting.

      5) The need for face-to-face discussions. Sending copies of the draft to interested parties and receiving their written comments may be sufficient.

   e. The auditor should be prepared for conflicts and questions.

      1) When the auditor has previously experienced difficulty with an individual, that individual's superior may be invited to attend.

      2) To be able to answer questions promptly, the auditor may wish to prepare notes.

      3) The auditor should be flexible on matters not affecting the substance of the matters communicated. However, the focus of discussions should always remain on the substantive issues.

         a) Additionally, the auditor should never negotiate the opinion.

f.   Disagreements are explained in the engagement communications.

g.   When the reviews result in significant changes, the other people with whom the draft was reviewed should have an opportunity to see, or be told of, the revisions.

h.   The auditor maintains careful records of the post-engagement meeting, of any objections, and of the manner in which conflicts were resolved.

i.   When copies of the draft are sent to concerned parties for review, the auditor

1) Asks for the timely return of the draft with any appropriate comments.
2) Sets a specific due date for the return of the draft.
3) Offers to meet with those who wish to discuss the draft further.

j.   Responses by clients about internal auditors' actions should go to both management and the internal auditors to ensure the accountability of the internal audit activity. This process is a way of

1) Judging the internal auditors' performance,
2) Improving future engagements by identifying areas of weak performance,
3) Bettering internal auditor-client relations through a greater sense of participation,
4) Minimizing conflicts, and
5) Helping clients to understand the difficulties faced by the internal auditors.

Stop and review! You have completed the outline for this subunit. Study multiple-choice question 12 on page 215.

9.6   APPROVE AND DISTRIBUTE REPORTS

> **Performance Standard 2440**
> **Disseminating Results**
>
> The chief audit executive must communicate results to the appropriate parties.

> **Interpretation of Standard 2440**
>
> The chief audit executive is responsible for reviewing and approving the final engagement communication before issuance and for deciding to whom and how it will be disseminated. When the chief audit executive delegates these duties, he or she retains overall responsibility.

1.   **Disseminating Results**

a.   Generally, final communications are distributed to persons having a business need for the results or responsibility for action plans. They include persons able to ensure due consideration of engagement results, that is, those who can take corrective action or ensure that it is taken. Organizational protocol also may dictate recipients.

1) The board ordinarily receives summary reports only.
2) Each communication should contain a distribution sheet listing the distributees and indicating with whom it has been reviewed in draft. Distributees may include the following:

a) The executive to whom the internal audit activity reports
b) The person or persons to whom replies will be addressed
c) Persons responsible for the activity or activities reviewed, e.g., auditee management
d) Persons required to take corrective action

b.   Results may be communicated orally or in writing, with the format varying with the recipient.

2. **Sensitive Information**

   a. The auditors may possess critically sensitive and substantial information with significant potential adverse consequences. If the new information is substantial and credible, the auditors normally communicate it on a timely basis to senior management and the board.

      1) The communication is typically through the internal audit activity's usual chain of command, i.e., from staff to supervisor to chief audit executive.

   b. If the CAE then concludes that senior management is exposing the organization to unacceptable risk and is not taking appropriate action, (s)he presents the information and differences of opinion to the board.

   c. Laws, regulations, or common practices may require immediate reporting of sensitive occurrences, e.g., fraudulent financial reporting or illegal acts, to the board.

   d. Auditors may need to consider communicating outside the chain of command or the organization (internal or external whistleblowing, respectively).

      1) Most whistleblowers act internally. However, those who act outside the organization typically mistrust its response, fear retaliation, or have health or safety concerns.

         a) If an internal auditor elects internal whistleblowing, (s)he must cautiously evaluate the evidence, the reasonableness of the conclusions, and the merits of possible actions. Such action may be appropriate if it results in responsible action by senior management or the board.

      2) The decision to communicate outside the chain of command should be based on a well-informed opinion that the wrongdoing is supported by the evidence and that a legal, professional, or ethical obligation requires action.

         a) The auditor must make a professional decision about his or her obligation to the employer.

   e. Public servants may be required to report illegal or unethical acts, and some laws protect citizen whistleblowers. Thus, auditors need to be aware of applicable laws and must obtain legal advice if uncertain of legal requirements or consequences.

      1) Members of The IIA and CIAs also follow the provisions of The IIA's Code of Ethics.

      2) An auditor's professional duty and ethical responsibility is to evaluate the evidence and the reasonableness of his or her conclusions. The auditor then decides whether further actions may be needed to protect

         a) The organization,
         b) Its stakeholders,
         c) The outside community, or
         d) The institutions of society.

      3) The auditor also needs to consider the duty of confidentiality. The advice of legal counsel and other experts may be needed.

   f. Information that is privileged, proprietary, or related to improper or illegal acts is disclosed in a separate communication and distributed to the board.

      1) If senior management is involved, report distribution is to the board.

3. **Communications Outside the Organization**

Implementation Standard 2440.A2

If not otherwise mandated by legal, statutory, or regulatory requirements, prior to releasing results to parties outside the organization the chief audit executive must:

- Assess the potential risk to the organization.
- Consult with senior management and/or legal counsel as appropriate.
- Control dissemination by restricting the use of the results.

---

    a. Auditors review guidance for disseminating information outside the organization. Such information could affect the organization's market value, reputation, earnings, or competitiveness. If guidance does not exist, auditors facilitate adoption of policies. These policies address

        1) Authorization requirements,

        2) The approval process,

        3) Guidelines for types of information that may be reported,

        4) Authorized recipients and what they may receive,

        5) Legal considerations, and

        6) Other information includible in outside communications (e.g., nature of assurance, opinions, guidance, advice, or recommendations).

    b. Requests for existing information are reviewed to determine its suitability for disclosure. A request for information that must be created or determined results in a new internal audit engagement.

        1) It may be possible to create a special-purpose report based on existing information that is suitable for outside disclosure.

    c. Outside dissemination considers

        1) The need for a written agreement;

        2) Identifying persons related to the report or information;

        3) Identification of objectives, scope, and procedures;

        4) Nature of the report or other communication; and

        5) Copyright issues.

    d. The internal auditor may discover information reportable to senior management or the board during an engagement that requires outside disclosure. As a result, the CAE needs to communicate suitably to the board.

    e. Engagements to generate internal audit reports or communications outside the organization need to be conducted in accordance with applicable standards. The report or other communication should refer to such standards.

EXAMPLE

An internal auditor discovered fraud committed by members of management and is unsure of whom to disclose this information.

In most cases of whistleblowing, whistleblowers will disclose sensitive information internally, even if not within the normal chain of command. If they trust the policies and mechanisms of the organization to investigate the problem, information can be shared with the appropriate internal parties. However, if the whistleblower doubts the problem will be properly investigated by the corporation, (s)he may consider disclosing the problem to an outside party.

Stop and review! You have completed the outline for this subunit. Study multiple-choice questions 13 through 16 beginning on page 215.

9.7 MONITOR ENGAGEMENT OUTCOMES

Performance Standard 2500
Monitoring Progress

The chief audit executive must establish and maintain a system to monitor the disposition of results communicated to management.

---

1. **Monitor Outcomes**

   a. Further guidance is provided in IG 2500, *Monitoring Progress*.

      1) In establishing and maintaining a monitoring system for engagement results, the CAE first considers the type of information and the detail the board and senior management expect.

      2) The CAE is guided by professional judgment and the expectations of the board and senior management in determining the timing and means of monitoring.

      3) At a minimum, the system should include recording (a) pertinent observations, (b) corrective action, and (c) current status.

         a) The factors that influence the nature of monitoring include the organization's size and complexity and the availability of exception tracking software.

   b. Specific characteristics of monitoring processes may include the following:

      1) The CAE establishes procedures to monitor the disposition of reported results. They include a(n)

         a) Time frame for management's response,

         b) Evaluation and verification of the response (if appropriate),

         c) Follow-up (if appropriate), and

         d) Communications process that reports unsatisfactory responses (including assumption of risk) to the appropriate senior management or the board.

      2) Observations and recommendations needing immediate action are monitored until correction or implementation, respectively.

      3) Observations and recommendations are addressed to managers responsible for corrective action.

      4) Management responses and action plans are received and evaluated during the engagement or within a reasonable time afterward. Responses need to be sufficient for the CAE to evaluate the adequacy and timeliness of proposed actions.

      5) The internal audit activity receives periodic updates from management to evaluate the status of its efforts to correct observations or implement recommendations.

      6) Information from other units involved in follow-up or correction is received and evaluated.

      7) The status of responses is reported to senior management or the board.

2. **Follow-Up Process**

Implementation Standard 2500.A1

The chief audit executive must establish a follow-up process to monitor and ensure that management actions have been effectively implemented or that senior management has accepted the risk of not taking action.

---

    a.   Follow-up is the element of monitoring that evaluates the adequacy, effectiveness, and timeliness of actions on reported observations and recommendations, including those by other auditors.

        1)   The **internal audit activity charter** defines the responsibility for follow-up. The CAE defines its nature, timing, and extent after considering the

               a)   Significance of what is reported,
               b)   Effort and cost of correction,
               c)   Effect of failure of correction,
               d)   Complexity of correction, and
               e)   Time period involved.

        2)   The CAE includes follow-up as part of the work schedule. Scheduling depends on the risk involved and the difficulty and timing of corrective action.

        3)   If action already taken suffices, follow-up may be part of the next engagement.

        4)   Auditors verify that actions remedy underlying conditions.

        5)   Follow-up should be documented.

        6)   Follow-up also includes determining whether senior management or the board has assumed the risk of not taking corrective action on reported observations.

    b.   The following is a more detailed description of the follow-up process:

        1)   The internal auditor should

               a)   Receive all replies by the engagement client to the engagement communications

               b)   Evaluate the adequacy of those replies

               c)   Be convinced that the action taken will cure the defects

        2)   The internal auditor is in the best position to carry out the follow-up responsibility. (S)he is

               a)   Better acquainted with the facts than senior management or other control centers in the organization

               b)   More objective than the operating manager who must take the corrective action

        3)   The responsibility for determining whether corrective action is adequate should include the authority to evaluate the adequacy of replies to engagement communications. The internal auditor should

               a)   Report to management when corrective actions are not timely or effective.

               b)   Submit periodic reports to management on open engagement observations and recommendations.

        4)   The adequacy of a response depends on the circumstances in each case. In general, a satisfactory response

               a)   Addresses itself to the complete problem, not just to specific items included in the internal auditor's sample.

               b)   Shows that action also has been taken to prevent a recurrence of the deficient condition.

    5)   In evaluating the reply, the internal auditor should be satisfied that the action promised is actually taken. The auditor should

        a)   Obtain copies of revised procedures issued to correct conditions.

        b)   Make any field tests needed to provide assurance that the condition has been corrected.

    6)   A formal system should be designed to keep engagements open until adequate corrective action is assured. For example,

        a)   Provisions should be made for the formal opening and closing of engagements.

        b)   The internal auditors should issue a formal statement of closure, supported by copies of replies to engagement communications and explanations of the action taken to ensure the adequacy and effectiveness of corrective measures.

           i)   Closure reports are directed to the chief audit executive.

        c)   Engagements should not be removed from the internal audit activity's open engagements listing until all required corrective actions have been taken and evaluated.

3.   **Acceptance of Excessive Risk**

    a.   The CAE is responsible for assessing the risk that remains after client management has taken action, or no action, to reduce its severity (i.e., residual risk).

Performance Standard 2600
<u>Communicating the Acceptance of Risks</u>

When the chief audit executive concludes that management has accepted a level of risk that may be unacceptable to the organization, the chief audit executive must discuss the matter with senior management. If the chief audit executive determines that the matter has not been resolved, the chief audit executive must communicate the matter to the board.

Interpretation of Standard 2600

The identification of risk accepted by management may be observed through an assurance or consulting engagement, monitoring progress on actions taken by management as a result of prior engagements, or other means. It is not the responsibility of the chief audit executive to resolve the risk.

---

    b.   Management decides the action to be taken in response to engagement results. The CAE assesses this action for timely resolution. The extent of follow-up also is a function of follow-up work done by others.

    c.   Senior management may assume the risk of noncorrection. The decisions on all significant engagement observations and recommendations are reported to the board.

Stop and review! You have completed the outline for this subunit. Study multiple-choice questions 17 through 20 beginning on page 216.

QUESTIONS

9.1 Communication with Clients

1. You are conducting an engagement to evaluate the organization's marketing effort. You agreed to keep the marketing vice president informed of your progress on a regular basis. What method should be used for those progress reports?

    A. Oral or written interim reports.

    B. Written reports signed by the chief audit executive.

    C. Copies of working paper summaries.

    D. Briefing by the appropriate marketing first-line supervisor.

Answer (A) is correct.
    REQUIRED: The method of progress reporting.
    DISCUSSION: Interim reports are oral or written and may be transmitted formally or informally. Interim reports are used to communicate information that requires immediate attention, to communicate a change in engagement scope for the activity under review, or to keep management informed of engagement progress when engagements extend over a long period.
    Answer (B) is incorrect. An oral report is acceptable. Answer (C) is incorrect. Engagement communications, not workpapers, should be submitted to engagement clients. Answer (D) is incorrect. The internal auditors, not a marketing supervisor, should submit engagement communications.

2. Which of the following are valid reasons to submit an interim report?

1. Communicating a change in engagement scope.
2. Updating management on progress during a long engagement.
3. Informing management of significant matters, even if unrelated to the engagement.
4. Addressing audit findings that will be excluded from the final report.

    A. 1 and 2 only.

    B. 1, 2, and 3 only.

    C. 3 and 4 only.

    D. 1, 2, 3, and 4.

Answer (B) is correct.
    REQUIRED: The valid reasons to submit an interim report.
    DISCUSSION: An interim report (oral or written) should be transmitted formally or informally to communicate (1) a change in the scope of the engagement, (2) the progress of a long-duration engagement, and (3) information needing immediate attention (even if not related to engagement objectives).
    Answer (A) is incorrect. Informing management of significant matters, even if unrelated to the engagement, also is a valid reason for submitting an interim report. Answer (C) is incorrect. Addressing audit findings to be excluded from the final report is not a valid reason for submitting an interim report. Thus, some less significant matters resolved during the engagement may be excluded from the final report. But all matters should be documented in the workpapers. Answer (D) is incorrect. Addressing audit findings to be excluded from the final report is not a valid reason for submitting an interim report. Thus, some less significant matters resolved during the engagement may be excluded from the final report. But all matters should be documented in the workpapers.

9.2 Observations and Recommendations

3. An engagement communication relating to an engagement performed at a bank categorizes observations as "deficiencies" for major problems and "other areas for improvement" for less serious problems. Which of the following excerpts is properly included under "other areas for improvement?"

    A. Many secured loans did not contain hazard insurance coverage for tangible property collateral.

    B. Loan officers also prepare the cashier's checks for disbursement of the loan proceeds.

    C. The bank is incurring unnecessary postage cost by not combining certain special mailings to checking account customers with the monthly mailing of their statements.

    D. At one branch a large amount of cash was placed on a portable table behind the teller lines.

Answer (C) is correct.
    REQUIRED: The excerpt properly included under "other areas for improvement" in an engagement communication.
    DISCUSSION: The attributes of engagement observations include effect, the risk or exposure, because the condition is inconsistent with the criteria. Moreover, the internal auditor must determine the degree of the risk or exposure. That the bank incurs unnecessary postage expense by not combining mailings warrants mentioning but does not constitute a serious risk or exposure.
    Answer (A) is incorrect. A lack of hazard insurance coverage for collateral is a serious risk or exposure for the bank that could have a material effect on its financial statements. Answer (B) is incorrect. Loan officers should not be permitted to prepare disbursement checks and grant loans to bank customers. These are duties that must be segregated to prevent possible employee defalcations. Answer (D) is incorrect. Failure to limit access to cash violates internal control policies assigning cash to specific individuals for accountability purposes.

4. While performing an operational engagement involving the firm's production cycle, an internal auditor discovers that, in the absence of specific guidelines, some engineers and buyers routinely accept vacation trips paid by certain of the firm's vendors. Other engineers and buyers will not accept even a working lunch paid for by a vendor. Which of the following actions should the internal auditor take?

A. None. The engineers and buyers are professionals. An internal auditor should not inappropriately interfere in what is essentially a personal decision.

B. Informally counsel the engineers and buyers who accept the vacation trips. This helps prevent the possibility of kickbacks, while preserving good internal auditor-engagement client relations.

C. Formally recommend that the organization establish a code of ethics. Guidelines of acceptable conduct, within which individual decisions may be made, should be provided.

D. Issue a formal engagement communication naming the personnel who accept vacations but make no recommendations. Corrective action is the responsibility of management.

Answer (C) is correct.
REQUIRED: The internal auditor's action upon discovering an absence of guidelines regarding employee-vendor relations.
DISCUSSION: The internal auditor may communicate recommendations for improvements, acknowledgments of satisfactory performance, and corrective actions. Recommendations are based on the internal auditor's observations and conclusions. They call for action to correct existing conditions or improve operations and may suggest approaches to correcting or enhancing performance as a guide for management in achieving desired results. Recommendations can be general or specific. Accordingly, the internal auditor's responsibility in these circumstances is to recommend adoption of a code of ethics.
Answer (A) is incorrect. Internal auditors are charged with the responsibility of evaluating what they examine and of making recommendations, if appropriate. Answer (B) is incorrect. Management is charged with the responsibility of making any corrections necessary within its department. Answer (D) is incorrect. Internal auditors should make recommendations if appropriate.

Question 5 is based on the following information. This information is to be included in a final communication made following an inventory control engagement for a tent and awning manufacturer. The issue relates to overstocked rope.

1. The quantity on hand at the time of the engagement represented a 10-year supply based on normal usage.
2. The organization had held an open house of its new factory 2 months prior to the engagement and had used the rope to provide safety corridors through the plant for visitors. This was not considered when placing the last purchase order.
3. Rope is reordered when the inventory level reaches a 1-month supply and is based on usage during the previous 12 months.
4. The quantity to be ordered should be adequate to cover expected usage for the next 6 months.
5. The purchasing department should review inventory usage and inquire about any unusual fluctuations before placing an order.
6. A public warehouse was required to store the rope.
7. The purchasing agent receives an annual salary of US $59,000.

---

5. Which of these statements should be in the effect section of the communication?

A. 2 only.

B. 3 only.

C. 5 only.

D. 6 only.

Answer (D) is correct.
REQUIRED: The statement that should be included in the effect section of the finding.
DISCUSSION: The effect attribute states the risk or exposure the organization and/or others encounter because the condition is not consistent with the criteria (the impact of the difference). In determining the degree of risk or exposure, internal auditors consider the effect their engagement observations and recommendations may have on the organization's operations and financial statements. Only statement 6 describes the negative results of the situation as it is.
Answer (A) is incorrect. Statement 2 should be in the cause section. Answer (B) is incorrect. Statement 3 should be in the criteria section. Answer (C) is incorrect. Statement 5 should be in the recommendations section.

6. A recommendation in a final engagement communication should address what attribute?

    A. Cause.

    B. Statement of condition.

    C. Criteria.

    D. Effect.

Answer (A) is correct.
    REQUIRED: The attribute of a recommendation.
    DISCUSSION: A recommendation must address the cause attribute to describe the necessary corrective action.
    Answer (B) is incorrect. The condition attribute simply describes "what is" to serve as a basis for comparison with given criteria. Answer (C) is incorrect. Criteria describe "what should be" and are compared with the statement of condition. Answer (D) is incorrect. The effect attribute addresses the importance of an observation.

9.3 Communicating Engagement Results

7. Which of the following is the most appropriate method of reporting disagreement between the internal auditor and the engagement client concerning engagement observations and recommendations?

    A. State the internal auditor's position because the report is designed to provide the internal auditor's independent view.

    B. State the engagement client's position because management is ultimately responsible for the activities reported.

    C. State both positions and identify the reasons for the disagreement.

    D. State neither position. If the disagreement is ultimately resolved, there will be no reason to report the previous disagreement. If the disagreement is never resolved, the disagreement should not be reported because there is no mechanism to resolve it.

Answer (C) is correct.
    REQUIRED: The most appropriate method of reporting disagreement between the auditor and the auditee about audit findings and recommendations.
    DISCUSSION: As part of the internal auditor's discussions with the engagement client, the internal auditor obtains agreement on the results of the engagement and on any necessary plan of action to improve operations. If the internal auditor and engagement client disagree about the engagement results, the engagement communications state both positions and the reasons for the disagreement. The engagement client's written comments may be included as an appendix to the engagement report in the body of the report or in a cover letter.

8. Which of the following is most appropriate for inclusion in the summary of a final engagement communication?

    A. Engagement client responses to recommendations.

    B. A concise statement of engagement observations.

    C. Reference to areas not covered by the engagement.

    D. Discussion of recommendations given in prior years' engagement communications.

Answer (B) is correct.
    REQUIRED: The most appropriate inclusion in the management summary of a formal audit report.
    DISCUSSION: A signed report is issued after the engagement's completion. Summary reports highlighting engagement results are appropriate for levels of management above the engagement client.
    Answer (A) is incorrect. Engagement client responses to recommendations are appropriately included in the body of the communication rather than in the summary. Answer (C) is incorrect. A reference to areas not covered by the engagement communications is appropriately included in the body of the communication rather than in the summary. Answer (D) is incorrect. A discussion of recommendations given in prior years' engagement communications is appropriately included in the body of the communication rather than in the summary.

9. An internal auditor found that employees in the maintenance department were not signing their time cards. This situation also existed during the last engagement. The internal auditor should

- A. Include this observation in the current engagement communication.
- B. Ask the manager of the maintenance department to assume the resulting risk.
- C. Withhold conclusions about payroll internal control in the maintenance department.
- D. Instruct the employees to sign their time cards.

Answer (A) is correct.
REQUIRED: The proper auditor action when the internal auditor discovers that employees do not sign their time cards.
DISCUSSION: Internal auditors must communicate results of engagements. Results include observations, conclusions, opinions, recommendations, and action plans. Observations (findings) are relevant statements of fact, which include whether a condition (current state) complies with established criteria (correct state). Accordingly, the internal auditor should include the observation in the current engagement communication.
Answer (B) is incorrect. Asking the manager of the maintenance department to assume the resulting risk is not within the internal auditor's authority, and it would not remedy the situation. However, the internal auditor should ascertain whether senior management has decided to assume the risk. Answer (C) is incorrect. The final engagement communication must contain conclusions about internal control of payroll in the maintenance department. Answer (D) is incorrect. The internal auditor should not supervise maintenance department employees.

9.4 Communication Qualities and Overall Opinions

10. Avoiding unnecessary technical language is best associated with which quality of communication addressed in the *Standards*?

- A. Accurate.
- B. Concise.
- C. Clear.
- D. Complete.

Answer (C) is correct.
REQUIRED: The quality best associated with avoiding unnecessary technical language.
DISCUSSION: Communications must be accurate, objective, clear, concise, constructive, complete, and timely (Perf. Std. 2420). Clear communications are easily understood and logical. Clarity can be improved by avoiding unnecessary technical language and providing all significant and relevant information (Inter. Std. 2420).
Answer (A) is incorrect. Accurate communications avoid errors and distortions. Answer (B) is incorrect. Concise communications avoid superfluous detail, redundancy, and wordiness. Answer (D) is incorrect. Complete communications lack nothing that is essential to the target audience and include all significant and relevant information and observations to support recommendations and conclusions.

11. The manner in which data and evidence is gathered, evaluated, and summarized for presentation should be done with care and precision. Which quality of communications does this statement best describe?

- A. Objective.
- B. Accurate.
- C. Timely.
- D. Constructive.

Answer (B) is correct.
REQUIRED: The quality of communications that is described.
DISCUSSION: Communications should be accurate, objective, clear, concise, constructive, complete, and timely (Perf. Std. 2420). Accurate communications are free from errors and distortions and are faithful to the underlying facts (Inter. Std. 2420).
Answer (A) is incorrect. Objective communications concern observations, conclusions, and recommendations that should be derived and expressed without prejudice, partisanship, personal interests, and the undue influence of others. Answer (C) is incorrect. Timely communications concern the timing of the presentation of engagement results, which should be set without undue delay and with a degree of urgency and so as to enable prompt, effective action. Answer (D) is incorrect. Constructive communications concern the contents and tone of the presentation, which should be useful, positive, and well-meaning and contribute to the objectives of the organization.

9.5 Exit Conference and Management's Response

12. Which of the following combinations of participants is most appropriate to attend an exit meeting?

A. The responsible internal auditor and representatives from management who are knowledgeable about detailed operations and who can authorize implementation of corrective action.

B. The chief audit executive and the executive in charge of the activity or function reviewed.

C. Staff internal auditors who conducted the field work and operating personnel in charge of the daily performance of the activity or function reviewed.

D. Staff auditors who conducted the field work and the executive in charge of the activity or function reviewed.

Answer (A) is correct.

REQUIRED: The combination of participants most appropriate to attend an exit meeting.

DISCUSSION: The level of participants in the discussions and reviews may vary by organization and nature of the report; they generally include those individuals who are knowledgeable of detailed operations and who can authorize the implementation of corrective action.

Answer (B) is incorrect. The CAE and the executive in charge of the activity reviewed might not be knowledgeable about the details. Answer (C) is incorrect. Staff auditors and operating personnel might not have the necessary perspectives or authority. Answer (D) is incorrect. The staff auditors might lack the proper perspective and authority.

9.6 Approve and Distribute Reports

13. An engagement performed at an organization's payroll department has revealed various control weaknesses. These weaknesses, along with recommendations for corrective actions, were addressed in the final engagement communication. This communication should be most useful to the organization's

A. Purchasing manager.

B. Audit committee of the board of directors.

C. Payroll manager.

D. President.

Answer (C) is correct.

REQUIRED: The person most likely to benefit from the receipt of a payroll department engagement communication.

DISCUSSION: The CAE distributes the final engagement communication to the management of the audited activity and to those persons in the organization who can ensure engagement results are given due consideration and take corrective action or ensure that corrective action is taken. A communication on control weaknesses in the payroll function should be most useful to the payroll manager because (s)he is in a position to take corrective action.

Answer (A) is incorrect. The purchasing manager is not responsible for the payroll department. Answer (B) is incorrect. The audit committee is not in operational control of the department. Answer (D) is incorrect. The president is not in operational control of the department.

14. The chief audit executive (CAE) or a designee is required to decide to whom the final engagement communication will be distributed. Observations concerning significant internal control weakness are included in an engagement communication on the accounts payable system of an organization whose securities are publicly traded. Which of the following is the most likely reason that the CAE has chosen to send copies of this engagement communication to the board and the external auditor?

A. The board and external auditor are normally sent copies of all internal audit engagement communications as a courtesy.

B. The board and external auditor will need to take corrective action based on the observations.

C. The activities of the board and external auditor may be affected because of the potential for misstated financial statements.

D. A regulatory agency's guidelines require such distribution.

Answer (C) is correct.

REQUIRED: The most likely reason for distributing copies of an engagement communication containing observations about significant control weaknesses in the accounts payable system.

DISCUSSION: The CAE distributes the final engagement communication to the management of the audited activity and to those persons in the organization who can ensure engagement results are given due consideration and take corrective action or ensure that corrective action is taken. The potential for misstated financial statements created by the internal control weaknesses should be of interest to the board and the external auditor.

Answer (A) is incorrect. Normal distribution is to management of the activity under review and others in a position to take corrective action or ensure that corrective action is taken. Answer (B) is incorrect. Operating management is responsible for taking corrective action. Answer (D) is incorrect. Such a requirement is unlikely.

15. An internal auditor has uncovered illegal acts committed by a member of senior management. Such information

    A.   Should be excluded from the internal auditor's engagement communication and discussed orally with the senior manager.

    B.   Must be immediately reported to the appropriate government authorities.

    C.   May be disclosed in a separate communication and distributed to all senior management.

    D.   May be disclosed in a separate communication and distributed to the board.

Answer (D) is correct.
    REQUIRED: The appropriate action when an internal auditor discovers illegal acts committed by a member of senior management.
    DISCUSSION: Certain information is not appropriate for disclosure to all report recipients because it is privileged, proprietary, or related to improper or illegal acts. Disclose such information in a separate report. Distribute the report to the board if the conditions being reported involve senior management.
    Answer (A) is incorrect. Although improper or illegal acts may be disclosed in a separate communication, the internal auditor should not discuss such information with individuals who have committed such acts. Answer (B) is incorrect. In general, internal auditors are responsible to their organization's management rather than outside agencies. In the case of fraud, statutory filings with regulatory agencies may be required. Answer (C) is incorrect. Such information should be communicated to individuals to whom senior managers report.

16. An internal audit activity's evaluation of sales contracts revealed that a bribe had been paid to secure a major contract. The strong possibility existed that a senior executive had authorized the bribe. Which of the following best describes the proper distribution of the completed final engagement communication?

    A.   The report should be distributed to the chief executive officer and the appropriate regulatory agency.

    B.   The report should be distributed to the board, the chief executive officer, and the independent external auditor.

    C.   The chief audit executive should provide the board a copy of the report and decide whether further distribution is appropriate.

    D.   The report should be distributed to the board, the appropriate law enforcement agency, and the appropriate regulatory agency.

Answer (C) is correct.
    REQUIRED: The proper distribution of the completed audit report if a senior executive may have authorized a bribe.
    DISCUSSION: Certain information is not appropriate for disclosure to all report recipients because it is privileged, proprietary, or related to improper or illegal acts. Disclose such information in a separate report. Distribute the report to the board if the conditions being reported involve senior management.

9.7 Monitor Engagement Outcomes

17. After an engagement report with adverse observations has been communicated to appropriate engagement client personnel, internal auditing's proper action is to

    A.   Schedule a follow-up engagement.

    B.   Implement corrective action indicated by the observations.

    C.   Examine further the data supporting the observations.

    D.   Assemble new data to support the observations.

Answer (A) is correct.
    REQUIRED: The proper action after an audit report with adverse findings has been communicated to appropriate auditee personnel.
    DISCUSSION: The CAE must establish and maintain a system to monitor the disposition of results communicated to management (Perf. Std. 2500).
    Answer (B) is incorrect. The internal audit activity ordinarily has no responsibility to implement corrective action. Answer (C) is incorrect. Data have already been examined. Answer (D) is incorrect. Data have already been examined.

18. Management is beginning to take corrective action on personnel department deficiencies reported during the last engagement performed by the internal audit activity. The internal auditor should

- A. Oversee the corrective action.
- B. Postpone the next engagement of the personnel department until the corrective action is completed.
- C. Refrain from judging whether the corrective action will remedy the deficiencies.
- D. Follow up to see that the corrective action satisfies the engagement recommendations.

Answer (D) is correct.
REQUIRED: The internal auditor's action regarding corrective action on personnel department deficiencies reported during the last internal audit.
DISCUSSION: The CAE must establish a follow-up process to monitor and ensure that management actions have been effectively implemented or that senior management has accepted the risk of not taking action (Impl. Std. 2500.A1).
Answer (A) is incorrect. Internal auditors should not perform operating functions. Answer (B) is incorrect. A follow-up engagement should be considered if engagement observations were especially significant. Moreover, no reason is given for postponing the next regular engagement. Answer (C) is incorrect. Internal auditors must determine that management actions have been effectively implemented or that senior management has accepted the risk of not taking action.

19. What action must the chief audit executive take when (s)he believes that senior management has accepted a level of residual risk that is unacceptable to the organization?

- A. Report the matter to the board for resolution.
- B. Report the matter to an external authority.
- C. Discuss the matter with external auditors.
- D. Discuss the matter with senior management.

Answer (D) is correct.
REQUIRED: The mandatory action when senior management has accepted residual risk unacceptable to the organization.
DISCUSSION: A CAE may believe that senior management has accepted a level of risk that may be unacceptable to the organization. The CAE then must discuss the matter with senior management. If the CAE determines that the matter is unresolved, (s)he must report the matter to the board (Perf. Std. 2600).
Answer (A) is incorrect. The CAE must report the matter to the board for resolution when a decision is not resolved after a discussion with senior management. Answer (B) is incorrect. The matter must be discussed with senior management. Answer (C) is incorrect. The CAE must discuss the matter with senior management.

20. When monitoring the progress of management's disposition of recommendations, the internal auditors should do all of the following, **except**

- A. Address observations and recommendations to appropriate management levels.
- B. Evaluate management responses to observations and recommendations.
- C. Create an open-ended time frame for completion of responses to observations and recommendations.
- D. Actively monitor the implementation of recommendations.

Answer (C) is correct.
REQUIRED: The inappropriate action by internal auditors who are monitoring the disposition of recommendations.
DISCUSSION: The chief audit executive must establish and maintain a system to monitor the disposition of results communicated to management. The system should include procedures for items such as (1) evaluation and verification of management's response to observations and recommendations and (2) communication of unsatisfactory responses or actions to appropriate levels of management. Procedures also should be prepared that address the time frame within which management's response to engagement observations and recommendations is required. An open-ended time frame does not communicate the necessary urgency of responses to observations and recommendations.
Answer (A) is incorrect. The internal audit activity effectively monitors progress by addressing engagement observations and recommendations to appropriate levels of management responsible for action. Answer (B) is incorrect. Evaluation of management responses to observations and recommendations is necessary to assure that actions agreed to were taken, and the actions taken have the intended results. Answer (D) is incorrect. Actively monitoring the implementation of recommendations helps to reduce delays during the implementation process.

Access the **Gleim CIA Premium Review System** featuring our SmartAdapt technology from your Gleim Personal Classroom to continue your studies. You will experience a personalized study environment with exam-emulating multiple-choice questions.

APPENDIX A
THE IIA GLOSSARY

This appendix contains the Glossary appended to the *Standards*.

Add Value – The internal audit activity adds value to the organization (and its stakeholders) when it provides objective and relevant assurance, and contributes to the effectiveness and efficiency of governance, risk management, and control processes.

Adequate Control – Present if management has planned and organized (designed) in a manner that provides reasonable assurance that the organization's risks have been managed effectively and that the organization's goals and objectives will be achieved efficiently and economically.

Assurance Services – An objective examination of evidence for the purpose of providing an independent assessment on governance, risk management, and control processes for the organization. Examples may include financial, performance, compliance, system security, and due diligence engagements.

Board – The highest level governing body (e.g., a board of directors, a supervisory board, or a board of governors or trustees) charged with the responsibility to direct and/or oversee the organization's activities and hold senior management accountable. Although governance arrangements vary among jurisdictions and sectors, typically the board includes members who are not part of management. If a board does not exist, the word "board" in the *Standards* refers to a group or person charged with governance of the organization. Furthermore, "board" in the *Standards* may refer to a committee or another body to which the governing body has delegated certain functions (e.g., an audit committee).

Charter – The internal audit charter is a formal document that defines the internal audit activity's purpose, authority, and responsibility. The internal audit charter establishes the internal audit activity's position within the organization; authorizes access to records, personnel, and physical properties relevant to the performance of engagements; and defines the scope of internal audit activities.

Chief Audit Executive – Chief audit executive describes the role of a person in a senior position responsible for effectively managing the internal audit activity in accordance with the internal audit charter and the mandatory elements of the International Professional Practices Framework. The chief audit executive or others reporting to the chief audit executive will have appropriate professional certifications and qualifications. The specific job title and/or responsibilities of the chief audit executive may vary across organizations.

Code of Ethics – The Code of Ethics of The Institute of Internal Auditors (IIA) are Principles relevant to the profession and practice of internal auditing, and Rules of Conduct that describe behavior expected of internal auditors. The Code of Ethics applies to both parties and entities that provide internal audit services. The purpose of the Code of Ethics is to promote an ethical culture in the global profession of internal auditing.

Compliance – Adherence to policies, plans, procedures, laws, regulations, contracts, or other requirements.

Conflict of Interest – Any relationship that is, or appears to be, not in the best interest of the organization. A conflict of interest would prejudice an individual's ability to perform his or her duties and responsibilities objectively.

Consulting Services – Advisory and related client service activities, the nature and scope of which are agreed with the client, and are intended to add value and improve an organization's governance, risk management, and control processes without the internal auditor assuming management responsibility. Examples include counsel, advice, facilitation, and training.

Control – Any action taken by management, the board, and other parties to manage risk and increase the likelihood that established objectives and goals will be achieved. Management plans, organizes, and directs the performance of sufficient actions to provide reasonable assurance that objectives and goals will be achieved.

Control Environment – The attitude and actions of the board and management regarding the importance of control within the organization. The control environment provides the discipline and structure for the achievement of the primary objectives of the system of internal control. The control environment includes the following elements:

- Integrity and ethical values.
- Management's philosophy and operating style.
- Organizational structure.
- Assignment of authority and responsibility.
- Human resource policies and practices.
- Competence of personnel.

Control Processes – The policies, procedures (both manual and automated), and activities that are part of a control framework, designed and operated to ensure that risks are contained within the level that an organization is willing to accept.

Core Principles for the Professional Practice of Internal Auditing – The Core Principles for the Professional Practice of Internal Auditing are the foundation for the International Professional Practices Framework and support internal audit effectiveness.

Engagement – A specific internal audit assignment, task, or review activity, such as an internal audit, control self-assessment review, fraud examination, or consultancy. An engagement may include multiple tasks or activities designed to accomplish a specific set of related objectives.

Engagement Objectives – Broad statements developed by internal auditors that define intended engagement accomplishments.

Engagement Opinion – The rating, conclusion, and/or other description of results of an individual internal audit engagement, relating to those aspects within the objectives and scope of the engagement.

Engagement Work Program – A document that lists the procedures to be followed during an engagement, designed to achieve the engagement plan.

External Service Provider – A person or firm outside of the organization that has special knowledge, skill, and experience in a particular discipline.

Fraud – Any illegal act characterized by deceit, concealment, or violation of trust. These acts are not dependent upon the threat of violence or physical force. Frauds are perpetrated by parties and organizations to obtain money, property, or services; to avoid payment or loss of services; or to secure personal or business advantage.

Governance – The combination of processes and structures implemented by the board to inform, direct, manage, and monitor the activities of the organization toward the achievement of its objectives.

Impairment – Impairment to organizational independence and individual objectivity may include personal conflict of interest; scope limitations; restrictions on access to records, personnel, and properties; and resource limitations (funding).

Independence – The freedom from conditions that threaten the ability of the internal audit activity to carry out internal audit responsibilities in an unbiased manner.

Information Technology Controls – Controls that support business management and governance as well as provide general and technical controls over information technology infrastructures, such as applications, information, infrastructure, and people.

Information Technology Governance – Consists of the leadership, organizational structures, and processes that ensure that the enterprise's information technology supports the organization's strategies and objectives.

Internal Audit Activity – A department, division, team of consultants, or other practitioner(s) that provides independent, objective assurance and consulting services designed to add value and improve an organization's operations. The internal audit activity helps an organization accomplish its objectives by bringing a systematic, disciplined approach to evaluate and improve the effectiveness of governance, risk management and control processes.

International Professional Practices Framework – The conceptual framework that organizes the authoritative guidance promulgated by The IIA. Authoritative guidance is composed of two categories – (1) mandatory and (2) recommended.

Must – The *Standards* use the word "must" to specify an unconditional requirement.

Objectivity – An unbiased mental attitude that allows internal auditors to perform engagements in such a manner that they believe in their work product and that no quality compromises are made. Objectivity requires that internal auditors do not subordinate their judgment on audit matters to others.

Overall Opinion – The rating, conclusion, and/or other description of results provided by the chief audit executive addressing, at a broad level, governance, risk management, and/or control processes of the organization. An overall opinion is the professional judgment of the chief audit executive based on the results of a number of individual engagements and other activities for a specific time interval.

Risk – The possibility of an event occurring that will have an impact on the achievement of objectives. Risk is measured in terms of impact and likelihood.

Risk Appetite – The level of risk that an organization is willing to accept.

Risk Management – A process to identify, assess, manage, and control potential events or situations to provide reasonable assurance regarding the achievement of the organization's objectives.

Should – The *Standards* use the word "should" where conformance is expected unless, when applying professional judgment, circumstances justify deviation.

Significance – The relative importance of a matter within the context in which it is being considered, including quantitative and qualitative factors, such as magnitude, nature, effect, relevance, and impact. Professional judgment assists internal auditors when evaluating the significance of matters within the context of the relevant objectives.

Standard – A professional pronouncement promulgated by the Internal Audit Standards Board that delineates the requirements for performing a broad range of internal audit activities and for evaluating internal audit performance.

Technology-based Audit Techniques – Any automated audit tool, such as generalized audit software, test data generators, computerized audit programs, specialized audit utilities, and computer-assisted audit techniques (CAATs).

APPENDIX B
THE IIA CIA EXAM SYLLABUS AND CROSS-REFERENCES

For your convenience, we have reproduced verbatim The IIA's CIA Exam Syllabus for this CIA exam part. Note that the "basic" cognitive level means the candidate must retrieve relevant knowledge from memory and/or demonstrate basic comprehension of concepts or processes. Those levels labeled "proficient" mean the candidate must apply concepts, processes, or procedures; analyze, evaluate, and make judgments based on criteria; and/or put elements or material together to formulate conclusions and recommendations. We also have provided cross-references to the study units and subunits in this book that correspond to The IIA's more detailed coverage. Please visit The IIA's website for updates and more information about the exam. Rely on the Gleim materials to help you pass each part of the exam. We have researched and studied The IIA's CIA Exam Syllabus as well as questions from prior exams to provide you with an excellent review program.

PART 2 – PRACTICE OF INTERNAL AUDITING

		Domain	Cognitive Level	Gleim Study Unit(s) or Subunit(s)
	Managing the Internal Audit Activity (20%)			
	1. Internal Audit Operations			
	A	Describe policies and procedures for the planning, organizing, directing, and monitoring of internal audit operations	**Basic**	**1.1-1.4**
	B	Interpret administrative activities (budgeting, resourcing, recruiting, staffing, etc.) of the internal audit activity	**Basic**	**1.2, 1.4**
	2. Establishing a Risk-based Internal Audit Plan			
	A	Identify sources of potential engagements (audit universe, audit cycle requirements, management requests, regulatory mandates, relevant market and industry trends, emerging issues, etc.)	**Basic**	**4.1**
	B	Identify a risk management framework to assess risks and prioritize audit engagements based on the results of a risk assessment	**Basic**	**4.1-4.2**
I	C	Interpret the types of assurance engagements (risk and control assessments, audits of third parties and contract compliance, security and privacy, performance and quality audits, key performance indicators, operational audits, financial and regulatory compliance audits)	**Proficient**	**2.1-2.8, 3.1-3.8**
	D	Interpret the types of consulting engagements (training, system design, system development, due diligence, privacy, benchmarking, internal control assessment, process mapping, etc.) designed to provide advice and insight	**Proficient**	**3.3-3.7**
	E	Describe coordination of internal audit efforts with the external auditor, regulatory oversight bodies, and other internal assurance functions, and potential reliance on other assurance providers	**Basic**	**1.5**
	3. Communicating and Reporting to Senior Management and the Board			
	A	Recognize that the chief audit executive communicates the annual audit plan to senior management and the board and seeks the board's approval	**Basic**	**4.3**
	B	Identify significant risk exposures and control and governance issues for the chief audit executive to report to the board	**Basic**	**4.3**
	C	Recognize that the chief audit executive reports on the overall effectiveness of the organization's internal control and risk management processes to senior management and the board	**Basic**	**4.3**
	D	Recognize internal audit key performance indicators that the chief audit executive communicates to senior management and the board periodically	**Basic**	**4.3**

		Domain	Cognitive Level	Gleim Study Unit(s) or Subunit(s)
II		**Planning the Engagement (20%)**		
		1. Engagement Planning		
	A	Determine engagement objectives, evaluation criteria, and the scope of the engagement	Proficient	5.2
	B	Plan the engagement to assure identification of key risks and controls	Proficient	5.1
	C	Complete a detailed risk assessment of each audit area, including evaluating and prioritizing risk and control factors	Proficient	5.1
	D	Determine engagement procedures and prepare the engagement work program	Proficient	5.4-5.5
	E	Determine the level of staff and resources needed for the engagement	Proficient	5.3
III		**Performing the Engagement (40%)**		
		1. Information Gathering		
	A	Gather and examine relevant information (review previous audit reports and data, conduct walk-throughs and interviews, perform observations, etc.) as part of a preliminary survey of the engagement area	Proficient	5.1, 6.3-6.5, 8.2
	B	Develop checklists and risk-and-control questionnaires as part of a preliminary survey of the engagement area	Proficient	5.1, 6.3
	C	Apply appropriate sampling (nonstatistical, judgmental, discovery, etc.) and statistical analysis techniques	Proficient	SU 7
		2. Analysis and Evaluation		
	A	Use computerized audit tools and techniques (data mining and extraction, continuous monitoring, automated workpapers, embedded audit modules, etc.)	Proficient	8.1, 8.4
	B	Evaluate the relevance, sufficiency, and reliability of potential sources of evidence	Proficient	6.1-6.2
	C	Apply appropriate analytical approaches and process mapping techniques (process identification, workflow analysis, process map generation and analysis, spaghetti maps, RACI diagrams, etc.)	Proficient	8.2
	D	Determine and apply analytical review techniques (ratio estimation, variance analysis, budget vs. actual, trend analysis, other reasonableness tests, benchmarking, etc.)	Basic	3.6, 8.3
	E	Prepare workpapers and documentation of relevant information to support conclusions and engagement results	Proficient	8.4-8.5
	F	Summarize and develop engagement conclusions, including assessment of risks and controls	Proficient	8.6
		3. Engagement Supervision		
	A	Identify key activities in supervising engagements (coordinate work assignments, review workpapers, evaluate auditors' performance, etc.)	Basic	8.5, 8.7

		Domain	Cognitive Level	Gleim Study Unit(s) or Subunit(s)
IV		**Communicating Engagement Results and Monitoring Progress (20%)**		
		1. Communicating Engagement Results and the Acceptance of Risk		
	A	Arrange preliminary communication with engagement clients	**Proficient**	**9.1**
	B	Demonstrate communication quality (accurate, objective, clear, concise, constructive, complete, and timely) and elements (objectives, scope, conclusions, recommendations, and action plan)	**Proficient**	**9.2-9.4**
	C	Prepare interim reporting on the engagement progress	**Proficient**	**9.1**
	D	Formulate recommendations to enhance and protect organizational value	**Proficient**	**9.2**
	E	Describe the audit engagement communication and reporting process, including holding the exit conference, developing the audit report (draft, review, approve, and distribute), and obtaining management's response	**Basic**	**9.3, 9.5-9.6**
	F	Describe the chief audit executive's responsibility for assessing residual risk	**Basic**	**9.7**
	G	Describe the process for communicating risk acceptance (when management has accepted a level of risk that may be unacceptable to the organization)	**Basic**	**4.3, 9.7**
		2. Monitoring Progress		
	A	Assess engagement outcomes, including the management action plan	**Proficient**	**9.7**
	B	Manage monitoring and follow-up of the disposition of audit engagement results communicated to management and the board	**Proficient**	**9.7**

APPENDIX C
THE IIA STANDARDS CITED IN PART 2

Gleim Subunit	Attribute Standard
3.4	1000 - Purpose, Authority, and Responsibility
3.5	1130 - Impairment to Independence or Objectivity
3.5	1210 - Proficiency
3.5	1220 - Due Professional Care

Gleim Subunit	Performance Standard
1.2	2000 - Managing the Internal Audit Activity
3.4, 4.1	2010 - Planning
4.3	2020 - Communication and Approval
1.4	2030 - Resource Management
1.2, 8.4	2040 - Policies and Procedures
1.5, 8.4	2050 - Coordination
4.3	2060 - Reporting to Senior Management and the Board
1.4	2070 - External Service Provider and Organizational Responsibility for Internal Auditing
1.1	2100 - Nature of Work
2.8, 3.1, 3.4	2120 - Risk Management
2.5, 2.8, 3.2, 3.4, 8.4	2130 - Control
5.1	2200 - Engagement Planning
3.5, 5.1	2201 - Planning Considerations
3.5, 5.1, 5.2	2210 - Engagement Objectives
3.5, 5.2	2220 - Engagement Scope
5.3	2230 - Engagement Resource Allocation
3.5, 5.4, 5.5	2240 - Engagement Work Program
6.1	2310 - Identifying Information
8.3	2320 - Analysis and Evaluation
3.5, 8.4, 8.5	2330 - Documenting Information
8.7	2340 - Engagement Supervision
9.3	2400 - Communicating Results
3.5, 9.3	2410 - Criteria for Communicating
9.4	2420 - Quality of Communications
9.4	2421 - Errors and Omissions
9.4	2430 - Use of "Conducted in Conformance with the *International Standards for the Professional Practice of Internal Auditing*"
9.4	2431 - Engagement Disclosure of Nonconformance
3.5, 9.6	2440 - Disseminating Results
9.4	2450 - Overall Opinions
3.5, 9.7	2500 - Monitoring Progress
9.7	2600 - Communicating the Acceptance of Risks

APPENDIX D
THE IIA EXAMINATION BIBLIOGRAPHY

The Institute has prepared a listing of references for Part 2 of the CIA exam as of October 2017, reproduced below. These publications have been chosen by the Professional Certifications Department as reasonably representative of the common body of knowledge for internal auditors. However, all of the information in these texts will not be tested. When possible, questions will be written based on the information contained in the suggested reference list. This bibliography is provided to give you an overview of the scope of the exam.

The IIA bibliography is reproduced for your information only. The texts you need to prepare for the CIA exam depend on many factors, including

1. Innate ability
2. Length of time out of school
3. Thoroughness of your undergraduate education
4. Familiarity with internal auditing due to relevant experience

CIA EXAM REFERENCES

Title/URL	Author	Year Published	Publisher
Internal Auditing: Assurance & Advisory Services, 4th Edition *URL: https://bookstore.theiia.org/Internal-Auditing-Assurance-Advisory-Services-fourth-edition-2*	Urton L. Anderson, Michael J. Head, Sridhar Ramamoorti, Cris Riddle, Mark Salamasick, Paul J. Sobel	2017	The Internal Audit Foundation
International Professional Practices Framework (IPPF), including ● Mission ● Definition of Internal Auditing ● Core Principles ● Code of Ethics ● *Standards* ● Implementation Guides ● Practice Guides ● Global Technology Audit Guides (GTAGs) *URL: http:bit.ly/1AilTOC*	The Institute of Internal Auditors, Inc.	Updated continually	The Institute of Internal Auditors, Inc.
Position Paper: The Role of Internal Auditing in Resourcing the Internal Audit Activity *URL: https://na.theiia.org/standards-guidance/ Public Documents/PP The Role of Internal Auditing in Resourcing the Internal Audit Activity.pdf*	The Institute of Internal Auditors, Inc.	2009	The Institute of Internal Auditors, Inc.
Sawyer's Guide for Internal Auditors, 5th and 6th Editions *URL: https://bookstore.theiia.org/sawyers-guide-for-internal-auditors-6th-edition-8-3*	L.B. Sawyer	2012	The Institute of Internal Auditors Research Foundation

AVAILABILITY OF PUBLICATIONS

The listing on the previous page presents only some of the current technical literature available, and The IIA does not carry all of the reference books. Quantity discounts are provided by The IIA. Visit bookstore.theiia.org or request a current catalog by phone or mail.

Internal Audit Foundation Bookstore
1650 Bluegrass Lakes Pkwy
Alpharetta, GA 30009-1616 U.S.A.
iiapubs@pbd.com
(877) 867-4957 (toll-free in U.S. and Canada) or (770) 280-4183

Contact the publisher directly if you cannot obtain the desired texts from The IIA or your local bookstore. Begin your study program with the Gleim CIA Review, which most candidates find sufficient. If you need additional reference material, borrow books mentioned in The IIA's bibliography from colleagues, professors, or a library.

APPENDIX E
ACCOUNTING CYCLES

On the following pages are five flowcharts and accompanying tables describing the steps in five basic accounting cycles and the controls in each step for an organization large enough to have an optimal segregation of duties.

NOTE: Except for manual checks and remittance advices, the flowcharts presented do not assume the use of either a paper-based or an electronic system. Each document symbol represents a business activity or control, whether manual or computerized.

NOTE: In the diagrams that follow, documents that originate outside the organization are separated by a thick border.

Sales-Receivables Cycle

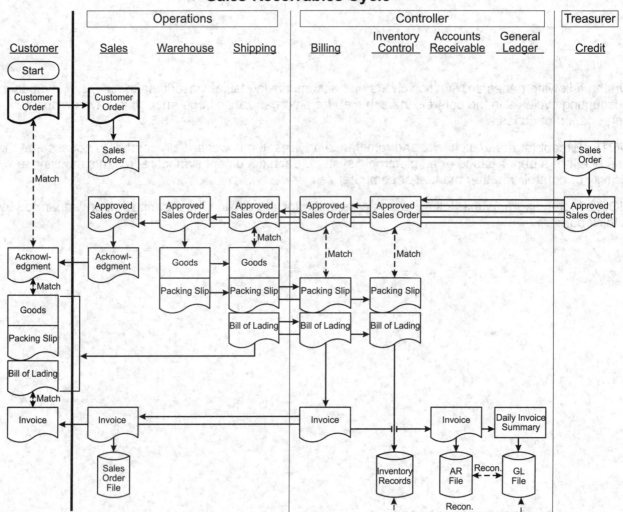

Figure E-1

Sales-Receivables Cycle

Function:	Authorization				Custody		Recording		
Department:	Customer	Sales	Credit	Billing	Shipping	Warehouse	Inventory Control	Accounts Receivable	General Ledger

Step	Business Activity	Embedded Control
1	Sales receives a **customer order** for merchandise, prepares a **sales order**, and forwards it to Credit.	Reconciling sequentially numbered sales orders helps ensure that customer orders are legitimate.
2	Credit performs a credit check on the customer. If the customer is creditworthy, Credit approves the **sales order**.	Ensures that goods are shipped only to actual customers and that the account is unlikely to become delinquent.
3	Credit sends the **approved sales order** to Sales, Warehouse, Shipping, Billing, and Inventory Control.	Notifies these departments that a legitimate sale has been made.
4	Upon receipt of an **approved sales order**, Sales sends an acknowledgment to the customer.	The customer's expectation of receiving goods reduces the chances of misrouting or misappropriation.
5	Upon receipt of an **approved sales order**, Warehouse pulls the merchandise, prepares a **packing slip**, and forwards both to Shipping.	Ensures that merchandise is removed from Warehouse only as part of a legitimate sale.
6	Shipping verifies that the goods received from Warehouse match the **approved sales order**, prepares a **bill of lading**, and sends the shipment to the customer.	Ensures that the correct goods are shipped.
7	Shipping forwards the **packing slip** and **bill of lading** to Inventory Control and Billing.	Notifies these departments that the goods have actually been shipped.
8	Upon receipt of the **packing slip** and **bill of lading**, Inventory Control matches them with the **approved sales order** and updates the inventory system.	Ensures that inventory unit counts are updated once the goods have actually been shipped. Updating inventory and GL files separately provides an additional accounting control when they are periodically reconciled.
9	Upon receipt of the **packing slip** and **bill of lading**, Billing matches them with the **approved sales order**, prepares an **invoice**, and sends it to the customer. If the invoice is paper-based, a **remittance advice** is included for use in the cash receipts cycle.	Ensures that customers are billed for all goods, and only those goods, that were actually shipped. Reconciling sequentially numbered invoice transactions helps prevent misappropriation of goods.
10	Sales receives the **invoice** from Billing and updates the sales order file.	Prevents double shipment of completed orders and allows follow-up of partially filled orders.
11	Accounts Receivable receives the **invoice** from Billing and posts a **journal entry** to the AR file.	Ensures that customer accounts are kept current.
12	Accounts Receivable prepares a **summary of all invoices** for the day and forwards it to General Ledger for posting of the total to the GL file.	Updating AR and GL files separately provides an additional accounting control when they are periodically reconciled.

Cash Receipts Cycle

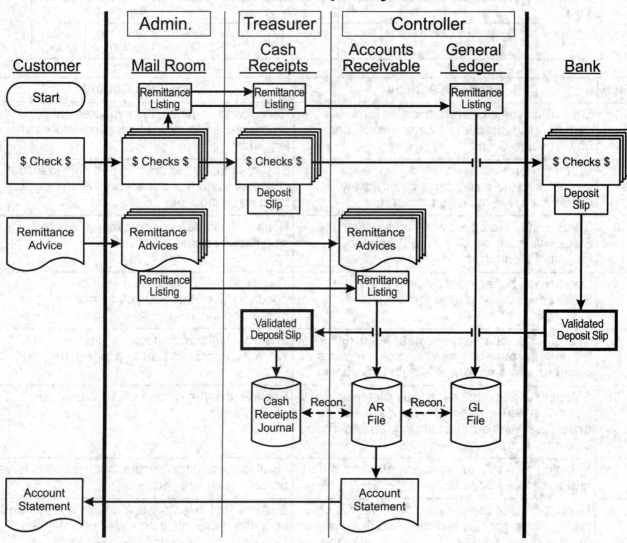

Figure E-2

Cash Receipts Cycle

Function:	Authorization		Custody		Recording	
Department:	Customer	Bank	Mail Room	Cash Receipts	Accounts Receivable	General Ledger

Step	Business Activity	Embedded Control
1	Mail Room opens customer mail. Two clerks are present at all times. Customer **checks** are immediately endorsed "For Deposit Only." **Remittance advices** are separated.	Reduces risk of misappropriation by a single employee.
2	Mail Room prepares a **remittance listing** of all **checks** received during the day and forwards it with the checks to Cash Receipts.	Remittance listing provides a control total for later reconciliation.
3	Cash Receipts prepares a **deposit slip** and deposits checks in Bank. Bank validates the **deposit slip**.	Bank provides independent evidence that the full amount was deposited.
4	Upon receipt of the **validated deposit slip**, Cash Receipts posts a **journal entry** to the cash receipts journal.	Ensures that the cash receipts journal is updated for the amount actually deposited.
5	Mail Room also sends the **remittance listing** to General Ledger for posting of the total to the GL file.	Updating AR and GL files separately provides an additional accounting control when they are periodically reconciled.
6	Mail Room also sends the **remittance listing** and **remittance advices** to Accounts Receivable for updating of customer accounts.	Ensures that customer accounts are kept current.
7	Accounts Receivable periodically sends **account statements** to customers showing all sales and payment activity.	Customers will complain about mistaken billings or missing payments.

Purchases-Payables Cycle

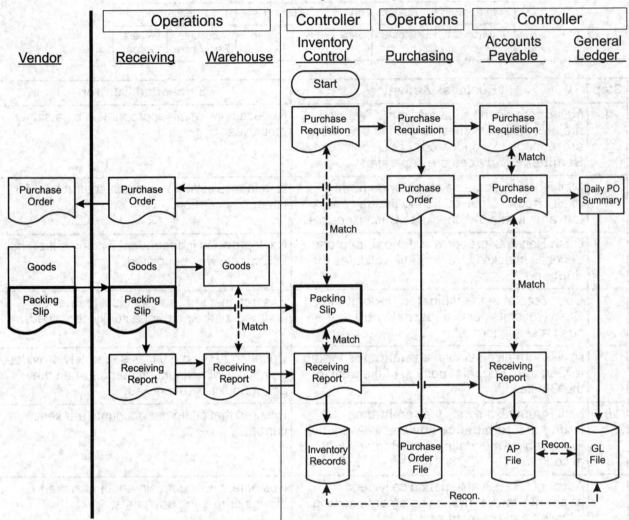

Figure E-3

Purchases-Payables Cycle

Function:	Authorization		Custody			Recording	
Department:	Inventory Control	Purchasing	Vendor	Receiving	Warehouse	Accounts Payable	General Ledger

Step	Business Activity	Embedded Control
1	Inventory Control prepares a **purchase requisition** when inventory approaches the reorder point and sends it to Purchasing and Accounts Payable.	Predetermined inventory levels trigger authorization to initiate purchase transaction.
2	Purchasing locates authorized vendor in vendor file, prepares a **purchase order**, and updates the purchase order file.	Ensures that goods are bought only from vendors who have been preapproved for reliability.
		Reconciling sequentially numbered purchase orders helps ensure that customer orders are legitimate.
3	Purchasing sends the **purchase order** to Vendor, Receiving, and Accounts Payable. Receiving's copy has blank quantities.	Vendor prepares merchandise for shipment.
		Receiving is put on notice to expect shipment.
		Accounts Payable is put on notice that liability to this vendor is about to increase.
4	Accounts Payable prepares a **summary of all purchase orders** issued that day and forwards it to General Ledger for posting of the total to the GL file.	Updating AP and GL files separately provides an additional accounting control when they are periodically reconciled.
5	Goods arrive at Receiving with a **packing slip**.	Because quantities are blank on Receiving's copy of the purchase order, employees cannot assume the order is correct as received and must count items.
6	Receiving prepares a **receiving report** and forwards it with the goods to Warehouse.	Detects discrepancies between the vendor packing slip and actual goods received.
7	Warehouse verifies that goods received match those listed on the **receiving report**.	Detects any loss or damage between Receiving and Warehouse.
8	Receiving sends the **receiving report** and **packing slip** to Inventory Control for matching with the **purchase requisition** and updating of inventory records.	Ensures that inventory records are current. Updating inventory and GL files separately provides an additional accounting control when they are periodically reconciled.
9	Receiving also sends the **receiving report** to Accounts Payable for matching with the **purchase order** and **purchase requisition** and updating of the AP file.	Ensures that vendor accounts are current.

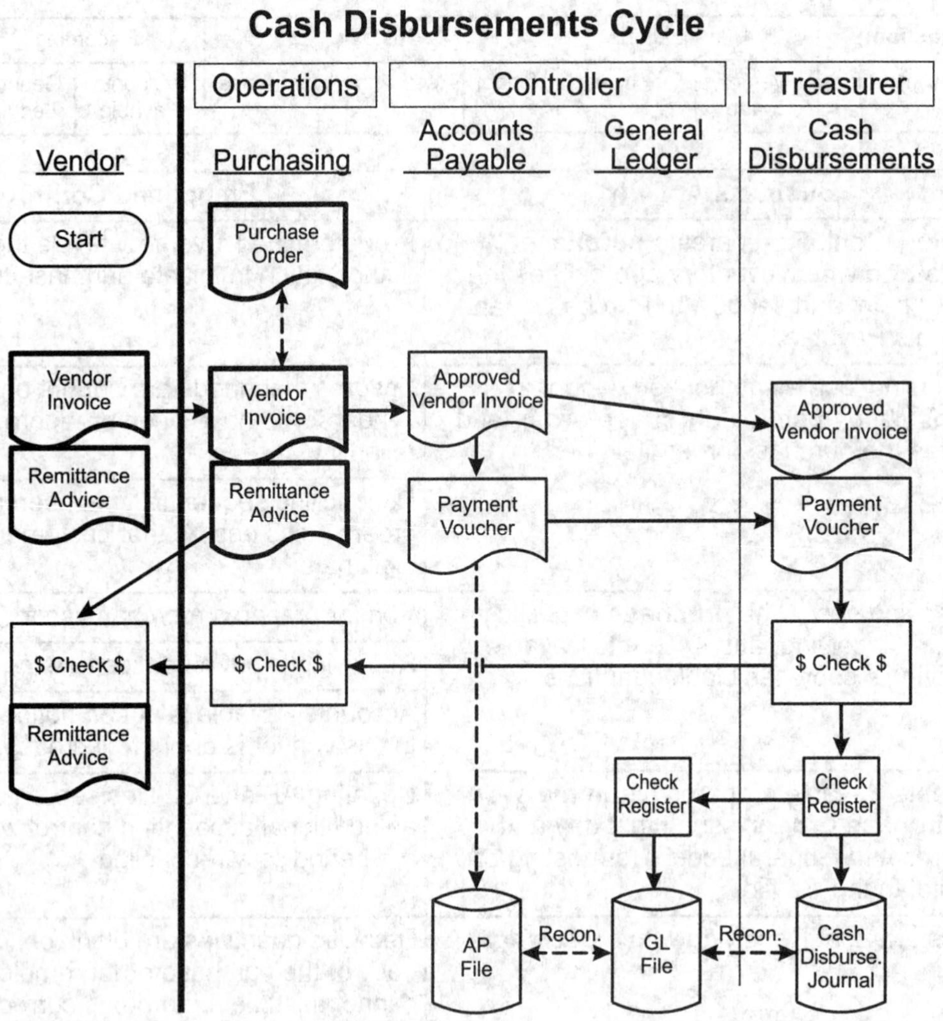
Cash Disbursements Cycle
Operations
Controller
Treasurer
Vendor
Purchasing
Accounts Payable
General Ledger
Cash Disbursements
Start
Purchase Order
Vendor Invoice
Vendor Invoice
Approved Vendor Invoice
Approved Vendor Invoice
Remittance Advice
Remittance Advice
Payment Voucher
Payment Voucher
$ Check $
$ Check $
$ Check $
Remittance Advice
Check Register
Check Register
AP File
Recon.
GL File
Recon.
Cash Disburse. Journal

Figure E-4

Cash Disbursements Cycle

Function:	Authorization		Custody	Recording	
Department:	Vendor	Purchasing	Cash Disbursements	Accounts Payable	General Ledger

Step	Business Activity	Embedded Control
1	Purchasing receives a **vendor invoice** and **remittance advice**. The remittance advice is separated and filed. The invoice is matched with the purchase order and approved for payment. The **purchase order** is marked as closed, and the approval is forwarded to Accounts Payable.	Ensures that vendors are timely paid for goods received and that Purchasing can follow up on partially filled orders.
2	Accounts Payable matches the **approved vendor invoice** with the AP file and issues a **payment voucher** to Cash Disbursements.	Ensures that the invoice is for goods actually received and that duplicate payment cannot be made.
3	Upon receipt of a **payment voucher** with an **approved vendor invoice**, Cash Disbursements issues a **check** and forwards it to Purchasing.	Ensures that payments are made only when goods have actually been received.
4	Purchasing sends the **remittance advice** with the **check** to Vendor.	Settles liability to Vendor.
5	Cash Disbursements prepares a **check register** of all checks issued during the day and posts a **journal entry** to the cash disbursements journal.	Ensures that the cash disbursements journal is updated for the total of checks requested.
6	The check register is also forwarded to General Ledger for posting of the total to the GL file.	Updating AP and GL files separately provides an additional accounting control when they are periodically reconciled.

Payroll Cycle

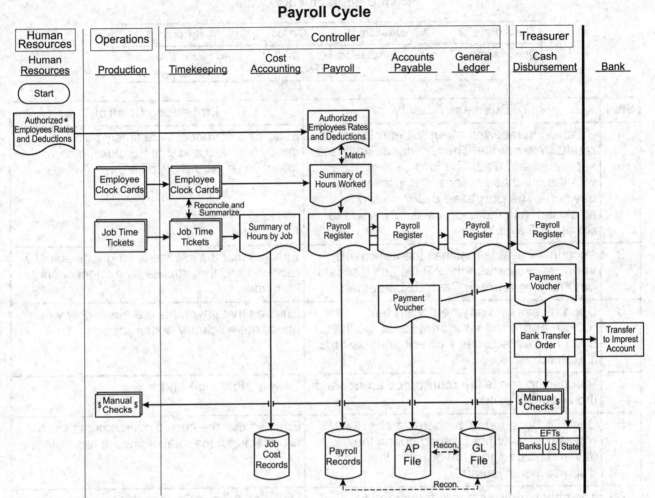

*Human resources receives only a list of authorized employee rates and deductions and does not have authority to change those rates.

Figure E-5

Payroll Cycle

Function:	Authorization		Custody		Recording				
Department:	Human Resources	Production	Cash Disbursements	Bank	Time-keeping	Cost Accounting	Payroll	Accounts Payable	General Ledger

Step	Business Activity	Embedded Control
1	Human Resources sends a **list of authorized employees**, pay rates, and deductions to Payroll.	Ensures that only actual persons are carried on the payroll and that rates of pay and withholding amounts are accurate.
2	Employees register the start and end times of their workdays on **clock cards**.	Mechanically or electronically captures employee work hours.
3	Employees record time worked on various tasks on **job time tickets**.	Allows accumulation of labor costs by job as well as tracking of direct and indirect labor.
4	At the end of the pay period, a production supervisor approves **clock cards** and **job time tickets** and forwards them to Timekeeping.	Ensures that employees worked only authorized hours.
5	Timekeeping reconciles the **clock cards** and **job time tickets**.	Ensures that employees are paid only for actual hours worked.
6	Timekeeping prepares a summary of **hours worked by job** and forwards it to Cost Accounting for updating of the job records.	Ensures that direct labor costs are appropriately assigned to jobs.
7	Timekeeping prepares a summary of **hours worked by employee** and forwards it to Payroll. Payroll matches it with the **authorized employee list**, prepares a **payroll register**, and updates the payroll records.	Ensures that employees are paid the proper amount.
8	Accounts Payable receives the **payroll register** from Payroll, prepares a **payment voucher**, and forwards it along with the payroll register to Cash Disbursements.	Ensures that a payable is accrued. Authorizes the movement of cash into the payroll imprest account.
9	Accounts Payable also forwards the **payroll register** to General Ledger for posting of the total to the GL file.	Updating AP and GL files separately provides an additional accounting control when they are periodically reconciled.
10	Cash Disbursements compares the **payment voucher** with the payroll register total and initiates appropriate **bank transfers**.	Ensures that the correct amount is transferred to the payroll imprest account and governmental authorities.
11	Cash Disbursements executes three **bank transfers**.	Use of an imprest payroll account allows idle funds to be invested and funds related to uncashed checks to be isolated.
		In the U.S., federal taxes withheld are transferred to the U.S. Treasury.
		In the U.S., state taxes withheld are transferred to the state government.
12	Employees paid by **manual check** are given checks by Treasury personnel, not by Payroll or their supervisors.	Ensures that Payroll or supervisory personnel cannot perpetrate fraud through the creation of fictitious employees.

APPENDIX F
GLOSSARY OF ACCOUNTING TERMS
U.S. TO BRITISH VS. BRITISH TO U.S.

U.S. TO BRITISH

Accounts payable	Trade creditors
Accounts receivable	Trade debtors
Accrual	Provision (for liability or charge)
Accumulated depreciation	Aggregate depreciation
Additional paid-in capital	Share premium account
Allowance	Provision (for diminution in value)
Allowance for doubtful accounts	Provision for bad debt
Annual Stockholders' Meeting	Annual General Meeting
Authorized capital stock	Authorized share capital
Bellweather stock	Barometer stock
Bylaws	Articles of Association
Bond	Loan finance
Capital lease	Finance lease
Certificate of Incorporation	Memorandum of Association
Checking account	Current account
Common stock	Ordinary shares
Consumer price index	Retail price index
Corporation	Company
Cost of goods sold	Cost of sales
Credit Memorandum	Credit note
Equity	Reserves
Equity interest	Ownership interest
Financial statements	Accounts
Income statement	Profit and loss account
Income taxes	Taxation
Inventories	Stocks
Investment bank	Merchant bank
Labor union	Trade union
Land	Freehold
Lease with bargain purchase option	Hire purchase contract
Liabilities	Creditors
Listed company	Quoted company
Long-term investments	Fixed asset investments
Long-term lease	Long leasehold
Merchandise trade	Visible trade
Mutual funds	Unit trusts
Net income	Net profit
Note payable	Bill payable
Note receivable	Bill receivable
Paid-in surplus	Share premium
Par value	Nominal value
Pooling of interests method	Merger accounting
Preferred stock	Preference share
Prime rate	Base rate
Property, plant, and equipment	Tangible fixed assets
Provision for bad debts	Charge
Purchase method	Acquisition accounting
Purchase on account	Purchase on credit
Retained earnings	Profit and loss account
Real estate	Property
Revenue	Income
Reversal of accrual	Release of provision
Sales on account	Sales on credit
Sales/revenue	Turnover
Savings and loan association	Building society
Shareholders' equity	Shareholders' funds
Stock	Inventory
Stockholder	Shareholder
Stock dividend	Bonus share
Stockholders' equity	Share capital and reserves or Shareholders' funds
Taxable income	Taxable profit
Treasury bonds	Gilt-edged stock (gilts)

BRITISH TO U.S.

British	U.S.
Accounts	Financial statements
Acquisition accounting	Purchase method
Aggregate depreciation	Accumulated depreciation
Annual General Meeting	Annual Stockholders' Meeting
Articles of Association	Bylaws
Authorized share capital	Authorized capital stock
Barometer stock	Bellweather stock
Base rate	Prime rate
Bill payable	Note payable
Bill receivable	Note receivable
Bonus share	Stock dividend
Building society	Savings and loan association
Charge	Provision for bad debts
Company	Corporation
Cost of sales	Cost of goods sold
Credit note	Credit Memorandum
Creditors	Liabilities
Current account	Checking account
Finance lease	Capital lease
Fixed asset investments	Long-term investments
Freehold	Land
Gilt-edged stock (gilts)	Treasury bonds
Hire purchase contract	Lease with bargain purchase option
Income	Revenue
Inventory	Stock
Loan finance	Bond
Long leasehold	Long-term lease
Memorandum of Association	Certificate of Incorporation
Merchant bank	Investment bank
Merger accounting	Pooling of interests method
Net profit	Net income
Nominal value	Par value
Ordinary shares	Common stock
Ownership interest	Equity interest
Preference share	Preferred stock
Profit and loss account	Income statement
Profit and loss account	Retained earnings
Property	Real estate
Provision for bad debt	Allowance for doubtful accounts
Provision (for diminution in value)	Allowance
Provision (for liability or charge)	Accrual
Purchase on credit	Purchase on account
Quoted company	Listed company
Release of provision	Reversal of accrual
Reserves	Equity
Retail price index	Consumer price index
Sales on credit	Sales on account
Share capital and reserves or Shareholders' funds	Stockholders' equity
Shareholder	Stockholder
Shareholders' funds	Shareholders' equity
Share premium	Paid-in surplus
Share premium account	Additional paid-in capital
Stocks	Inventories
Tangible fixed assets	Property, plant, and equipment
Taxable profit	Taxable income
Taxation	Income taxes
Trade creditors	Accounts payable
Trade debtors	Accounts receivable
Trade union	Labor union
Turnover	Sales/revenue
Unit trusts	Mutual funds
Visible trade	Merchandise trade

INDEX

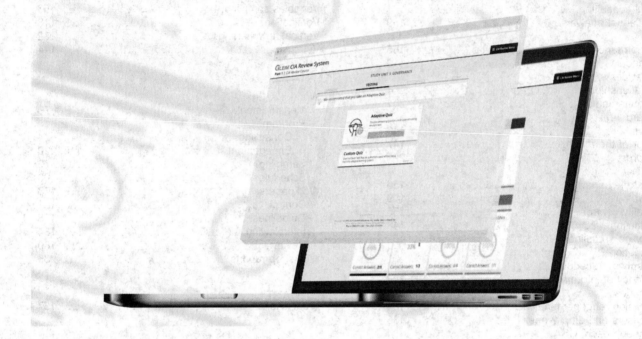